STOCHASTIC MODELS OF NEURAL NETWORKS

Frontiers in Artificial Intelligence and Applications

Volume 102

Published in the subseries
Knowledge-Based Intelligent Engineering Systems
Editors: L.C. Jain and R.J. Howlett

Recently published in KBIES:

Recently published in FAIA:

ISSN 0922-6389

Stochastic Models of Neural Networks

Claudio Turchetti

Department of Electronics, Artificial Intelligence and Telecommunications
Università Politecnica delle Marche, Italy

IOS
Press

Ohmsha

Amsterdam • Berlin • Oxford • Tokyo • Washington, DC

ISBN 1 58603 388 3 (IOS Press)
ISBN 4 274 90626 4 C3055 (Ohmsha)
Library of Congress Control Number: 2003113123

Publisher
IOS Press
Nieuwe Hemweg 6B
1013 BG Amsterdam
The Netherlands
fax: +31 20 620 3419
e-mail: order@iospress.nl

Distributor in the UK and Ireland
IOS Press/Lavis Marketing
73 Lime Walk
Headington
Oxford OX3 7AD
England
fax: +44 1865 75 0079

Distributor in the USA and Canada
IOS Press, Inc.
5795-G Burke Centre Parkway
Burke, VA 22015
USA
fax: +1 703 323 3668
e-mail: iosbooks@iospress.com

Distributor in Japan
Ohmsha, Ltd.
3-1 Kanda Nishiki-cho
Chiyoda-ku, Tokyo 101-8460
Japan
fax: +81 3 3233 2426

Stochastic Models of Neural Networks

Claudio Turchetti

Department of Electronics, Artificial Intelligence and Telecommunications
Università Politecnica delle Marche, Italy

IOS
Press

Ohmsha

Amsterdam • Berlin • Oxford • Tokyo • Washington, DC

ISBN 1 58603 388 3 (IOS Press)
ISBN 4 274 90626 4 C3055 (Ohmsha)
Library of Congress Control Number: 2003113123

Publisher
IOS Press
Nieuwe Hemweg 6B
1013 BG Amsterdam
The Netherlands
fax: +31 20 620 3419
e-mail: order@iospress.nl

Distributor in the UK and Ireland
IOS Press/Lavis Marketing
73 Lime Walk
Headington
Oxford OX3 7AD
England
fax: +44 1865 75 0079

Distributor in the USA and Canada
IOS Press, Inc.
5795-G Burke Centre Parkway
Burke, VA 22015
USA
fax: +1 703 323 3668
e-mail: iosbooks@iospress.com

Distributor in Japan
Ohmsha, Ltd.
3-1 Kanda Nishiki-cho
Chiyoda-ku, Tokyo 101-8460
Japan
fax: +81 3 3233 2426

To my daughter Francesca,
who opened my mind to the beauty of the world

Preface

Artificial Neural Networks, or more simply neural networks, are the main objects of a new science, named *neural computing* (or *neurocomputing*), which aims to define a paradigm of the information processing adopted by the human brain.

Neural computing is one of the most exciting and rapidly expanding disciplines of current research, involving people from a wide range of scientific areas, i.e. mathematics, physics, engineering, physiology and computer science, to mention just a few.

Although the study of the processing mechanism of the human brain has ancient origins (it is known that some Greek philosophers such as Plato and Aristotle suggested explanations of the brain and thinking process) only over the last 60 years or so, has research in this field produced any relevant results.

The first milestone in the study of the human brain mechanism is a paper by Mc Culloch and Pitts [1], in which they derived theorems related to models of neural systems based on the physical knowledge of the biological structures. In such a model the activity of the neuron is an 'all-or-none' process with a certain fixed number of synapses.

The second important contribution in this field of research is due to D.O. Hebb who, in 1949, published a book entitled "The Organization of Behavior" [2], in which he suggested the method of updating synaptic weights that we now refer to as 'Hebbian'. Hebb made some postulates among which he stated that, in a neural network, information is stored in the weight of the synapses (connections).

Thereafter, in 1968, an important paper by F. Rosenblatt [3] defined a neural network structure called the *perceptron*. As the perceptron is capable of learning to classify certain pattern sets by modifying its connections, it was described as a *learning machine*.

Another milestone was established by B. Widrow and M. Hopf, who, in 1960, published a paper [4] that from an engineering point of view, may be considered one of the most important papers on neural network technology.

The main contributions of this paper are the introduction of a device called *Adaline* (Adaptive Linear), which consists of a single neuron with an arbitrary number of inputs, and the implementation in hardware of the neural structure they suggested.

It is hard, and out of the scope of this book, to describe what happened in the subsequent nearly 40 years, as a vast number of scientific papers on neural modeling have been published.

The structure of the brain

Recently even more accurate methods available for biomedical investigation have made it possible to acquire a deeper, but not exhaustive, knowledge of the biological neural networks anatomy.

The human brain is a formidable complex structure having the capability of performing many activities, such as pattern recognition, perception, control and so on.

The neuron is the basic unit of the brain, acting as an analogue processing unit. In the brain there are approximately 100 billion (10^{11}) neurons, each of these connected to about ten thousand (10^4) others. The neuron plays several functional roles many of which are not completely understood, even though the basic details are relatively clear.

A neuron is composed of the cell nucleus or *soma* and a set of branching fibers, named *processes*, which serve as interconnections to other neurons (to form the distributed processing network) and muscle tissues for controlling muscle activity. The processes are classified into *dendrites* and *axons*. Dendrites are input connections through which the neuron receives signals from other neurons. The axon, usually just one per neuron, serves as its primary output device. An axon is a long fiber acting as a transmission line that may branch out to 10^3 different points. The connecting points between an axon and the dendrite of a receiving neuron are called *synapses*. There are approximately 10^{13} to 10^{14} synapses in the human brain, thus forming a dense network of neural connections with the 100 billion neurons.

The neurons interact with each other by transmitting electrical signals through a complex electrochemical process. When a series of impulses is received at the input of a neuron and the electrical potential on the cell membrane raises above a critical threshold, the neuron fires an electrical pulse down its axon to the receiving neurons connected with it. Otherwise the neuron will remain in its inactive, quiet state.

Along with these studies on the neural network physiology, several others have been carried out at the same time on the computing methods adopted by the human brain, aiming at, among other things, the realization of artificial neural machines inspired by biological one. Such research, was developed on the basis of phenomenological events rather than on a profound knowledge of the physics of computing mechanisms actually adopted by the biological networks, has produced a lot of interesting results on the nature of such a processing approach [5-11].

State-of-the-art

As the human being has conceived a very powerful artificial computing machine, i.e. the digital computer, it is natural to ask whether the brain behaves like a computer.

At present we may consider the following assertions and their argumentation as plausible, making a clear distinction between neural networks and digital computers.

i) Biological neural systems do not behave like a digital computer, i.e. do not apply the principles of digital computation.

This assertion is justified by the fact that neurons cannot be threshold-logic circuits, since the accuracy and stability of such circuits is not adequate to define Boolean functions.

As a consequence the biological brain must use signal processing elements and mechanism that are essentially analog in nature. Other differences between the two computing systems are inherent in their physical realization. Signals in neural systems are approximately 100-millivolt nerve impulses lasting nearly a millisecond, while digital computers work with 1-3 volt signal levels switching at fractions of nanosecond intervals. The average nerve cell dissipates power in the 10^{-12} -watt range, i.e. several orders less than the one dissipated on average by a logic gate in a digital computer.

ii) The computation mechanism adopted by the human brain is completely different to the one adopted by a digital computer since no machine instructions or control codes occur in neural computing. As a consequence the brain does not implement recursive computation and it does not solve problems in an algorithmic way.

The knowledge acquired from biological systems as well as the above statements constitute some of the main motivations for the very impressive development of artificial neural processing which has occurred in the last 25 years. A great variety of neural network models, that could hardly be summarized, and whose exhaustive discussion is beyond the purpose of this book, have been published in a very rich scientific paper production. Nevertheless it is currently accepted that these models have several properties in common with biological networks.

A well-known property that neural networks possess is their ability to learn from experience. This property is closely related to the approximating capability, in that learning from a set of examples can be regarded as synthesizing an approximation of a multidimensional function [12].

Recent works have demonstrated that Multilayer Perceptrons (MLP's) [13-15], Radial Basis Function Networks (RBF's) [16], and Approximate Identity Neural Networks (AINN's) [17-18] possess this property with reference to some classes of functions. These results show that neural networks of these kinds are capable of approximating, arbitrarily well, any function belonging to a certain class, with the degree of accuracy depending on the learning algorithm and on the number of neurons available.

Specific theorems for each of the three cases considered, i.e. MLP's, RBF's, and AINN's networks, are reported in [13-15], [16], and [17-18] respectively.

Other important properties, that won't be discussed in this book, are *Adaptivity* and *Fault Tolerance.*

Artificial neural networks have been implemented both in software and hardware and they are demonstrated to be useful in an incredible number of practical applications. Some examples of these are pattern recognition, knowledge data bases for stochastic information, optimization computation, robot control, decision making and signal processing, however the reader is referred to specialized books for complete discussions of them.

Nowadays the study of artificial neural networks has been developing along two main directions. The first one aims at understanding the anatomy and physiology of the human brain in order to define models, as adherent as possible to the physical behavior of it. Unfortunately, at present, as the invasive methods of experimental inspection are not adequate to be applied directly on the biological systems, it is not a simple task to gain insight of the brain mechanism from non-invasive observations.

The second direction, the research on artificial neural networks proceeds along, is essentially theoretical and it aims at establishing new general concepts of neural computing. The computing scheme of a neural network should be based on the distributed and parallel structure of the brain, and able to easily solve problems like visual perception, speech recognition, cognitive activity and so on, which require a large amount of resources and are scarcely efficient if implemented with the computing method usually adopted by digital computers.

This new scientific field, named neural computing or simply neurocomputing, is irrespective of the physical nature of networks, able to implement such a computing approach. As a consequence, an artificial neural network represents just one of the several models to which the principles of parallel information processing apply.

With regard to this field, it is worth underlining the pioneering work by S. I. Amari [6] which has significantly contributed to its development.

A new model of neural computing

From what is said above, it follows that one of the main features of neural networks, allowing them to collect information from environment, is their ability of learning by experience.

However it must be recognized that the surrounding environment in which a neural system operates, carrying out its actions, is mostly stochastic. The randomness of both signals and events with which a neural network interacts, is not only due to the superimposition of a noise to a non-random signal, i.e. the "truth" signal. Instead it is clear that the signals are inherently stochastic in that a predictable component of the signal cannot be identified.

The human speech, pronounced by one or more speakers, is a well known example of stochastic signals, since the same word corresponds to a set of infinite different realizations.

It is hard to accept the idea that the human brain might be able to process and memorize mathematical models of the events that occur in the surrounding environment, as if they were expressed through the deterministic laws we use to manage events in the scientific approach. This method has been developed over a relative short lapse of time (hundreds of years) when compared with the time the human brain had required to define its powerful structure (thousands of years). In an environment essentially non predictable, it is certainly more realistic to model the events as stochastic processes, rather than to treat them as deterministic. The human brain should have acquired, over its lengthy evolution, very advanced skillfulness at treating stochastic processes.

In view of these assertions, in this book both biological and artificial neural networks will be considered as systems capable of processing stochastic processes. Two fundamental aspects will be treated and deepened in the book: the first regards the process of memorizing the stochastic processes and it is related to the learning capability of neural networks, the second addresses the problem of defining a model for neural computing.

In order to memorize and process these kinds of signals a neural network should be able to learn realizations of the stochastic process under observation. Hence from a mathematical point of view the learning process can be viewed as a problem of approximating random functions. To this end classes of neural networks with this capability, named Stochastic Neural Networks (SNN's), acting as universal approximators of stochastic processes, will be defined.

Stochastic neural networks are known in the literature mainly as paradigms for solving optimization problems, due to their ability in circumventing the major inconvenience of the currently used Newton-based algorithms, i.e. trapping the solution in local minima.

Usually stochastic networks are classified as
- networks using stochastic activation function (also known as *Boltzmann machines*);
- networks using stochastic weights.

A *Boltzmann machine* [19-20] is a neural network with symmetric recurrent connections, and using a probabilistic mechanism in the firing of neurons.

In the study of *networks using stochastic weights* [21-22] the connection weights may be regarded as if they are determined randomly and we find those properties which hold for almost all randomly generated networks under the same probability law.

It is worth noting that with reference to the networks defined above, Boltzmann machines are stochastic in their own nature, while regarding to the networks of the second kind, although they behave deterministically, it is effective to train them as if they were stochastic. Nevertheless networks using stochastic weights may be viewed as input-output mapping depending on random variables. Thus they may be considered as random variables dependent on one (or more) parameter and in fact as stochastic processes.

As it will appear later, studying neural networks from this point of view is particularly fruitful since they display new interesting properties when they themselves are treated as stochastic processes.

The aim of this book is to investigate the properties of such networks to be viewed as sources of random functions. In particular, as it is natural to ask whether approximating properties similar to those valid for deterministic function hold for random function too, this will be the main objective of this book.

In order to simplify the treatment of this subject, we will refer solely to the class of Approximate Identity Neural Networks (AINN's) because they exhibit a linear dependence on the random coefficients that characterize their statistical behavior.

A natural extension of the theory developed here is the generalization of the results to the MLP and RBF networks, but involving further mathematical problems not easily solvable, due to the nonlinearity of such networks with respect to random coefficients.

This book is intended to provide a treatment of the theory and applications of such a class of neural networks on the basis of recent developments on this subject [23-24]. The mathematical frameworks on which the theory is founded embrace the approximation of non-random functions by dense sets of functions as well as the theory of stochastic processes. With regard to the first aspect earlier results has been reported with reference to the works of Poggio [12] and Park [16] for radial basis function networks, Cybenko [13], Funahashi [14], and Hornik [15] with reference to multilayer feedforward networks, and by Conti [17] with reference to approximate identity neural networks. As far as the other aspect is concerned, a section of the book is intended to cover, in a self-consistent way, the basic properties of random functions. The treatment of stochastic processes is carried out by using several well known results of the elementary geometry of Hilbert space, following a point of view introduced earlier in the stochastic process theory by Kolmogorov [25], Cramer [26], and other authors [27-29]. Particular emphasis is devoted to the canonical decompositions of stochastic processes which prove to be very successful in the representation of large classes of random functions either stationary or non-stationary [28]. On the basis of these results it is shown that some classes of artificial neural networks exist such that they are capable of providing arbitrary approximation, in the mean square sense, to prescribed stochastic processes [23]. The networks so defined constitute a model for neural processing consistent with the need for learning from a stochastic environment. As the problem of learning is of central importance a large part of the book is devoted to this topic within the framework of the estimation of stochastic processes. Particular attention is given to elucidate the main features of stochastic neural networks: among these, the properties of generalization and representation of input-output transformations are the most significant.

Finally an approach for neural computing based on the composition of stochastic processes, and fundamentally different from the one adopted in digital computers, will be discussed.

A brief description of the chapters of the book is given in more detail here.

Description of the chapters of the book

Chapter 1

This chapter introduces the mathematical model of wide classes of Artificial Neural Networks (ANN's), i.e. Multilayer Perceptron Networks (MLP's), Radial Basis Function Networks (RBF's) and Approximate Identity Neural Networks (AINN's). With regard to the third class of nets some theoretical results on their capability of approximating functions and some implementation examples with electrical solid-state circuits will be reported.

Chapter 2

This chapter reports some fundamental concepts and results of the *stochastic process* theory. As a result the *canonical representation* for processes belonging to a wide class of nonstationary processes is stated and demonstrated.

Chapter 3

The aim of this chapter is to define the *Stochastic Neural Networks* and to investigate their properties with regard to the space of functions they generate, rather than their ability in solving global optimization problems, in which they are usually used.

One of the main objectives of this chapter is to demonstrate that a significant property of these networks is their ability in approximating stochastic processes belonging to certain specific classes.

Chapter 4

The scope of this chapter is to define some suitable architectures for the implementation of stochastic networks and to discuss several application examples showing the learning capability of the stochastic networks so defined.

Chapter 5

The aim of this chapter is twofold. Firstly the process of modeling and memorizing physical events considered as stochastic processes will be considered. Secondly the problem of neural computing with an approach fundamentally different to the one currently adopted in digital computers will be addressed and discussed.

References

[1] McCulloch, W. C., & Pitts, W. (1943). *A Logical Calculus of the Ideas Immanent in Nervous Activity*. Bulletin of Mathematical Biophysics, 5, 115–133.

[2] Hebb, D. O. (1949) *The Organization of Behavior*. New York: John Wiley.

[3] Rosenblatt, F. (1958). *The Perceptron: a Probabilistic Model for Information Storage and Organization in the Brain*. Psychology Review, 65, 386–408.

[4] Widrow, B., & Hopf, M. E. (1960). *Adaptive Switching Circuits*. 1960 IRE Convention Record: Part 4 - Computers: Man-Machine Systems, Los Angeles, 96–104.

[5] Kohonen, T. (1988). *An Introduction to Neural Computing*. Neural Networks, 1, pp. 3–16.

[6] Amari, S. I. (1990). *Mathematical Foundations of Neurocomputing*, Proceedings of the IEEE, 78 (9), 1443–1463.

[7] Mead, C. (1989). *Analog VLSI and Neural Systems*. Reading, MA: Addison Wesley.

[8] Beale, R., & Jackson, T. (1990). *Neural Computing: An Introduction*. Institute of Physics Publishing.

[9] Haykin, S. (1994). *Neural Networks*. Prentice-Hall, USA.

[10] Dayhoff, J. E. (1990). *Neural Network Architectures*. New York: Van Nostrand Reinhold.

[11] Taylor, J. G. (1966). *Neural Networks and Their Applications*, John Wiley and Sons.

[12] Poggio, T. & Girosi, F. (1990). *Networks for Approximation and Learning*. Proceedings of IEEE, 78 (9), 1481–1497.

[13] Cybenko, G. (1989). *Approximation by Superposition of Sigmoidal Function*. Math. Control, Systems, Signal, 2, 303–314.

[14] Funahashi, K. (1989). *On the Approximate Realisation of Continuous Mappings by Neural Networks*. Neural Networks, 2, 183–192.

[15] Hornik, K., Stinchcombe, M., & White, H. (1989). *Multilayer Feedforward Networks are Universal Approximators*. Neural Networks, 2, 395–403.

[16] Park, J., & Sandberg, I. W. (1991). *Universal Approximation Using Radial-Basis-Function Networks*. Neural Computation, 3, 246–257.

[17] Conti, M., Orcioni, S., & Turchetti, C. (1994). *A Class of Neural Networks Based on Approximate Identity for Analog IC's Hardware Implementation*. IEICE Transactions on Fundamentals of Electronics, Communications and Computer Sciences, E77-A (6), 1069–1079.

[18] Conti, M., & Turchetti, C. (1994). *Approximation of Dynamical Systems by Continuous-Time Recurrent Approximate Identity Neural Networks*. Neural, Parallel & Scientific Computations, 2, 299–322.

[19] Amari, S., Kurata, K., & Nagaoka, H. (1992). *Information Geometry of Boltzmann Machine*. IEEE Transactions on Neural Networks, 3 (2), 260–271.

[20] Simon Foo, Y.-P., & Takefuji, Y. (1988). *Stochastic Neural Networks for solving Job-Shop Scheduling: Part 1. Problem Representation*. IEEE Proceedings of International Conference on Neural Networks, Vol. 2, 275–282, San Diego, CA, USA, July 1988.

[21] Zhao, J., & Shawe-Taylor, J. (1996). *A Recurrent Network with Stochastic Weights*. IEEE Proceedings of International Conference on Neural Networks, Vol. 2, 1302–1307, Washington, DC, USA, June 1996.

[22] Amari, S., & Maginu, K. (1988). *Statistical Neurodynamics of Associative Memory*. Neural Networks, 1, 63–73.

[23] Turchetti, C., Conti, M., Crippa, P., & Orcioni, S. (1998). *On the Approximation of Stochastic Processes by Approximate Identity Neural Networks*. IEEE Transactions on Neural Networks, 9 (6), 1069–1085.

[24] Belli, M. R., Conti, M., Crippa, P., & Turchetti, C. (1999). *Artificial Neural Networks as Approximators of Stochastic Processes*. Neural Networks, 12, 647–658.

[25] Kolmogorov, A. N. (1941). *Stationary Sequences in Hibert Spaces*. Bull. Math. Univ. Moscow, (2).

[26] Cramer, H., & Leadbetter M. R. (1967). *Stationary and Related Stochastic Processes*. New York: John Wiley.

[27] Doob, J. L. (1990). *Stochastic Processes*. New York: John Wiley & Sons.

[28] Gihman, I. I., & Skorohod, A.V. (1974). *The Theory of Stochastic Processes*. Berlin: Springer-Verlag.

[29] Prohorov, Y. V., & Rozanov, Y. A. (1969). *Probability Theory*. Berlin: Springer-Verlag.

Acknowledgments

Firstly I would like to thank Prof. L. Jain (University of South Australia, Adelaide, Australia) for inviting me to write this book for the IOS Press series Frontier in Artificial Intelligence and Applications.

I am also indebted to Dr. Paolo Crippa (Department of Electronics, Artificial Intelligence and Telecommunications, Università Politecnica delle Marche, Ancona, Italy) for his precious cooperation in writing the book. Although he does not appear as coauthor, much of the material presented in the book has been discussed with him, and the final version of the manuscript greatly benefits from his scientific and technical support.

I am particularly grateful to my wife, who was very patient with me throughout the writing process of the book.

Contents

*We believe in the possibility of a theory which
is able to give a complete description of reality,
the laws of which establish relations between the
things themselves and not merely between their
probabilities ...
God does not play dice.*

Albert Einstein

CHAPTER ONE

NEURAL NETWORKS AS APPROXIMATORS OF DETERMINISTIC FUNCTIONS

This chapter introduces the mathematical model of wide classes of Artificial Neural Networks (ANN's) by focusing, in particular, on the class of Approximate Identity Neural Networks (AINN's) based on the Approximate Identity (AI) functions. With regard to this class of nets some theoretical results on their capability of approximating functions have been reported. From an application point of view, networks of this kind are particularly suitable for implementation with electrical solid-state circuits, as some examples of hardware realization will show.

1.1.   Artificial Neural Networks (ANN's)

Generally speaking a neural network is a mathematical model of the biological neural systems. For the comprehension of the neural computing mechanism, defining a paradigm that models some of the operations of the human brain is of major concern. On the other hand, from an application point of view, the realization of networks acting as biological networks is particularly attractive. In the latter case, as the main objective is not merely to define a mathematical model, but instead to realize an actual network (e.g. an electrical network), such networks will be called Artificial Neural Networks (ANN's). In the context of this book the term ANN's will be used with this meaning.

The treatment of the book will be referred to the class of multi-input single-output feedforward neural networks with three layers whose general scheme is reported in Fig. 1. A neural network belonging to this class is represented mathematically by a linear combination of nonlinear elementary functions and thus takes the form

$$S_n(\boldsymbol{x}) = \sum_{i=1}^{n} w_i \sigma_i(\boldsymbol{x}) , \quad \boldsymbol{x} \equiv \left[x_1, x_2, \cdots, x_r\right]^T \in \mathbb{R}^r \tag{1.1}$$

where w_i are constants to be adjusted in the learning stage, $\sigma_i(\boldsymbol{x})$ are non linear elementary functions named *neurons*, and $\mathbb{R}$ is the usual space of real numbers. The first layer of this network consists of the inputs whose number is equivalent to the number r of independent variables in (1.1). The second layer is composed of nonlinear "hidden" units fully connected to the first layer. The output layer consists of one linear unit whose constants w_i are the unknown coefficients of the expansion (1.1). The name *hidden layer* refers to the fact that the outputs of neurons belonging to such layer are hidden from the user who only observes the output of the network. The form of functions $\sigma_i(\boldsymbol{x})$ defines specific classes of networks. We will consider three different neural networks, depending on the elementary functions $\sigma_i(\boldsymbol{x})$ chosen, which are particularly suitable for the purposes of the book: Multilayer Perceptron nets (MLP's), Radial Basis Function nets (RBF's), and Approximate Identity nets (AINN's).

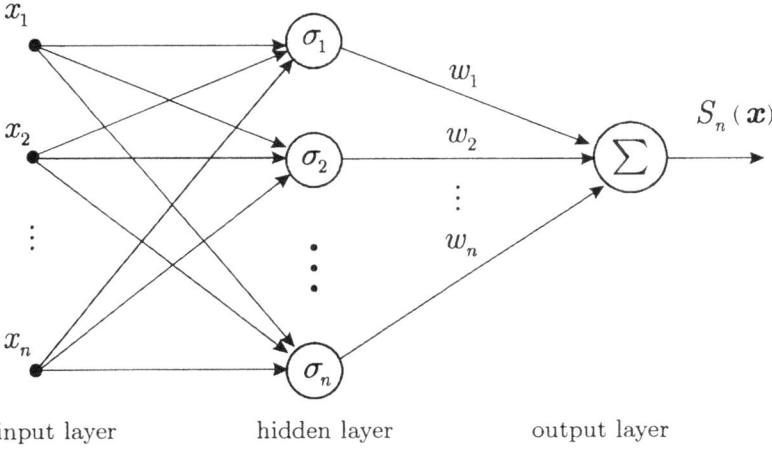

input layer   hidden layer   output layer

Figure 1.   Three-layers feedforward neural network

1.2.   Multilayer Perceptron Nets (MLPs)

This class of networks is characterized by the model of *single layer perceptron* [1] which takes a linear combination of inputs giving the output

$$\sigma_i\left(\boldsymbol{x}\right) = \sigma\left(\boldsymbol{y}_i^T \cdot \boldsymbol{x} + \vartheta_i\right) \tag{1.2}$$

where σ is a nonlinear function, named *neural activation function*, which acts on input signals $\boldsymbol{x}$ weighted by the synaptic connection weights $\boldsymbol{y}_i$, and ϑ_i is the bias (or threshold). Various neural network models differ for the activation function used. The most commonly are

sigmoid : $\sigma\left(u\right) = \dfrac{1}{1 + \exp(-u)}$,

hyperbolic tangent: $\sigma\left(u\right) = \tanh(u)$,

threshold: $\sigma\left(u\right) = \begin{cases} 1 & u \geq 0 \\ -1 & u < 0 \end{cases}$.

These three activation functions are depicted in Fig. 2.

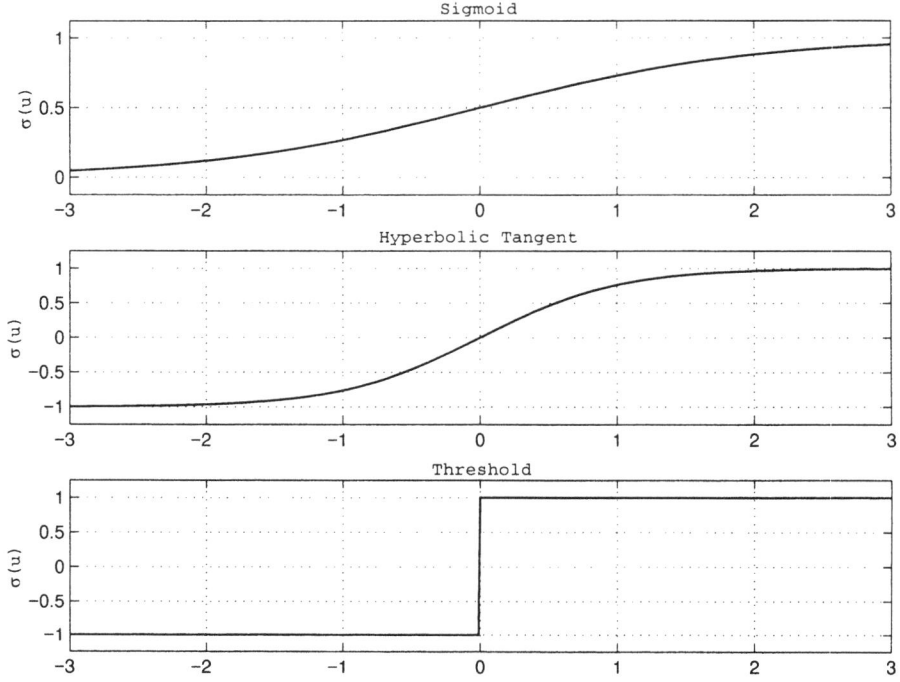

Figure 2. Examples of neural activation functions

1.3.   Radial Basis Function Nets (RBF's)

A Radial Basis Network (RBF) is a feed-forward neural network using a *radial basis activation function*. Thus in this case the elementary functions in (1.1) can be written as

$$\sigma_i(\boldsymbol{x}) = K\left(\frac{\boldsymbol{x} - \boldsymbol{z}_i}{q_i}\right) \tag{1.3}$$

where K is a radially symmetric kernel function, which has the general form

$$K\left(\frac{\|\boldsymbol{x} - \boldsymbol{z}_i\|}{q_i}\right) = K\left(\frac{d_i}{q_i}\right) \tag{1.4}$$

being $\|\boldsymbol{x} - \boldsymbol{z}_i\| = d_i$ the usual distance between the vectors $\boldsymbol{x}$ and $\boldsymbol{z}_i$. Such a function is symmetric with respect to the center point $\boldsymbol{z}_i$ and has a sharpness depending on q_t.

Several examples of one-dimensional radial basis functions are given in Fig. 3.

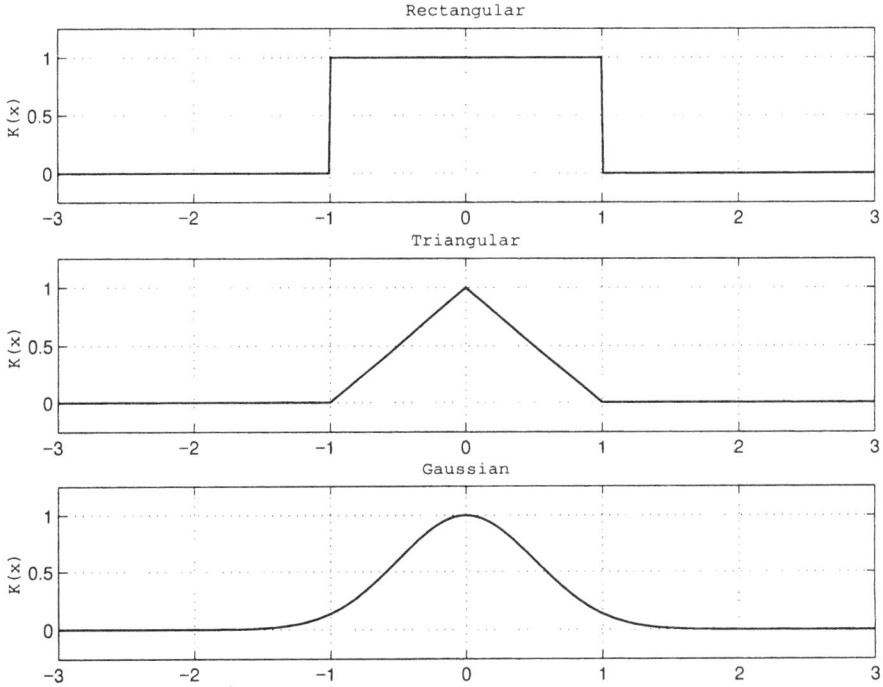

Figure 3. Examples of one-dimensional radial basis functions

A remarkable property of these networks is their capability in solving regularization problem, i.e. hypersurface reconstruction from sparse data points. This is a typical ill-posed problem in which the inverse of a transformation between finite and infinite dimensional spaces has to be determined. It is shown in [2] that specific forms of the RBF's functions (1.4) correspond to regularization operators that render the problem of surface reconstruction from a discrete set of examples, well posed.

1.4.   Approximate Identity Neural Networks (AINN's)

The class of *Approximate Identity Neural Networks* (AINN's) is based on the functions whose properties are summarized in the following.

Here the notation $\int dt$ will be used to denote the Lebesgue integral, while the symbol L_2 is adopted for the usual space of square integrable functions.

Let $\{k_\nu(x)\}_{\nu=1}^{\infty}$, $k_\nu(\cdot) : \mathbb{R} \to \mathbb{R}$ be a sequence of functions with either a discrete or continuous parameter ν: we call the sequence an *Approximate Identity* (AI) if it satisfies the following conditions:

P1)
$$\int_{-\infty}^{+\infty} k_\nu(x)\,dx = 1 \ , \qquad \text{for any } \nu \ ; \tag{1.5}$$

P2) for any $\varepsilon > 0$ and $\delta > 0$, there exists a number Γ such that for $\nu \geq \Gamma$ it results

$$\int_{|x|>\delta} |k_\nu(x)|\,dx \leq \varepsilon \ . \tag{1.6}$$

An example of functions satisfying these properties is given by (see for instance [13])

$$k_\nu(x) = \nu\,k(\nu x) \tag{1.7}$$

where k is such that

$$\int_{-\infty}^{+\infty} k(x)\,dx = 1 \ . \tag{1.8}$$

The typical behavior of an AI sequence is depicted in Fig. 4, showing that the area   under $k_\nu(x)$ is mostly concentrated around the origin as the index ν increases.

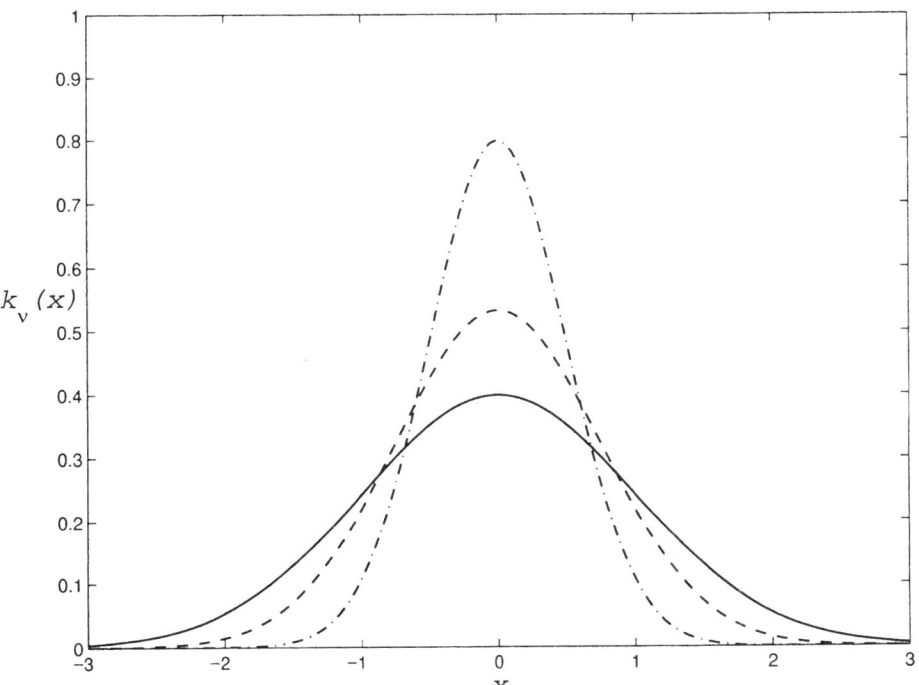

Figure 4. Typical shapes of AI functions

The importance of AI's steams from the property that, for a given function $f(x) \in L_2$, a sequence $f_\nu(x)$ of functions can be defined as the convolution of $f(x)$ and $k_\nu(x)$,

$$f_\nu(x) = f * k_\nu = \int_{-\infty}^{+\infty} f(z) k_\nu(x - z) dz , \qquad (1.9)$$

which approximates well $f(x)$. This result is stated by the following

Theorem 1.1. Suppose $f \in L_2$, then the convolution $f * k_\nu$ is defined almost everywhere for each ν, it is in class L_2, and

$$\underset{\nu \to \infty}{\text{l.i.m.}} f * k_\nu = f . \qquad (1.10)$$

where $\underset{\nu \to \infty}{\text{l.i.m.}}$ denotes the mean square limit (see the note at the end of Appendix).

Proof of this theorem can be found in [13] with reference to uniform

convergence. However, as it is well known, uniform convergence implies
convergence in mean square, so that (1.10) holds.

The one-dimensional AINN's are represented by finite sums of the form

$$S_n(x) = \sum_{i=1}^{n} a_i k_\nu (x - x_i) , \qquad x \in T \tag{1.11}$$

where $k_\nu(\cdot)$ are AI functions and a_i, ν, n, x_i is a set of unknown parameters.
These networks can be graphically represented by the scheme reported in Fig. 5.

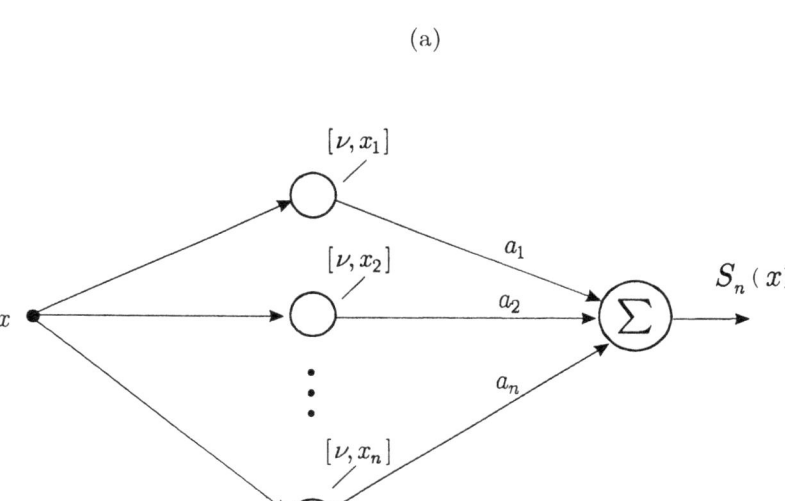

(a)

(b)

Figure 5. (a) Single neuron, (b) one-dimensional AINN

1.5.   Neural Networks as Approximators of Deterministic

Input-Output Mappings

A well-known property that neural networks own is their ability in approximating some classes of input-output functions. This property is closely related to the learning capability, in that learning an input-output mapping from a set of examples can be regarded as synthesizing an approximation of a multidimensional function [2].

Recent works have demonstrated that Multilayer Perceptrons [3-5], Radial Basis Function Networks [6] and Approximate Identity Neural Networks [7] possess this property with reference to some classes of functions. These results show that neural networks of these kinds are capable of approximating arbitrarily well any function belonging to a certain class, the degree of accuracy depending on the learning algorithm and on the number of neurons available. The approximation property of such networks can be established in a unified framework as follows.

Let us indicate with A the set of functions $S_n(x)$ given by (1.1), i.e. $S_n \in A$. The property of approximating a function $f(x)$ belonging to a set M, $f \in M$, by the summation (1.1), is equivalent to the property that the set A is dense in M (see Appendix A of Chap. 2 for a definition of *dense set*).

In symbols, for any $\varepsilon > 0$ and $f \in M$, there is an element S_n belonging to A for which $d(f, S_n) < \varepsilon$, being $d(\cdot, \cdot)$ the distance between two functions.

Specific theorems for each of the three cases considered, i.e. MLP's, RBF's, and AINN's networks, are reported in [3], [6], and [7] respectively. It is worth noting that the set M of the functions to be approximated depends on the function $\sigma_i(x)$ defining the class of the networks.

Here we won't report the proofs of this property for the MLP's and the RBF's, for which the reader is referred to specific papers, whereas in the subsequent sections we will derive in detail some results with regard to the AINN's solely.

1.6.   Approximating Properties of the AINN's

The approximating capabilities of AINN's are demonstrated by the following theorem.

Theorem 1.2. Let $k_\nu(\cdot)$ be AI functions, and a_i, $x_i \in \mathbb{R}$, then the finite sums of the form

$$S_n(x) = \sum_{i=1}^{n} a_i k_\nu (x - x_i) \tag{1.12}$$

are dense in L_2. In symbols

$$\forall\, \varepsilon > 0, \ \exists\, n, \nu \text{ depending on } \varepsilon \ \Rightarrow \ \|f(x) - S_n(x)\| < \varepsilon \tag{1.13}$$

where $f(x)$ is a real-valued function in L_2 and $\|\cdot\|$ is the usually L_2-norm.

Detailed proof of this theorem is reported in the Appendix for easy reference. The approximating property of the AINN's previously demonstrated for the real functions, can be extended to the complex functions. In such a case, given the complex functions $f(x) = f_1(x) + i f_2(x)$, $g(x) = g_1(x) + i g_2(x)$, the distance $d(f, g)$ is defined through the L_2-norm

$$\begin{aligned}
\|f(x) - g(x)\|^2 &= \int_{\mathbb{R}} |f(x) - g(x)|^2 \, dx \\
&= \int_{\mathbb{R}} |f_1(x) - g_1(x)|^2 \, dx + \int_{\mathbb{R}} |f_2(x) - g_2(x)|^2 \, dx
\end{aligned} \tag{1.14}$$

Therefore in this case the AINN assumes the complex form

$$S_n(x) = \sum_{l=1}^{n} a_l k_\nu (x - x_l) + i \sum_{m=1}^{n} a_m k_\nu (x - x_m) \,, \tag{1.15}$$

in order that the approximating property holds for complex function too.

(1.15) can be rewritten as

$$S_n(x) = \sum_{l=1}^{n} c_l k_\nu (x - x_l) \tag{1.16}$$

where the coefficients

$$c_l = a_l + i\, a_m \tag{1.17}$$

are complex.

Another important property of AI's, directly derived from the ones we have stated above is the following

P3)   If $k_\nu(x)$ is an AI on $\mathbb{R}$, then the product

$$v_\nu \left(\boldsymbol{x} \right) = k_\nu \left(x_1 \right) k_\nu \left(x_2 \right) \cdots k_\nu \left(x_m \right) , \tag{1.18}$$

where $\boldsymbol{x} = \left[x_1, x_2, \cdots, x_m \right]$, is an AI on $\mathbb{R}^m$. It is straightforward to show that properties P1 and P2 hold for this function.

1.7.   Hardware Implementation of ANN's

One of the main goals in *Artificial Intelligence* is to replicate the behavior of biological neural systems with artificial networks by using low-cost, reliable and reproducible technologies. Additionally, due to the large complexity of neural networks (of the order of 10^{11} elementary neurons), managing large size networks with small volume occupancy, constitutes an essential feature required in the implementation of ANN's. At present the only technology available owning such features is the technology of semiconductor devices and in particular the Very Large Scale Integrated (VLSI) circuits technology, capable of fabricating in an area of nearly 1 cm square 10^9 elementary devices.

Thus with these considerations in mind we may state that to effectively implement an Artificial Neural Network, it should have an architecture compatible with VLSI technology. Furthermore among analog and digital circuits, an analog solution seems to be the most promising since it is able to guarantee a higher parallelism, which is one of the main features of biological neural networks [15].

A lot of works have been produced in this field so far, showing the potential of VLSI technologies for the implementation of neural networks. However, since this subject is out of the scope of the book, the reader interested in deepening this aspect is referred to the specialized texts [15-17] and papers [18]-[19].

1.7.1. The Functions $\delta_\nu \left(x; \sigma \right)$

From the theory derived in Sect.1.6, we maintain that Approximate Identities have suitable properties for approximating a measurable function. Even though several different functions with AI properties exist within this class, from an application point of view it is convenient to choose one, which may be implemented with an analog, possibly integrated, circuit. As we will see in the Sect. 1.7.3 devoted to Integrated Circuits (IC's) implementation, the function we will analyze here is particularly fit for being implemented with analog IC's.

For this purpose let

$$\delta_\nu(x;\sigma) = a_\nu\, \omega_\nu(x;\sigma) \tag{1.19}$$

with

$$\omega_\nu(x;\sigma) = \tanh\left(\frac{\nu x + \sigma}{2}\right) - \tanh\left(\frac{\nu x - \sigma}{2}\right), \qquad x \in \mathbb{R}, \ \sigma \in \mathbb{R}^+, \ \nu \in \mathbb{R}^+ , \tag{1.20}$$

then the functions $\delta_\nu(x;\sigma)$ belong to the class of AI functions on $\mathbb{R}$.

Proof:

P1) -   To prove property P1 it is necessary to determine the coefficient a_ν such that

$$\int_{-\infty}^{+\infty} \delta_\nu(x;\sigma)\,dx = 1 . \tag{1.21}$$

The improper integral in (1.21) is equivalent to

$$\int_{-\infty}^{+\infty} \delta_\nu(x;\sigma)\,dx = a_\nu \frac{2}{\nu} \lim_{c\to\infty}\left\{\ln\left(\frac{1 + e^{-\nu x}e^{-\sigma}}{e^{-\sigma} + e^{-\nu x}}\right)\right\}_{-c}^{+c} = a_\nu \frac{2}{\nu}\ln e^{2\sigma} = a_\nu \frac{4\sigma}{\nu}, \tag{1.22}$$

From (1.21) and (1.22) it results

$$a_\nu = \frac{\nu}{4\sigma} , \tag{1.23}$$

therefore

$$\delta_\nu(x;\sigma) = \frac{\nu}{4\sigma}\left\{\tanh\left(\frac{\nu x + \sigma}{2}\right) - \tanh\left(\frac{\nu x - \sigma}{2}\right)\right\} . \tag{1.24}$$

P2) -   It is straightforward to show that $\delta_\nu(x;\sigma) = (\nu/2)\, k(\nu x/2)$ where $k(x) = (1/2\sigma)\left[\tanh\left(x + \sigma/2\right) - \tanh\left(x - \sigma/2\right)\right]$. Thus it suffices to check whether $\int_{-\infty}^{+\infty} k(x)\,dx < \infty$ (see e.g. [13]). This can be easily verified by taking into account eq. (1.21).

P3) -   By using the property stated by (1.18) we can define an approximate identity $\Delta_\nu(\boldsymbol{x};\sigma)$ on $\mathbb{R}^m$ as the product of the functions $\delta_\nu(x;\sigma)$, that is

$$\Delta_\nu(\boldsymbol{x};\sigma) = \delta_\nu(x_1;\sigma)\delta_\nu(x_2;\sigma)\cdots\delta_\nu(x_m;\sigma) = (a_\nu)^m\, \omega_\nu(x_1;\sigma)\omega_\nu(x_2;\sigma)\cdots\omega_\nu(x_m;\sigma)$$
$$= (a_\nu)^m\, \Omega_\nu(\boldsymbol{x},\sigma), \qquad \boldsymbol{x} \in \mathbb{R}^m . \tag{1.25}$$

1.7.2. The $\delta_\nu(x;\sigma)$ Approximate Identity Neural Networks Architecture

Having defined the approximating scheme based on AI functions we will apply the results of the theory previously discussed to show the equivalence between the approximating functions of the kind given by (1.12) and a class of neural networks.

By combining (1.12) and (1.25) we obtain

$$S_n(\boldsymbol{x}) = \sum_{i=1}^{n} b_i \Omega_\nu(\boldsymbol{x} - \boldsymbol{\vartheta}_i, \sigma) \quad, \qquad \boldsymbol{x} \in \mathbb{R}^m \ . \tag{1.26}$$

The architecture of the neural network corresponding to (1.26) is made up of three layers and it is shown in the 3-dimensional input case in Fig. 6. The hidden layer is formed by elements implementing the functions $\Omega_\nu(\boldsymbol{x}, \sigma)$ as products of one-dimensional functions $\omega_\nu(x)$. The basic elements for implementing the m-dimensional function $S_n(\boldsymbol{x})$ are:

i)   the generic block driven by only one input corresponding to the one-dimensional AI $\omega_\nu(x;\sigma)$;

ii)   the multiplier which allows the m-dimensional AI's to be obtained according to the property P3;

iii)   the adder implementing the summation in (1.26).

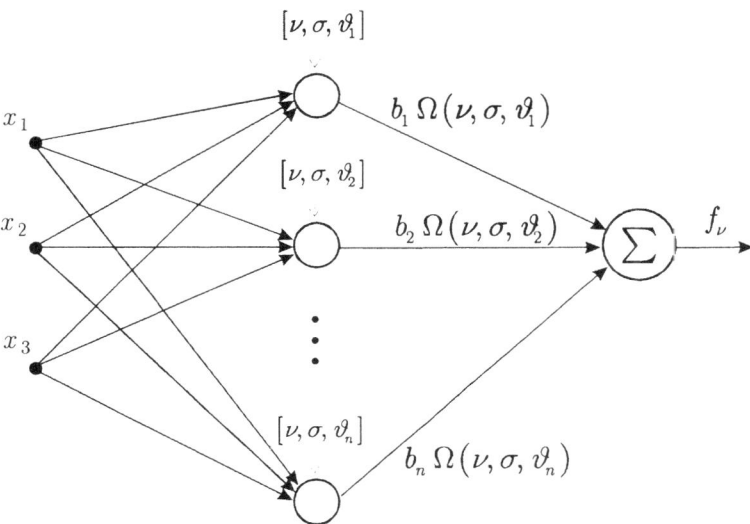

Figure 6.   Architecture of the AINN (3-dimensional input case)

Learning

Learning capability of a neural network is related to the property of approximating classes of functions to any degree of accuracy. When a set of "examples" is given, learning an input-output mapping with an AINN is equivalent to searching values of parameters b_j, ν, σ, ϑ_j such that (1.26) approximates the set of examples with a given error. The approximating function in this case is given by

$$
\tilde{f}(\boldsymbol{x}, \boldsymbol{w}) = \sum_{j=1}^{n} b_j \Omega_\nu\left(\boldsymbol{x} - \vartheta_j, \sigma\right) = \sum_{j=1}^{n} b_j \prod_{i=1}^{m} \omega_{ij} =
$$
$$
= \sum_{j=1}^{n} b_j \prod_{i=1}^{m} \left\{ \tanh\left(\frac{\nu_{ij}\left(x_i - \vartheta_{ij}\right) + \sigma_{ij}}{2}\right) - \tanh\left(\frac{\nu_{ij}\left(x_i - \vartheta_{ij}\right) - \sigma_{ij}}{2}\right) \right\} , \tag{1.27}
$$

where $\boldsymbol{w}$ represents the vector of parameters b_j, ν_j, ϑ_j, σ_j, $j = 1, \cdots, n$ to be determined.

The learning problem may be stated as follows; let

$$
S = \left\{ \left(\boldsymbol{x}_k, f(\boldsymbol{x}_k)\right) \in \mathbb{R}^m \times \mathbb{R} \mid k = 1, \cdots, p \right\} \tag{1.28}
$$

be a set of data we want to approximate by means of the function $\tilde{f}(\boldsymbol{x}, \boldsymbol{w})$, and let $d(\cdot, \cdot)$ be the distance between two functions defined in a suitable way, thus the parameters $\boldsymbol{w}$ are adjusted so that the distance is minimized, i.e.

$$
\min_{\boldsymbol{w}} \ d\left(f, \tilde{f}\right) . \tag{1.29}
$$

A manageable relationship for the distance $d(\cdot, \cdot)$ is the global quadratic error

$$
\mathcal{E} = \frac{1}{2} \sum_{k=1}^{p} \mathcal{E}_k = \frac{1}{2} \sum_{k=1}^{p} \left[f(\boldsymbol{x}_k) - \tilde{f}(\boldsymbol{x}_k, \boldsymbol{w})\right]^2 , \tag{1.30}
$$

where $\mathcal{E}_k$ is the error for each input pattern. The learning problem in this case is equivalent to choosing the parameters $\boldsymbol{w}$ that minimize $\mathcal{E}$.

In software implementation of neural networks of this kind, a commonly used algorithm for solving learning problem is the method of *steepest descent* in which the incremental changes Δw_i of parameters are proportional to the derivatives $\partial \mathcal{E} / \partial w_i$. However, when analog hardware implementation of such a network is demanded, to avoid implementation of partial derivatives a more suitable algorithm may be used. A simple way to do this is to change the coefficients accordingly to the input pattern changes so that, in this way, the changes Δw_i are proportional to $\partial \mathcal{E}_k / \partial w_1$. In particular for parameters b_j the partial derivative $\partial \mathcal{E}_k / \partial b_j$ can be evaluated using the chain rule

$$\frac{\partial \mathcal{E}_k}{\partial b_j} = \frac{\partial \mathcal{E}_k}{\partial \tilde{f}} \frac{\partial \tilde{f}}{\partial b_j} \tag{1.31}$$

where

$$\frac{\partial \mathcal{E}_k}{\partial \tilde{f}} = -\left[f(\boldsymbol{x}_k) - \tilde{f}(\boldsymbol{x}_k, \boldsymbol{w}) \right], \tag{1.32}$$

$$\frac{\partial \tilde{f}}{\partial b_j} = \omega_{1j} \cdots \omega_{mj} = \prod_{i=1}^{m} \omega_{ij} = \Omega_j(\boldsymbol{x}_k). \tag{1.33}$$

Putting

$$\Delta b_j = \eta \left[f(\boldsymbol{x}_k) - \tilde{f}(\boldsymbol{x}_k, \boldsymbol{w}) \right] \Omega_j(\boldsymbol{x}_k), \tag{1.34}$$

where η is a positive-valued constant that regulates the amount of adjustments made with each gradient move, it also results

$$\Delta b_j = -\eta \frac{\partial \mathcal{E}_k}{\partial b_j}, \tag{1.35}$$

i.e. the changes Δb_j are proportional to $\partial \mathcal{E}_k / \partial b_j$. It has been proved in [14] that, if a sufficiently small learning parameter η is chosen, this algorithm minimizes the global error $\mathcal{E}$ defined in (1.30). Furthermore this approach reduces the network complexity since the algorithm does not require that the whole pattern be memorized at the input, as is necessary when global error is minimized.

The learning algorithm is summarized in Fig. 7 where the same approach has been used for adjusting the other parameters ν_{ij}, σ_{ij}, ϑ_{ij} during the learning stage.

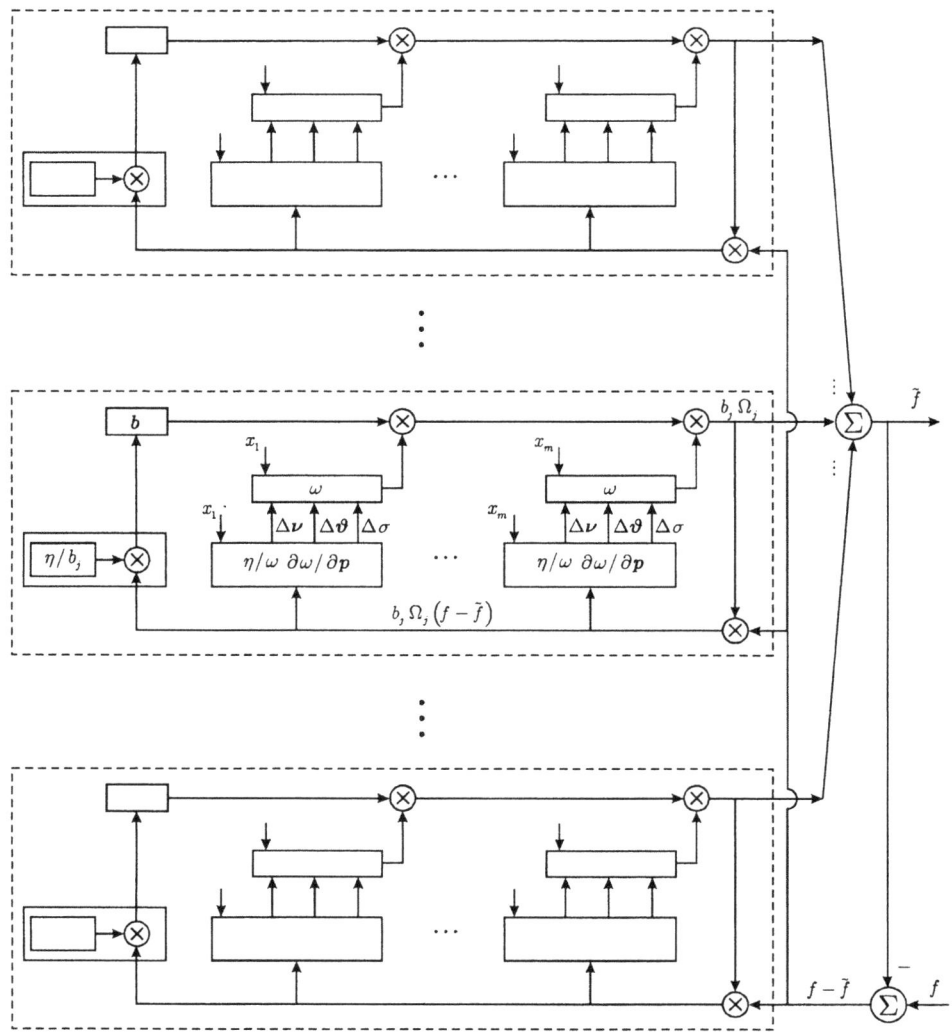

Figure 7. Schematic diagram of the steepest descent learning algorithm
$$\left(\boldsymbol{p}\equiv\left(\boldsymbol{\nu}_{_{J}},\boldsymbol{\vartheta}_{_{J}},\sigma_{_{J}}\right)\right)$$

1.7.3. Analog IC's Implementation of AINN's

Within the class of AI sequences, the functions $\delta_{_{\nu}}\left(x;\sigma\right)$, defined as the difference of two hyperbolic tangents, are particularly suitable for implementation with semiconductor devices and thus for exploiting the feasibility of VLSI neural networks.

Among different viable solutions the most promising are the ones which use Bipolar Junction Transistors (BJT's) and Metal-Oxide Silicon (MOS) devices. This is essentially due to the fact that the I-V characteristic of these largely used Integrated Circuits (IC's) solid-state devices are, under certain conditions, inherently exponential, thus making it possible to implement the $\delta_\nu(x;\sigma)$ function with a suitable combination of such devices.

Let us first consider AINN's implementation by Bipolar Junction Transistors. It is well known that BJT exhibits, under forward active mode [20], a collector-current I_C exponentially depending on the emitter-base voltage V_{BE}, *in formulae*

$$I_C = I_S \, e^{V_{BE}/v_T} \tag{1.36}$$

being I_S the saturation current of the emitter-base junction and v_T the thermal voltage. By assuming all transistors operate in such a condition, let us refer to the circuit of Fig. 8, which is made up of two differential BJT pairs Q1-Q2 and Q3-Q4, an input amplifier having a gain voltage of $-n$ and an output transresistance amplifier.

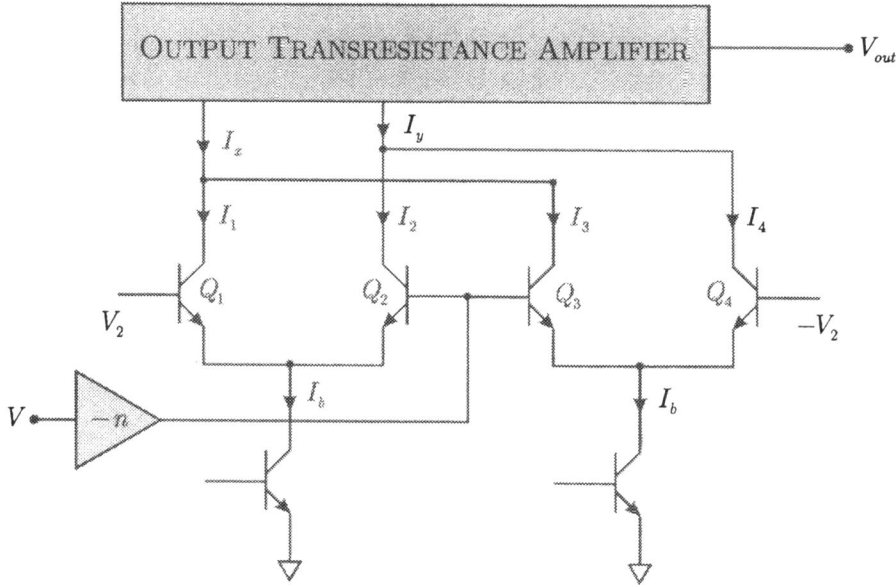

Figure 8. Schematic of the circuit for the implementation of the functions $\delta_\nu(x;\sigma)$

Using (1.36) for the currents I_1, I_2, I_3 and I_4, and assuming the output amplifier behaves linearly in the range of interest, it is straightforward to show that

$$V_{out} = A_R \left(I_x - I_y \right) = A_R I_b \left[\tanh \left(\frac{\nu V + V_\Delta}{2 v_T} \right) - \tanh \left(\frac{\nu V - V_\Delta}{2 v_T} \right) \right] \qquad (1.37)$$

where A_R is the transresistance gain of the output amplifier. Defining the normalized voltages $\sigma = V_\Delta / v_T$, $x = V / v_T$ and setting $A_R I_b = \nu / 4\sigma$, (1.37) expresses the same function as the one given by (1.19) and (1.20), showing that there is close correspondence between the AINN's mathematical model and circuits of the Fig.8 kind.

Metal-Oxide-Semiconductor-Field-Effect-Transistor (MOSFET) represents another valuable candidate for implementing neural networks by IC's technologies [15], especially because large size networks could be realized with small area occupancy, thanks to the high density integration capability of this technology.

Essentially, MOS transistors operating in the so-called sub-threshold regime and in saturation (i.e. with the gate potential less than the threshold voltage and the drain current non dependent on the drain voltage) behave like a BJT, that is with drain current I_D exponentially depending on the gate voltage V_G alone. Furthermore, the current in this region of operation is extremely low (it ranges from nearly 10^{-6} to 10^{-12} A), implying a remarkable advantage both in terms of power dissipation and integration density.

Thus the circuit of Fig.8, is adequate for neural networks implementation either using BJT or MOS transistors.

1.8.   Application Examples of AINN's

Neural networks and, in particular, AINN's are useful for solving problems in several fields of interest. In order to give an overview of the capabilities of such networks some case studies will be discussed in detail in this paragraph. The results of this section have been obtained with reference to a $\delta_\nu (x;\sigma)$ AINN, with $(3m + 1) \times n$ coefficients to be determined. Learning unknown parameters has been performed by solving an optimization problem with the steepest descent method, in which the partial derivatives in the Jacobian are numerically estimated.

1.8.1. Function Approximation

As a first example showing the AINN capability of learning measurable functions, we consider the approximation of a seventh degree polynomial

$$f(x) = x(x-1)^2(x-1.5)(x-3)^3 + 0.5x^2 .\tag{1.38}$$

Having chosen an approximating function $\tilde{f}$ with $n = 4$, the optimization algorithm based on a quasi-Newton method requires 80 iterations to reach an average percentage error, defined as $|f - \tilde{f}| / (f_{max} - f_{min}) \times 100$, of 0.96 %.

As an example of two-dimensional function approximation we refer to the so-called spiral function defined by

$$f(x,y) = \cos(\phi)\tag{1.39}$$

where

$$x = \rho \cos(\theta + \phi)$$
$$y = \rho \sin(\theta + \phi)\tag{1.40}$$
$$\rho = 0.2\,\theta$$

with $-1 \leq x \leq 1$, $-1 \leq y \leq 1$.

An average error of 2.08 % was achieved with a 10-neurons network, and it may be reduced by simply adding extra neurons to the network.

Another typical function for testing the approximating capabilities of a neural network, is the so-called "Mexican hat" function, which is expressed analytically as

$$f(x_1, x_2) = \left[2 - 4(x_1^2 + x_2^2)\right]\exp\left[-(x_1^2 + x_2^2)/0.72\right]\tag{1.41}$$

Figure 9 shows the shape of the function obtained with 530 points. A 4-neurons network gives rise to the approximating function reported in Fig. 10, with an average error on f of 0.12 %.

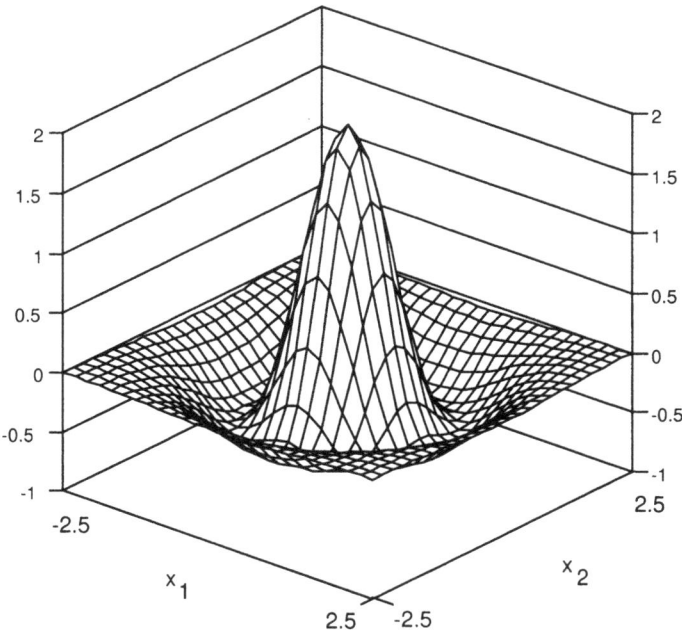

Figure 9.   The 'Mexican hat' function

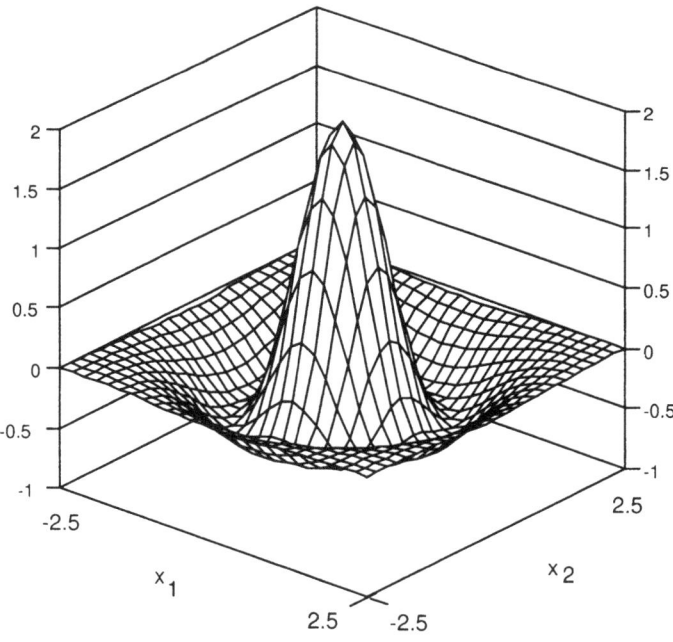

Figure 10.   The approximation of the 'Mexican hat' function with a 4-neurons AINN

Sensitivity to parameter variations

In analog neural network implementation the insensitiveness to parameter variations is of great concern. For this purpose the Root Mean Square Error (RMSE) defined as

$$RMSE = \left\{ \frac{1}{pq} \sum_{k=1}^{p} \sum_{j=1}^{q} \left[f_j\left(\boldsymbol{x}_k\right) - \tilde{f}_j\left(\boldsymbol{x}_k, \boldsymbol{w}\right) \right]^2 \right\}^{1/2} , \qquad (1.42)$$

where q is the output dimension and p is the number of the input patterns, may be assumed as a degree of insensitiveness.

As a result, the first example shows an RMSE of 0.122 corresponding to a parameter variation of 1 %. This value, if compared to the value of 0.098 achieved in the optimum point, proves that the network exhibits a low sensitivity to parameter variations. Also in the second and third example the sensitivity is low, since the RMSE increases from 0.061 to 0.078 and from 0.003 to 0.013, respectively, with the same parameter variation of 1 %. This means that analog circuit implementation of AINN allow parameter variations without appreciably affecting their expected behavior.

A comparison with other existing networks (RBF's and MLP's) has been made, in order to highlight some features of the proposed architecture. Figures 11 (a), (b), and (c) report the RMSE versus the number of parameters for the three networks considered in the examples of polynomial, spiral, and Mexican hat function, respectively.

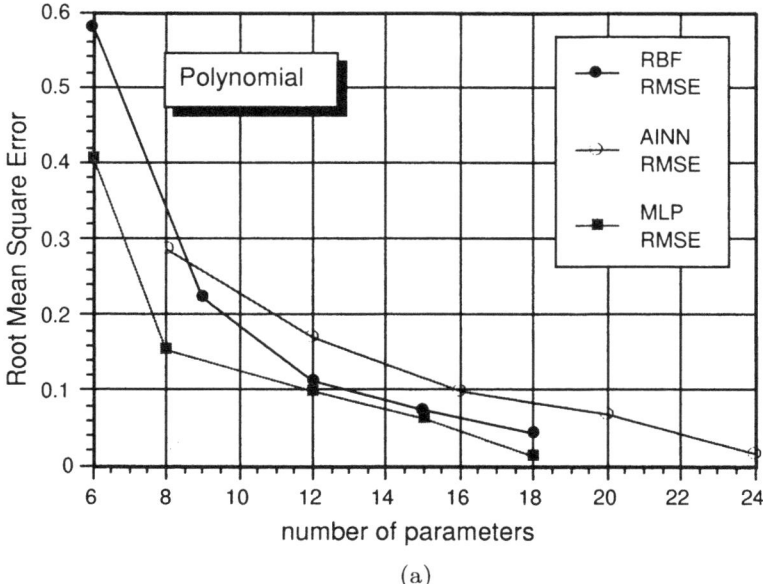

(a)

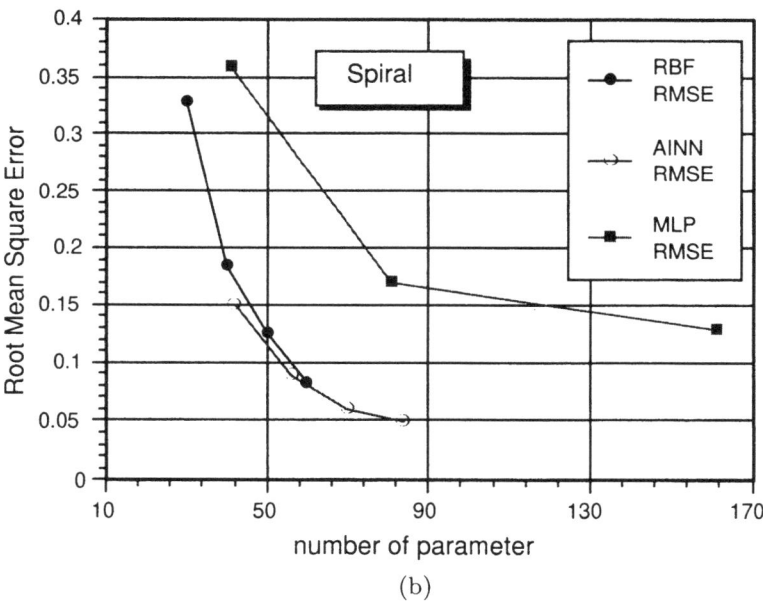

(b)

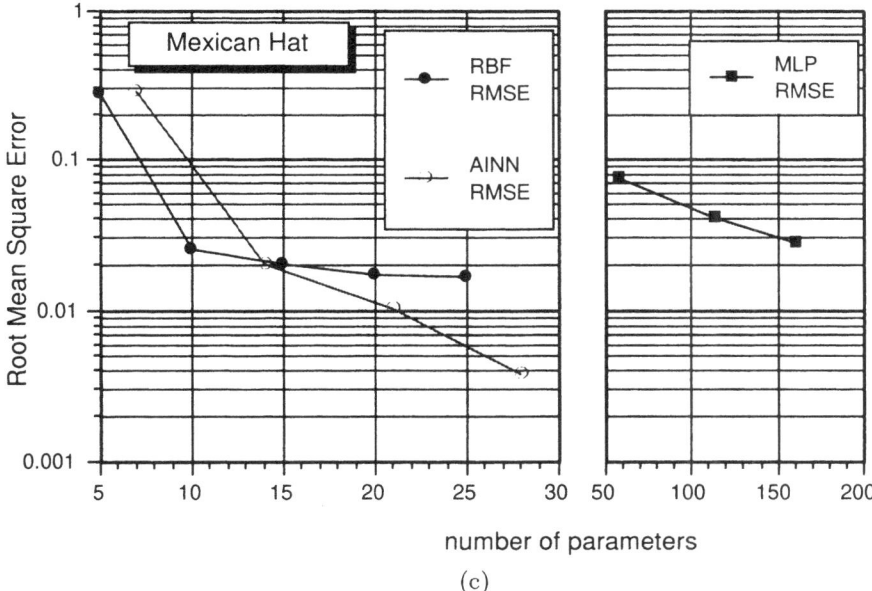

number of parameters

(c)

Figure 11. RMSE as a function of number of parameters for AINN compared with MLP and RBF for the examples: (a) polynomial function, (b) spiral function, (c) Mexican hat function.

1.8.2. Character Recognition

This case study deals with the recognition of the decimal numbers represented by 10 patterns on a 7×7 pixels array according to the PC-CGA graphic character set (see Fig. 12 (a)).

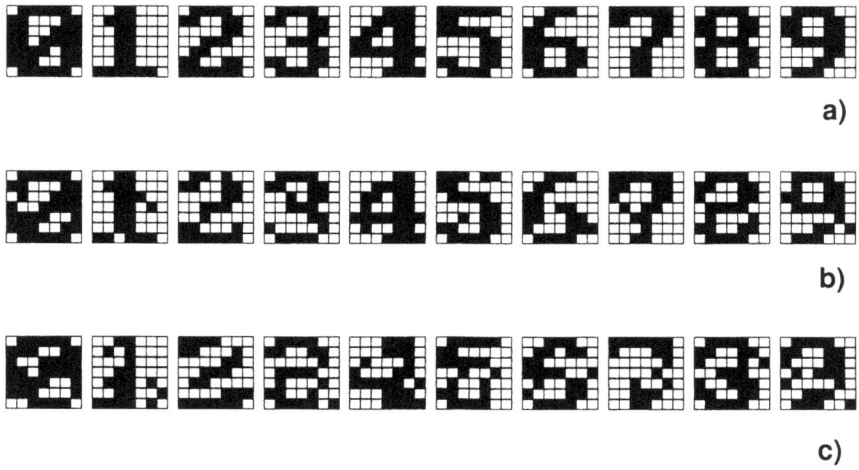

a)

b)

c)

Figure 12. Character recognition example input patterns of 7×7 pixels: (a) noiseless characters, (b) with 6% noise (HD = 3), (c) with 12% noise (HD = 6)

The architecture chosen for this application has a neuron with 1 output and 49 inputs for each pattern to be recognized, and a total number of 493 parameters to be set. To simplify learning and to improve the convergence rate without affecting accuracy, the parameters c_j, ν_{ij} and σ_{ij}, $i = 1, \cdots, 49$, $j = 1, \cdots, 10$ have been set to c, ν, and σ respectively, while choosing the centroids ϑ_{ij} of each neuron as the values of corresponding pixels of noiseless patterns. Thus the network has been trained with input patterns affected by a superimposed noise of 5 %, corresponding to an average Hamming Distance (HD) of 2.5. Figure 13 shows the RMSE as a function of the iteration number for the AINN under consideration, compared with the one achieved with a Multi-Layer Perceptron network having 773 weights initially set to trial values.

A more severe test may be performed, once the training stage is concluded, by increasing the noise superimposed on the patterns. The results of the test are shown in Table I. Each pattern with added noise is considered as *correctly recognized* provided the corresponding output is higher than a given threshold. On the contrary, it is *incorrectly recognized* when the output, although assuming a value above the threshold, does not correspond to the pattern with the superimposed noise. Finally the pattern is considered *rejected* if no outputs (indicated as "Rejected 0" in table 1) or more than one output (indicated as "Rejected +1") are higher than the threshold.

Figures 12 (b) and 12 (c) show noisy patterns with a Hamming Distances from noiseless characters of 3 and 6 respectively.

Table I

Approximate Identity Neural Network

	HD=0	1	2	3	4	5	6	7
Correctly Recogn.	10	195	499	991	998	0	0	0
Rejected 0	0	0	0	0	0	1000	999	1000
Rejected +1	0	5	1	9	2	0	1	0
Incorrectly Recogn.	0	0	0	0	0	0	0	0
Total	10	200	500	1000	1000	1000	1000	1000

Multi-Layer Perceptron

	HD=0	1	2	3	4	5	6	7
Correctly Recogn.	10	200	500	999	997	989	978	944
Rejected 0	0	0	0	0	0	7	13	32
Rejected +1	0	0	0	0	0	0	3	2
Incorrectly Recogn.	0	0	0	1	3	4	6	22
Total	10	200	500	1000	1000	1000	1000	1000

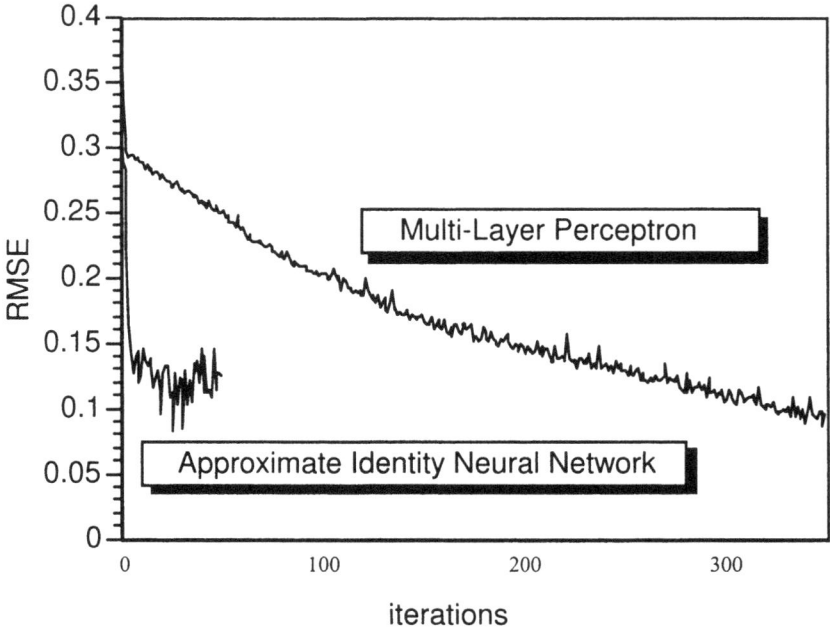

Figure 13. Root Mean Square Error as a function of iterations for AINN compared with Multi-Layer Perceptron Neural Network

1.8.3. Implementation of AINN's Using Analog BJT Circuits

In Sect.1.7.3 we showed a circuital configuration for the implementation of a neuron based on the $\delta_{\nu}(x;\sigma)$ function. Starting from this elementary circuit more complex networks may be built up to show the feasibility of analog solid-state AINN's.

Figure 14 shows the schematic diagram of an AINN with N neurons implemented with BJT's and Operational Amplifiers in a Printed Circuit Board (PCB). The main blocks of the circuit are: the N identical circuits that implement the $\delta_{\nu}(x;\sigma)$ elementary function in the summation (1.27), and the trasconductance amplifier that converts the difference $I_x - I_y$ to the output voltage V_{out}.

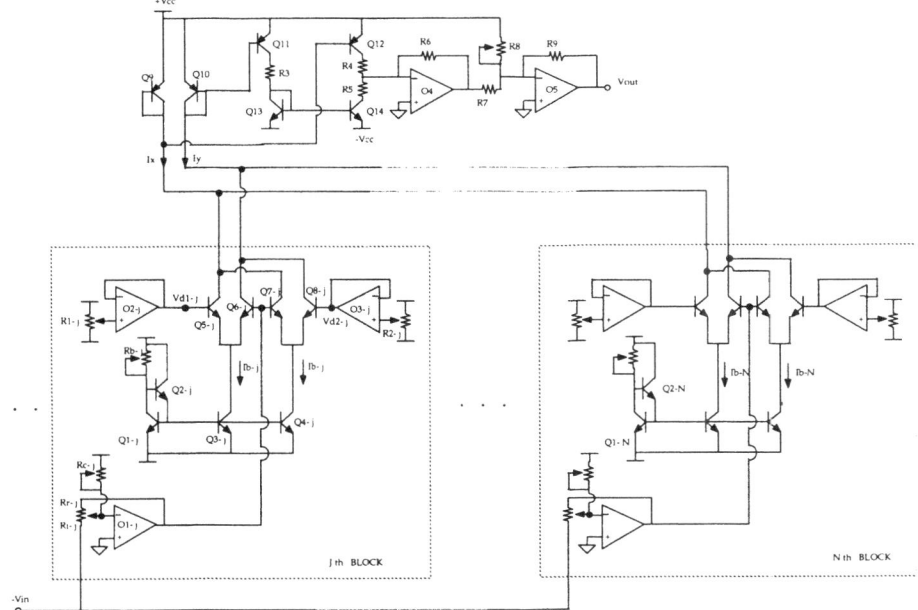

Figure 14. Schematic diagram of the PCB circuit for the synthesis of a typical wave of a piano note

The circuit, built up with standard components, has proven to be useful for the synthesis of a typical wave of a piano note with a fundamental frequency of 2 kHz. Four neurons suffice to achieve a desired average error less than 2 %, even though a smaller error may be obtained with a larger number of neurons.

Figures 15 show experimental data achieved from measurements on the PCB circuit. In particular the complete synthesized wave is reported in Fig. 15 (a) while Figs. 15 (b), (c), (d), and (e) report the four components corresponding to the four neurons of the neural network. Finally a comparison between the desired values of the piano note and the circuit response showing an average error of 1.6 % is reported in Fig. 16.

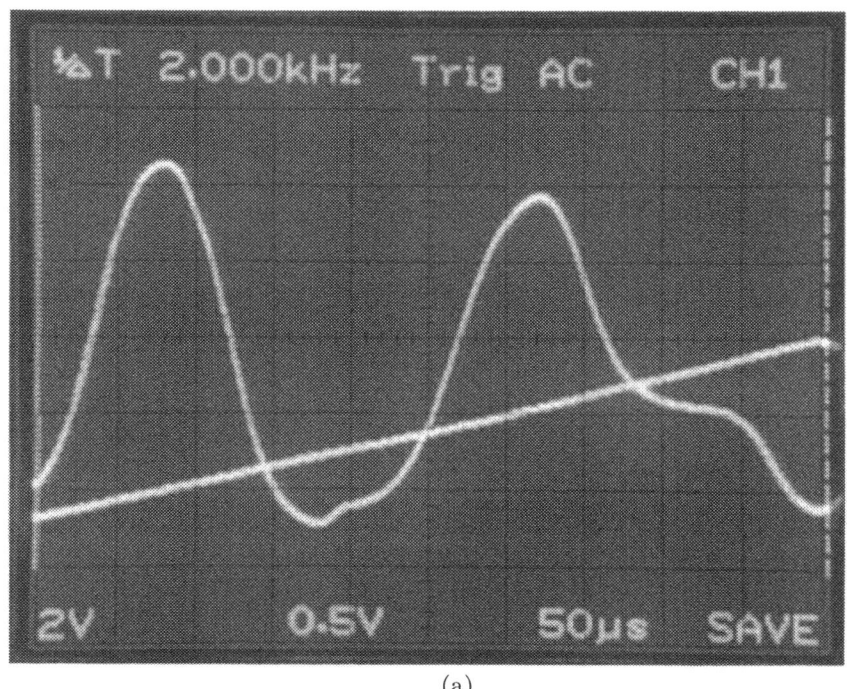

(a)

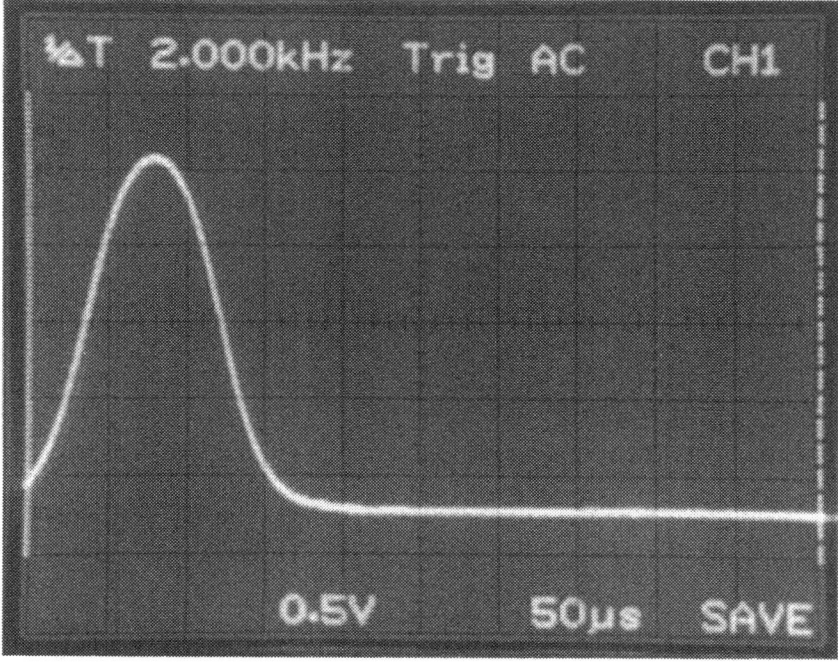

(b)

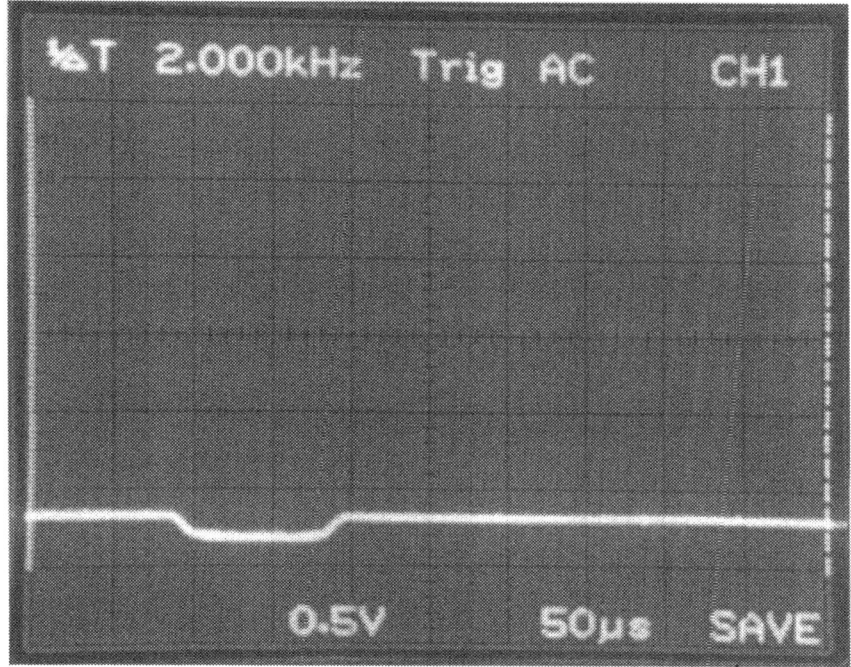

(c)

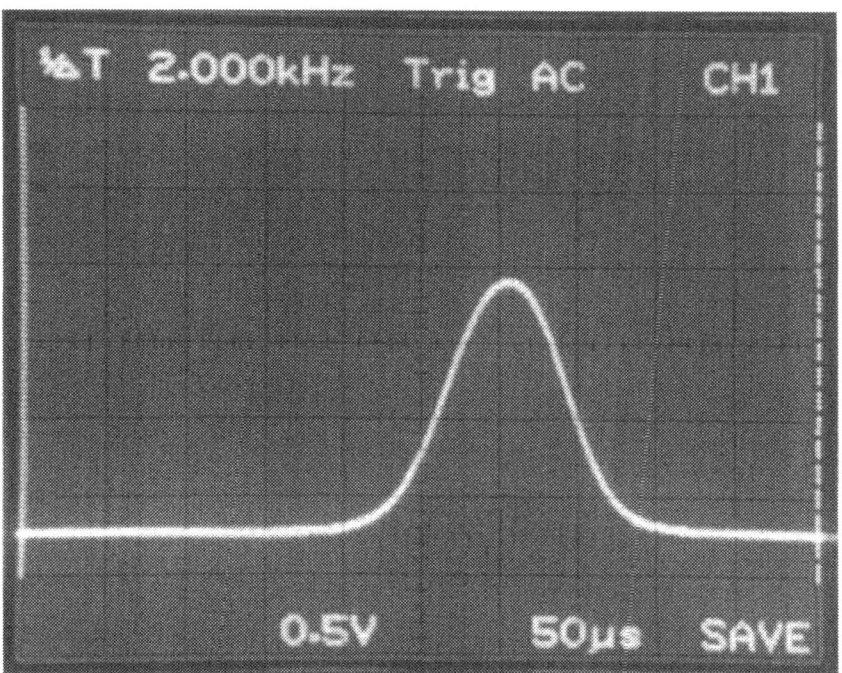

(d)

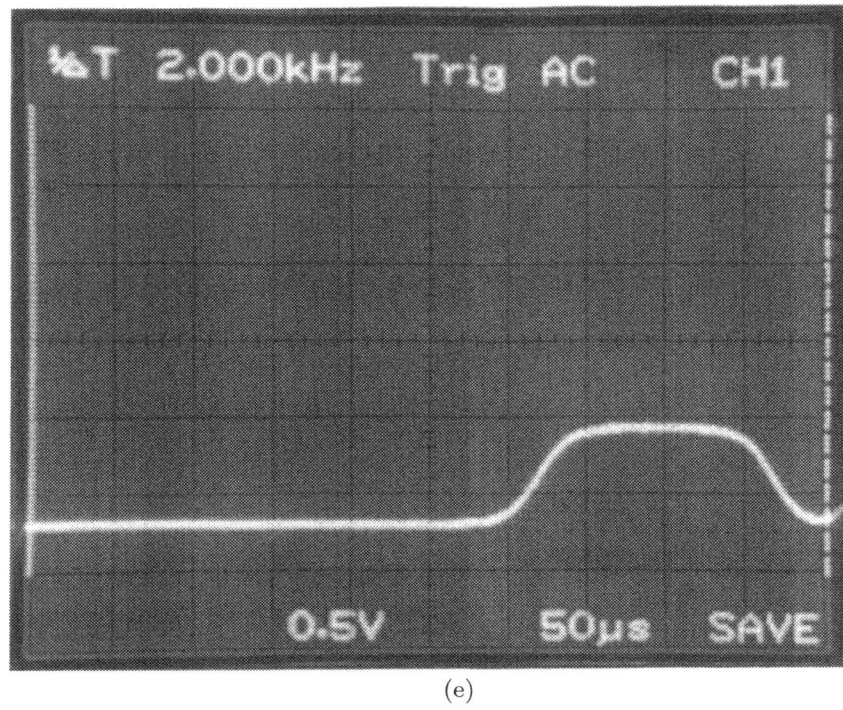

(e)

Figure 15. Experimental results showing (a) the approximation of the complete signal, (b), (c), (d), (e) the four components corresponding to the four neurons

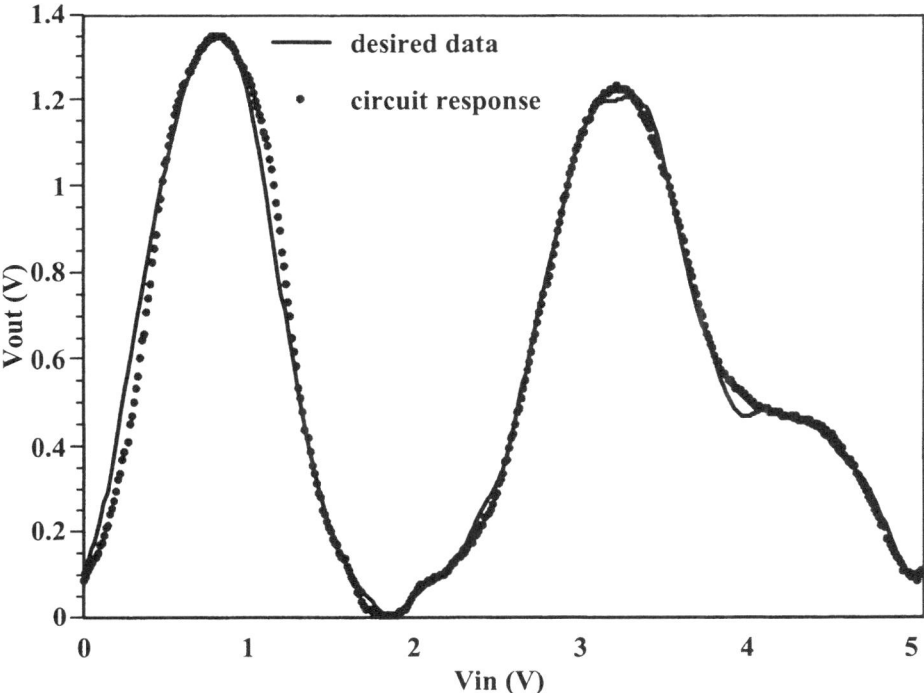

Figure 16. Comparison between circuit response and desired values

Appendix A

Proof of Theorem 1.2

We have to show that the set of functions $S_n(x)$ is dense in L_2, according to the definition reported in Appendix A of Chap. 2.

Let us consider the distance $\|f - S_n\|$ between f and S_n, we can write

$$\|f - S_n\| = \|f - f_\nu + f_\nu - S_n\| \leq \|f - f_\nu\| + \|f_\nu - S_n\| \tag{1.43}$$

where

$$f_\nu(x) = f * k_\nu = \int_{-\infty}^{+\infty} f(z) k_\nu(x - z) dz = \int_{-\infty}^{+\infty} g(x, z) dz \tag{1.44}$$

being $g(x, z)$ L_2-measurable for every t, as $f_\nu(x)$ is in class L_2 (see the statement of theorem 1.1).

From theorem 1.1, given $\varepsilon > 0$, a number ν exists such that

$$\|f - f_\nu\| < \varepsilon / 2 . \tag{1.45}$$

Now we want to show that it also results

$$\|f_\nu - S_n\| < \varepsilon / 2 . \tag{1.46}$$

From measurability of $g(x, z)$, it follows that for any $x \in T$ a sequence of *step functions* (or *simple functions*) $g_n(x, z)$ exist such that

$$\lim_{n \to \infty} g_n(x, z) = g(x, z) , \qquad \forall\, x \in T , \tag{1.47}$$

Here $g_n(x, z)$ is defined as

$$g_n(x, z) = \sum_{h=-\infty}^{+\infty} c_h \, \chi_{E_n^{(h)}}(z) , \qquad z \in \mathbb{R} \tag{1.48}$$

where $E_n^{(h)}$ are disjoint intervals of the real axis satisfying

$$\bigcup_h E_n^{(h)} \equiv \mathbb{R} \tag{1.49}$$

and

$$\chi_{E_n^{(h)}}(z) = \begin{cases} 1 & \text{if} \quad z \in E_n^{(h)} \\ 0 & \text{if} \quad z \notin E_n^{(h)} \end{cases} \tag{1.50}$$

is the *indicator* of $E_n^{(h)}$.

This is a known result of functional analysis, but for the reader's convenience proof of it will be reported in the following.

Suppose $g(x, z)$ is a measurable function and denoted by $\chi_n^{(h)}(z)$ the indicator of the (measurable) set

$$E_n^{(h)} = \left\{ \tau : \quad \frac{h}{2^n} \leq g(x, z) < \frac{h+1}{2^n} \right\} , \quad x \in T , \tag{1.51}$$

where h and $n > 0$ are integers defining a partition of the range of the function $g(x, z)$.

Let us set

$$f_n(z) = \sum_{h=-\infty}^{+\infty} \frac{h}{2^n} \chi_n^{(h)}(z) , \quad (n = 1, 2, \cdots) , \tag{1.52}$$

thus the functions $f_n(z)$ so defined are obviously simple functions. Furthermore $\left| g(x, z) - f_n(z) \right| < \frac{1}{2^n}$ and hence $\lim_{n \to \infty} f_n(z) = g(x, z)$.

With reference to the same partition, we consider the function

$$g_n(x, z) = \begin{cases} f(z_h) k_\nu (x - z_h) & z_h \in E_n^{(h)} \\ 0 & \text{otherwise} \end{cases} \tag{1.53}$$

which can also be written as

$$g_n(x, z) = \sum_{h=-\infty}^{+\infty} f(z_h) k_\nu (x - z_h) \chi_n^{(h)}(z) . \tag{1.54}$$

where z_h is any point of $E_n^{(h)}$. Thus it is easy to show that

$$\left| g(x, z) - g_n(x, z) \right| < \frac{1}{2^n} \tag{1.55}$$

since for $z = z_h$ we have

$$\frac{h}{2^n} \leq g(x, z_h) < \frac{h+1}{2^n}, \tag{1.56}$$

and thus

$$\lim_{n \to \infty} g_n(x, z) = g(x, z) \ . \tag{1.57}$$

From the definition of integral (see e.g. [12]) it results

$$
\begin{aligned}
\int_T g(x, z)\, dz &= \lim_{n \to \infty} \int_T g_n(x, z)\, dz \\
&= \lim_{n \to \infty} \int_T \sum_{h=-\infty}^{+\infty} f(z_h) k_\nu(x - z_h) \chi_n^{(h)}(z)\, dz \\
&= \lim_{n \to \infty} \sum_{h=-n}^{+n} \int_T f(z_h) k_\nu(x - z_h) \chi_n^{(h)}(z)\, dz \\
&= \lim_{n \to \infty} \sum_{h=-n}^{+n} f(z_h) k_\nu(x - z_h) \Delta z_h^{(n)}
\end{aligned}
\tag{1.58}
$$

where $\Delta z_h^{(n)}$ is the measure of the interval $E_n^{(h)}$. Putting $a_h^{(n)} = f(z_h) \Delta z_h^{(n)}$ we can write

$$
\begin{aligned}
S_n(x) &= \sum_{h=-n}^{+n} f(z_h) k_\nu(x - z_h) \Delta z_h^{(n)} \\
&= \sum_{h=-n}^{+n} a_h^{(n)} k_\nu(x - z_h)
\end{aligned}
\tag{1.59}
$$

Hereinafter the index n on $a_h^{(n)}$ will be omitted and the dependence on n implicitly assumed

$$S_n(x) = \sum_{h=-n}^{+n} a_h\, k_\nu(x - z_h) \ . \tag{1.60}$$

From the above relationships it follows

$$f(x) = \int_T g(x, z)\, d\tau = \lim_{n \to \infty} S_n(x) \ . \tag{1.61}$$

As the uniform convergence implies convergence in m.s. (see the note at the end of Appendix), thus given $\varepsilon > 0$ an index $N(\varepsilon, \nu)$ can be chosen such that for $n > N$ it results

$$\left\| f_\nu(x) - S_n(x) \right\| < \varepsilon / 2 \ , \tag{1.62}$$

so that we get

$$\left\| f - f_\nu \right\| + \left\| f_\nu - S_n \right\| < \varepsilon / 2 + \varepsilon / 2 = \varepsilon \ , \tag{1.63}$$

and this concludes the proof of the theorem.

It is worth noting that the index N depends not only on ε but also on ν, and since ν is itself dependent on ε we have

$$N\left(\varepsilon, \nu\left(\varepsilon\right)\right) . \tag{1.64}$$

Once the relationship $\nu\left(\varepsilon\right)$ is determined from

$$\left\| f - f_\nu \right\| < \varepsilon / 2 \tag{1.65}$$

the dependence $N\left(\varepsilon, \nu\left(\varepsilon\right)\right)$ on ε is known by

$$\left\| f_\nu\left(x\right) - S_n\left(x\right) \right\| < \varepsilon / 2 . \tag{1.66}$$

NOTE

If the sequence $h_n\left(x\right)$ converges uniformly to $h\left(x\right)$, then for any ε there exists N such that $n > N$, $\left| h\left(x\right) - h_n\left(x\right) \right| < \varepsilon$ for all x in $[a,b]$. Therefore

$$\int_a^b \left| h\left(x\right) - h_n\left(x\right) \right|^2 dx < \int_a^b \varepsilon^2 dx = \varepsilon^2\left(b - a\right) \tag{1.67}$$

so the integral can be made arbitrarily small by the choice of ε. This is just the statement that

$$\lim_{n \to \infty} \int_a^b \left| h\left(x\right) - h_n\left(x\right) \right|^2 dx = 0 . \tag{1.68}$$

or, with the notation currently used in functional analysis

$$\underset{n \to \infty}{\text{l.i.m.}} \, h_n\left(x\right) = h\left(x\right) . \tag{1.69}$$

References

[1]   Kohonen, T. (1988). *Self-Organisation and Associative Memory.* Germany: Springer-Verlag.

[2]   Poggio, T. & Girosi, F. (1990). *Networks for Approximation and Learning.* Proceedings of IEEE, 78 (9), 1481–1497.

[3]   Cybenko, G. (1989). *Approximation by Superposition of Sigmoidal Function.* Math. Control, Systems, Signal, 2, 303–314.

[4]   Funahashi, K. (1989). *On the Approximate Realisation of Continuous Mappings by Neural Networks.* Neural Networks, 2, 183–192.

[5]   Hornik, K., Stinchcombe, M., & White, H. (1989). *Multilayer Feedforward Networks are Universal Approximators.* Neural Networks, 2, 395–403.

[6]   Park, J., & Sandberg, I. W. (1991). *Universal Approximation Using Radial-Basis-Function Networks.* Neural Computation, 3, 246–257.

[7]   Conti, M., & Turchetti, C. (1994). *Approximation of Dynamical Systems by Continuous-Time Recurrent Approximate Identity Neural Networks.* Neural, Parallel & Scientific Computations, 2, 299–322.

[8]   Conti, M., Orcioni, S., & Turchetti, C. (1994). *A Class of Neural Networks Based on Approximate Identity for Analog IC's Hardware Implementation.* IEICE Transactions on Fundamentals of Electronics, Communications and Computer Sciences, E77-A (6), 1069–1079.

[9]   Doob, J. L. (1990). *Stochastic Processes.* New York: John Wiley & Sons.

[10] Gihman, I. I., & Skorohod, A.V. (1974). *The Theory of Stochastic Processes.* Berlin: Springer-Verlag.

[11] Prohorov, Y. V., & Rozanov, Y. A. (1969). *Probability Theory.* Berlin: Springer-Verlag.

[12] Halmos, P. R. (1974). *Measure Theory.* New York: Springer-Verlag.

[13] Wheeden, R. L., & Zygmund, A. (1977). *Measure and Integral.* New York: Marcel Dekker.

[14] Rumelhart, D. E., Hinton, G. E., & Williams, R. J. (1986). *Learning Internal Representations by Error Propagation.* In Rumelhart & McClelland (Eds.), *Parallel Distributed Processing: Exploration in Microstructures of Cognition,* Vol. 1: Foundations. MIT Press, Cambridge MA.

[15] Mead, C. (1989). *Analog VLSI and Neural Systems,* Reading MA: Addison-

Wesley Publishing Company.

[16] Ismail, M., & Fiez, T. (1994). *Analog VLSI – Signal and Information Processing.* New York: McGraw Hill.

[17] Ramacher, U., & Rückert, U. (1991). *VLSI Design of Neural Networks.* Boston MA: Kluwer Academic Publishers.

[18] Schemmel, J., Shurmann, F., Hohmann, S., & Meier, K. (2002). *An Integrated Mixed-Mode Neural Network Architecture for Megasynapse ANNs.* Proceedings of the International Joint Conference on Neural Networks, Vol. 3, 2704–2709, Honululu HI, May 2002.

[19] Ota, Y. (2002). *VLSI Structure for Static Image Processing with Pulse-Coupled Neural Network.* Proceedings of the 28th Annual Conference of the Industrial Electronics Society IECON 02, Vol. 4, 3221–3226, Sevilla, Spain, Nov. 2002.

[20] Gray, P. R., & Meyer, R. G. (1984). *Analog Integrated Circuits,* New York: John Wiley & Sons.

Stochastic Models of Neural Networks
C. Turchetti
IOS Press, 2004

The generation of random numbers is too
important to be left to chance.

Robert R. Coveyou, Oak Ridge National
Laboratory

CHAPTER TWO

RANDOM PROCESSES

This chapter introduces, in a non exhaustive way, some fundamental concepts and results of the *stochastic process* theory not commonly available in standard texts. As a result, the theorem due to Karhunen (1947) establishing a *canonical representation* for processes belonging to a wide class of nonstationary processes is stated and demonstrated.

Such a representation constitutes the model that will be used in subsequent chapters for the definition of *stochastic neural networks*, thus assuming a central role in the theory of this class of neural networks.

For a complete treatment of this subject some good references are the books by Doob(1962), Cramer and Leadbetter (1967), Gihman and Skorohod (1974).

2.1.   Basic Concept of Probability Theory

2.1.1. The Probability Space

The probability theory is a mathematical apparatus dealing with numbers associated to *events*. The problem of experimentally determining such numbers is no concern of the theory being an estimation issue. Intuitively, an event is one of the possible outcomes (or elementary events) of an experiment. Refer, as an example, to the classical throw of an ordinary six-sided die. Several different events can be defined in this particular experiment, each one resulting as a *set* of elementary events (for instance the event "The number on the top face of the die is even" include three elementary events). Thus *set theory* plays a central role in probability theory.

In the language of set theory, the totality of admissible events represents a class **S** of sets.

Thus, for instance, if E is a set and **S** is a class of sets,

$$E \in \mathbf{S} \qquad (2.1)$$

means that the set E belongs to (is a member of, is an element of) the class **S**.

Hereinafter we will use the usual symbols $\cup$, $\cap$, E', $\in$ for union, intersection, complementing, and belonging respectively, and the symbol $\mathbb{R}$ for the set of real numbers.

The class of admissible events **S** must satisfy some properties of consistency. In particular denoting with Ω the space of all elementary events ω that may occur, $\omega \in \Omega$, the following properties hold:

a)   the space of elementary events Ω belongs to **S**: $\Omega \in \mathbf{S}$;

b)   if a subspace E of Ω belongs to **S**, then so its complement:
$E \in \mathbf{S} \Rightarrow E' \in \mathbf{S}$;

c)   if a countable number of subsets belongs to **S**, then so is their union:
$E_i \in \mathbf{S} \Rightarrow \bigcup\limits_{i=1}^{\infty} E_i \in \mathbf{S}$.

In the set theory such a class, **S**, is called a σ-*algebra* of sets (or a Boolean σ-algebra of sets) and the pair $(\Omega, \mathbf{S})$ is called a *measurable space*. Recall that a

σ-algebra differs from an *algebra* in that the former is closed under formation of countable infinite unions, while the latter is only closed under finite unions. It is worth noticing that for situations concerning simple gambling games such as the rolling die, in which the total number of possible events is finite, an algebra is adequate, while in more general situations it is necessary to refer to a σ-algebra.

Thus in consequence of the above considerations we maintain that the probability theory consists of the study of the σ-algebra of sets (some authors use the term Borel field).

As mentioned at the beginning of the chapter, the probability of a certain event is a number associated with the event. In other words, probability is a numerically valued function $\mathcal{P}$ of events E, (the sets of a σ-algebra). The function $\mathcal{P}$ cannot be completely arbitrary, being subject to the condition of additivity for disjoint sets and to the values 0 and 1 for the empty set $\varnothing$ and the certain event Ω, respectively.

Formally

a) $\mathcal{P}(\varnothing) = 0$;

b) $\mathcal{P}(\Omega) = 1$;

c) $\mathcal{P}\left(\bigcup_{i=1}^{\infty} E_i\right) = \sum_{i=1}^{\infty} \mathcal{P}(E_i)$, if all $E_i \in \mathbf{S}$ are disjoint sets, i.e. $E_i \cap E_j = \varnothing$

for all $i \neq j$.

In mathematical language the function $\mathcal{P} : \mathbf{S} \rightarrow [0,1]$ so defined is a *measure* and is called a *probability measure* defined on $(\Omega, \mathbf{S})$. Accordingly, numerical probability is a measure $\mathcal{P}$ on a σ-algebra $\mathbf{S}$ of subsets of a set Ω, such that $\mathcal{P}(\Omega) = 1$.

From the above considerations we conclude that probability theory is, from a mathematical point of view, a branch of measure theory. The three entities Ω, $\mathbf{S}$, and $\mathcal{P}$ together, that is the triple $(\Omega, \mathbf{S}, \mathcal{P})$, is called a *probability space*.

To sum up we give the following

Definition 2.1 -   A space of elementary events or probability space $(\Omega, \mathbf{S}, \mathcal{P})$ is a measurable space of elements $\omega \in \Omega$ that are called *elementary events* or *elementary outcomes*, together with a probability measure $\mathcal{P}(A)$ on the σ-algebra $\mathbf{S}$ ($A \in \mathbf{S}$) such that it results:

$$\mathcal{P}(\Omega) = 1 \ . \tag{2.2}$$

The set A is called event, while $\mathcal{P}(A)$ is the *probability* of the event A.

2.1.2. Random Variables

Let $(X, \mathbf{B})$ be a measurable space (or *phase space*), i.e. a set X and a σ-algebra $\mathbf{B}$.

Definition 2.2 - A complex-valued measurable function $x = x(\omega) : \Omega \to X$, on the space of the elementary events $(\Omega, \mathbf{S}, \mathcal{P})$ with values in $(X, \mathbf{B})$ is called a *random variable* (r.v) in the phase space $(X, \mathbf{B})$.

Figure 17 depicts the correspondence established by mapping $x = x(\omega) : \Omega \to X$.

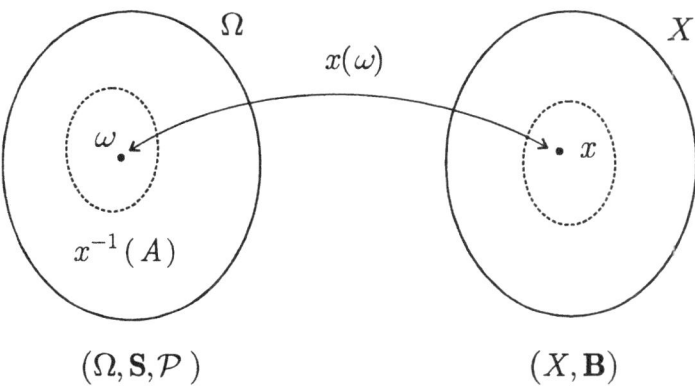

Figure 17. Mapping between the space of elementary events $(\Omega, \mathbf{S}, \mathcal{P})$ *and the measurable space* $(X, \mathbf{B})$ *induced by the random variable* $x(\omega)$

By the probability distribution of this r.v. x we mean the set function $\mathcal{P}_x = \mathcal{P}_x(A)$ on the σ-algebra $\mathbf{B}$ of the phase-space, defined by

$$\mathcal{P}_x(A) = \mathcal{P}\left\{\omega \,\Big|\, x(\omega) \in A\right\}, \qquad A \in \mathbf{B}. \tag{2.3}$$

The probability distribution $\mathcal{P}_x$ represents a probability measure in the phase space $(X, \mathbf{B})$. The previous relationship may also be rewritten

$$\mathcal{P}_x(A) = \mathcal{P}\{x^{-1}(A)\} \tag{2.4}$$

where $x^{-1}(A)$ is the *inverse image* of the set A.

Thus given the probability measure $\mathcal{P}$ on the σ-algebra **S**, the transformation $x(\omega)$ induces a measure $\mathcal{P}_x$ (*induced measure* or *measure induced by* $\mathcal{P}$) on the σ-algebra **B**.

The definition of probability distribution implies that the measure of A is equal to the one of $x^{-1}(A)$. Figure 18 shows a graphical interpretation of these concepts in the case of one-dimensional function.

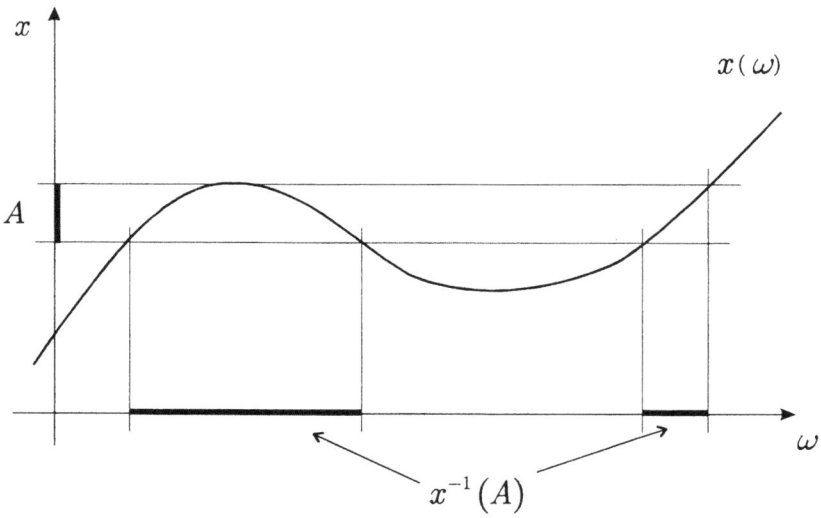

Figure 18. The inverse image $x^{-1}(A)$ of the set A through the transformation $x(\omega)$

Note that measurability of $x(\omega)$ is necessary to ensure that to every measurable set A, a measurable set $x^{-1}(A)$ corresponds. Equivalently a measurable function $x(\omega)$ has the property that for every λ the set

$$\left\{\omega \,\middle|\, x(\omega) \le \lambda\right\} \tag{2.5}$$

is measurable.

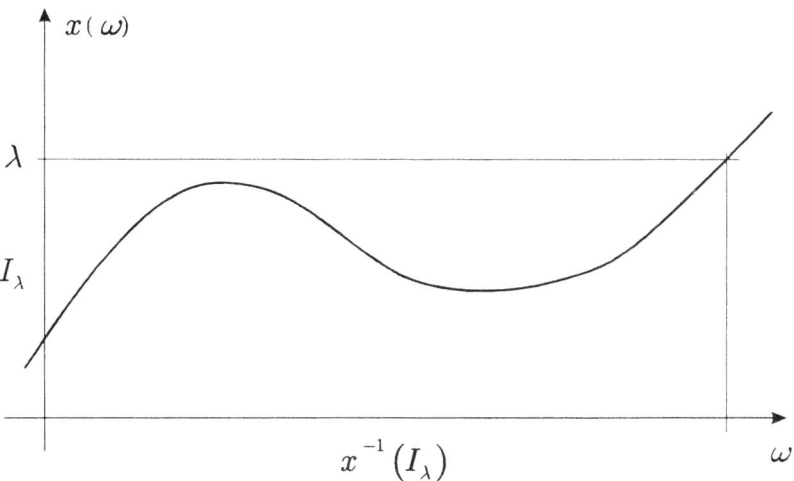

Figure 19.   The set I_λ and its inverse image $x^{-1}(I_\lambda)$ through the transformation

$$x(\omega)$$

Thus it results

$$\mathcal{P}_x\{x \le \lambda\} = \mathcal{P}\{\omega \mid x(\omega) \le \lambda\} \tag{2.6}$$

or

$$\mathcal{P}_x(I_\lambda) = \mathcal{P}\left(x^{-1}(I_\lambda)\right), \tag{2.7}$$

by putting

$$I_\lambda = \{x \le \lambda\}, \quad x^{-1}(I_\lambda) = \{\omega \mid x \in I_\lambda\}. \tag{2.8}$$

The sets I_λ and $x^{-1}(I_\lambda)$ are shown with reference to the r.v. $x(\omega)$ in Fig. 19. The probability $\mathcal{P}\left(x^{-1}(I_\lambda)\right)$ defines a non-decreasing function of λ by

$$\mathcal{P}_x\{x(\omega) \le \lambda\} = F(\lambda) \tag{2.9}$$

since it results $F(\lambda_1) \le F(\lambda_2)$, $\lambda_1 < \lambda_2$. An example of $F(\lambda)$ behavior is given in Fig. 20.

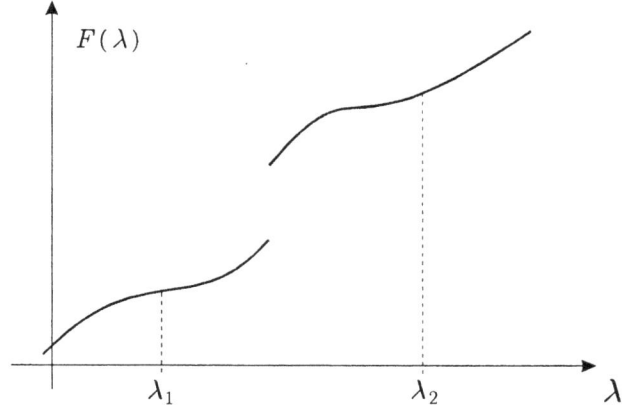

Figure 20. Typical behavior of the function $F(\lambda)$

For a finite right-open interval $\Delta\lambda = [\lambda_1, \lambda_2)$ we have

$$\mathcal{P}_x\{\lambda_1 \leq x < \lambda_2\} = F(\lambda_2) - F(\lambda_1) = \int_{\lambda_1}^{\lambda_2} dF(\lambda) = \mu(\Delta\lambda) \qquad (2.10)$$

where the integral is a Stieltjes integral (see Appendix A for its definition). Such a function defines a *Stieltjes probability measure* $\mu(\Delta\lambda)$ of sets $\Delta\lambda = [\lambda_1, \lambda_2)$.

Provided $F(\lambda)$ is absolutely continuous, that is, the number of points at which $F(\cdot)$ is not differentiable is countable, then

$$dF(\lambda) = f(\lambda)d\lambda , \qquad (2.11)$$

at all λ at which the derivative exists, and

$$F(\lambda) = \int_{-\infty}^{\lambda} f(\mu)d\mu . \qquad (2.12)$$

$F(\lambda)$ is called distribution function of the r.v. $x(\omega)$, while $f(\lambda)$ is the *probability density function (pdf)*.

Obviously all these concepts can be generalized in the case of multivariate random variables, and the reader is referred to specialized books for a complete treatment of this subject.

2.1.3. Characteristic Function

Let x be an r.v. with pdf $f_X(x)$. The *characteristic function* of x, $\Phi_X(u)$, is defined by

$$\Phi_X(u) = E\left\{e^{iux}\right\} = \int_{-\infty}^{+\infty} e^{iux} f_X(x)\, dx \qquad (2.13)$$

where u is arbitrary and has real values, and $E\{\cdot\}$ denotes the expectation. Therefore the characteristic function $\Phi_X(u)$ simply represents the Fourier-Transform (FT) of the pdf $f_X(x)$. Since a density function is absolutely integrable, its associated characteristic function always exists. The density function is uniquely determined in terms of characteristic function by the inverse FT

$$f_X(x) = \frac{1}{2\pi}\int_{-\infty}^{+\infty} e^{-iux}\Phi_X(u)\, du \; , \qquad (2.14)$$

so that the functions $\Phi_X(u)$ and $f_X(x)$ form a Fourier-Transform pair.

The one-dimensional *Gaussian* or *Normal* density is defined in terms of the expectation m and the variance σ^2 as

$$f_X(x) = \frac{1}{\sigma(2\pi)^{1/2}}\, e^{-\frac{(x-m)^2}{2\sigma^2}} \qquad (2.15)$$

and its characteristic function is given by

$$\Phi_X(u) = \frac{1}{\sigma(2\pi)^{1/2}}\int_{-\infty}^{+\infty} e^{iux} e^{-\frac{(x-m)^2}{2\sigma^2}}\, dx \; . \qquad (2.16)$$

Defining the new variable

$$\omega = \frac{x-m}{\sqrt{2\pi}\sigma} \; , \qquad (2.17)$$

the integral in (2.16) reduces to

$$\begin{aligned}
\Phi_X(u) &= e^{ium}\int_{-\infty}^{+\infty} e^{i\left(u\sqrt{2\pi}\sigma\right)\omega} e^{-\pi\omega^2}\, d\omega \\
&= e^{ium}\int_{-\infty}^{+\infty} e^{i2\pi t\omega} e^{-\pi\omega^2}\, d\omega
\end{aligned} \qquad (2.18)$$

where

$$t = u \frac{\sigma}{\sqrt{2\pi}} \, . \tag{2.19}$$

By using the well known correspondence

$$\mathfrak{F}\left\{e^{-\pi t^2}\right\} \rightleftarrows e^{-\pi \omega^2} \, , \tag{2.20}$$

where $\mathfrak{F}\{\cdot\}$ denotes the FT, (2.18) results in

$$\Phi_X(u) = \exp\left[imu - \frac{1}{2}\sigma^2 u^2\right] \, . \tag{2.21}$$

Random variables $x_1, \cdots, x_n$ are called Gaussian or Normally distributed, if the joint density is of the form

$$f_X(\boldsymbol{x}) = f_{X_1, \cdots, X_n}(x_1, \cdots, x_n) = \frac{(\det \mathbf{C})^{1/2}}{(2\pi)^{n/2}} \exp\left[-\frac{1}{2}\sum_{k,j=1}^{n} c_{kj}(x_k - m_k)(x_j - m_j)\right] \tag{2.22}$$

where $m_k = E\{x_k\}$, and the matrix $\mathbf{C} = [c_{kj}]$ with determinant $\det \mathbf{C}$ is the inverse of the $n \times n$ covariance matrix $\boldsymbol{\Lambda} = [b_{kj}]$ of $\boldsymbol{x}$ defined by

$$b_{kj} = E\left\{(x_k - m_k)(x_j - m_j)\right\} \, . \tag{2.23}$$

In matrix form

$$f_X(\boldsymbol{x}) = \frac{(2\pi)^{-n/2}}{(\det \boldsymbol{\Lambda})^{1/2}} \exp\left[-\frac{1}{2}(\boldsymbol{x} - \boldsymbol{m})^T \boldsymbol{\Lambda}^{-1}(\boldsymbol{x} - \boldsymbol{m})\right] \tag{2.24}$$

with

$$\boldsymbol{m}^T = [m_1, \cdots, m_n] \, . \tag{2.25}$$

The joint characteristic function is then given by

$$\Phi_X(\boldsymbol{u}) = \exp\left[i\,\boldsymbol{m}^T\boldsymbol{u} - \frac{1}{2}\boldsymbol{u}^T\boldsymbol{\Lambda}\boldsymbol{u}\right] \, . \tag{2.26}$$

2.1.4. The Hilbert Space of Square-Integrable Random Variables

The theory of *Hilbert spaces* plays a fundamental role in functional analysis and its mathematical development is so well established that plenty of results widely applicable in several fields have been derived so far.

Among others, many problems concerning stochastic processes can be treated as problems in the geometry of Hilbert space, so that the theory of random processes may benefit from this powerful mathematical tool.

As is well-known, a Hilbert space is an *inner product vector space* which, as a metric space, is complete. Thus the first item to be defined, in order to treat random variables as elements of a Hilbert space, is the inner product between two r.v.'s.

Consider a fixed probability space $(\Omega, \mathbf{S}, \mathcal{P})$. A complex-valued r.v. $x = x(\omega)$ defined on this space is *square integrable* if

$$E\{x\} = 0 , \quad E\{|x|^2\} < \infty . \tag{2.27}$$

The set of square-integrable r.v.'s together with addition and scalar multiplication defined in the obvious way, form a *vector space* $\mathbf{H}$. The inner product of two r.v.'s x and y is defined by the relation

$$\langle x, y \rangle_{\mathcal{P}} = E\{x\bar{y}\} \tag{2.28}$$

where the bar denotes the conjugate complex quantity, and the norm of the variable x is

$$\|x\| = \langle x, \bar{x} \rangle_{\mathcal{P}}^{1/2} = E\{|x|^2\}^{1/2} . \tag{2.29}$$

If two variables x_1 and x_2 are such that

$$E\left\{|x_1 - x_2|^2\right\} = 0 , \tag{2.30}$$

x_1 and x_2 are 'almost' the same in the sense that $x_1 = x_2$ with probability one

$$\mathcal{P}(x_1 = x_2) = 1 . \tag{2.31}$$

This statement means that r.v.'s x_1, x_2 are equal in the entire space of the definition except for a set of $\mathcal{P}$-measure zero. Then x_1 and x_2 are said to be *equivalent* r.v.'s and we write $x_1 = x_2$ a.s. (almost surely).

Having defined the inner product, it follows that the distance between two r.v.'s x and y is

$$d(x,y) = \|x - y\| = \left[E\left\{ (x-y)^2 \right\} \right]^{1/2} . \qquad (2.32)$$

The other property to be dealt with in defining a Hilbert space is the *completeness*, which is related to the concept of the convergence of sequences.

According to the definition of distance given above, we say that a sequence x_n converges to x if $d(x_n, x) \to 0$ i.e. if $E\left\{ (x_n - x)^2 \right\} \to 0$.

This kind of convergence is called convergence in *quadratic mean (q.m)* or *mean square (m.s.)*, and formally is stated by the following

Definition 2.3 -   A sequence of r.v.'s $\{x_n\}$ converges in m.s. to an r.v. x as $n \to \infty$ if

$$\lim_{n \to \infty} \|x_n - x\| = 0 . \qquad (2.33)$$

Convergence in m.s. is often expressed by

$$x_n \xrightarrow{\text{m.s.}} x \qquad \text{or} \qquad \underset{n \to \infty}{\text{l.i.m.}} \ x_n = x \qquad (2.34)$$

where the symbol l.i.m. denotes the limit in quadratic mean.

Finally, it can be shown that the space **H** of square-integrable r.v.'s is *complete* in the norm defined above, meaning that for every sequence of points x_1, x_2, $\cdots$ such that $\|x_m - x_n\| \to 0$ as $m, n \to \infty$, there is a point $x \in \mathbf{H}$ such that $\|x_n - x\| \to 0$.

Since to prove completeness is a difficult task, the reader interested in the proof is referred to Kingman [9].

Thus we say that the set **H** of all square-integrable random variables will form a Hilbert space, the *Hilbert space of second order r.v.'s*, which is often denoted by $L_2(\Omega, \mathbf{S}, \mathcal{P})$ or just $L_2(\mathcal{P})$.

2.1.5. Second-Order Stochastic Processes as Curves in Hilbert Space

Let us consider complex-valued random variables $\varphi = \varphi(\omega)$ defined on a fixed probability space $(\Omega, \mathbf{S}, \mathcal{P})$. A *stochastic process* (s.p.) (or *random function*) is a family of complex valued random variables $\varphi(t) = \varphi(t, \omega)$ depending on the parameter $t \in T \subset \mathbb{R}$. In the following, the notation $\{\varphi_t, \ t \in T\}$, or simply $\{\varphi_t\}$ when the t domain is unambiguously defined, will also be used for an s.p. If we assume that T is an interval, thus $\{\varphi_t, \ t \in T\}$ becomes a continuous parameter family, and the process is called a continuous parameter process.

For each fixed $\omega \in \Omega$ the function $\xi(\cdot, \omega) = \{\xi(t, \omega), \ t \in T\}$ of the parameter $t \in T$ with values in the phase space $(X, \mathbf{B})$ is called a *trajectory* or *realization* (also called *sample function*) of the s.p. $\xi(t)$.

Since an s.p. is a family of random variables $x(t) = x(t, \omega)$, we suppose that for every $t \in T$ we have $E\{x(t)\} = 0$, $E\{x(t)^2\} < \infty$ so that $x(t)$ is a point in the Hilbert space $\mathbf{H}$. When t varies over T, we get a one-parameter family of points or a *curve* $\mathcal{C}$ in $\mathbf{H}$.

The concept of mean-square convergence of a sequence of r.v.'s can be extended to a second order s.p. $x(t)$ where t is continuous over a finite interval.

As in the analysis of ordinary functions, this extension leads to the notion of continuity and, in this case, continuity in mean square.

Moreover, the concept of mean-square convergence is at the heart of the important definition of stochastic integral, as will be seen in Sect. 2.2.7.

In the following, unless explicitly declared, we will only refer to second order s.p.'s.

2.1.6. The Mean and the Covariance Functions

The *mean function* $m(t)$ of a complex-valued second order s.p. $\xi(t) = \eta(t) + i\zeta(t)$ is defined as

$$m(t) = E\{\xi(t)\} = E\{\eta(t)\} + i E\{\zeta(t)\}. \tag{2.35}$$

If

$$E\left\{\left|\xi\left(t\right)\right|^{2}\right\} = E\left\{\eta^{2}\left(t\right)\right\} + E\left\{\varsigma^{2}\left(t\right)\right\} \tag{2.36}$$

is finite for all t, then $m(t)$ is a finite, complex-valued, non random function of t.

As it is usually simpler to refer to the process $\tilde{\xi}(t) = \xi(t) - m(t)$, since it has for every t the mean zero, this assumption will be assumed throughout the book.

The *covariance function* $B(t,s)$ of the s.p. $\xi(t)$ is defined as

$$B(t,s) = E\left\{\xi(t)\overline{\xi(s)}\right\} . \tag{2.37}$$

By the Schwartz inequality it results

$$\left|B(t,s)\right|^{2} \leq E\left\{\left|\xi(t)\right|^{2}\right\} E\left\{\left|\xi(s)\right|^{2}\right\} \tag{2.38}$$

so that $B(t,s)$ is finite for all t and s.

The covariance function also has the properties

$$B(s,t) = \overline{B(t,s)} \tag{2.39}$$

and

$$B(t,t) = E\left\{\left|\xi(t)\right|^{2}\right\} \geq 0. \tag{2.40}$$

Every covariance function has the fundamental property of being a *non-negative definite function*, meaning that for a finite set of time points $t_1, \cdots, t_n$ and arbitrary complex numbers $z_1, \cdots, z_n$, the form

$$\sum_{j,k=1}^{n} B\left(t_j, t_k\right) z_j \overline{z_k} = E\left\{\sum_{j,k=1}^{n} \xi\left(t_j\right)\overline{\xi\left(t_k\right)} z_j \overline{z_k}\right\} = E\left\{\left|\sum_{j=1}^{n} \xi\left(t_j\right) z_j\right|^{2}\right\} \geq 0 \tag{2.41}$$

is always real and non-negative.

Given any function $B(t,s)$ having these properties, we can always find a stochastic process $\xi(t)$ having $B(t,s)$ as covariance function.

We say that $\xi(t)$ is a *wide-sense stationary* random process if the covariance function $B(t,s)$ depends on the difference $t - s$ only

$$B(t,s) = B(t-s) \tag{2.42}$$

or in another way if the function

$$B(s+t,s) = E\left\{\xi(s+t)\overline{\xi(s)}\right\} \tag{2.43}$$

is independent of s .

It is worth noting the difference with the class of *strictly stationary processes.* A strictly stationary process $\{x_t,\ t \in T\}$ is one with the multivariate distribution of the r.v.'s $x_{t_1+h},\ \cdots,\ x_{t_n+h}$ which is independent of h , i.e. it remains the same as time passes.

It can be shown that, in general, different random processes with quite different behavior in occurring realizations may have the same covariance function. As a consequence the covariance function is by no means a complete characteristic of a random function. Instead it is well known that a *Gaussian process* is completely characterized by its mean and covariance functions. Thus for two Gaussian processes $x(t)$, $y(t)$ to be identical it suffices that they have the same mean and covariance functions.

This important process will be formally defined and discussed in Sect. 2.3.9.

2.2.   Stochastic Measure and Integral

In the theory of stochastic processes the definition of stochastic integral and its related concept of stochastic measure is of central importance, integration being the most suitable tool for representing stochastic processes, since they are in general not differentiable. Intuitively speaking, as the usual definition of integral on the real axis can be viewed as a linear combination of the measures of elementary disjoint intervals, a stochastic integral is a linear combination of orthogonal r.v.'s associated with the intervals and defining the so-called stochastic measure.

An interesting aspect of this approach is that a stochastic measure can be derived from stochastic processes belonging to the so-called class of orthogonal increments processes, including the subclass of independent increment processes of which Brownian motion represents a well-known example.

2.2.1. Processes with Independent Increments

A process $\{y(\lambda),\ \lambda \in \Lambda \subset \mathbb{R}\}$ with *independent increments* is one whose random variables $\{y_\lambda\}$ have the property that, if $\lambda_1 < \cdots < \lambda_n$, the differences

$$y_{\lambda_2} - y_{\lambda_1},\ \ \cdots\ , y_{\lambda_n} - y_{\lambda_{n-1}} \tag{2.44}$$

are mutually independent.

Recall that the independence of two r.v.'s implies that the jpdf may be written as a product of the respective marginal pdf's, while two r.v.'s x and y are termed *uncorrelated* if

$$E\{x\overline{y}\} = E\{x\} E\{\overline{y}\} \ . \tag{2.45}$$

Thus two independent variables are also uncorrelated, but the vice-versa is not true.

2.2.2. Processes with Orthogonal Increments

A process $\{y(\lambda), \ a \leq \lambda \leq b \ ; \ a, b \in \mathbb{R}\}$ is said to have *orthogonal increments* (o.i.) if

$$E\left\{\left|y_{\lambda_2} - y_{\lambda_1}\right|^2\right\} < \infty \tag{2.46}$$

and

$$E\left\{\left[y(\lambda_2) - y(\lambda_1)\right]\overline{\left[y(\lambda_4) - y(\lambda_3)\right]}\right\} = 0 \quad , \qquad \lambda_1 < \lambda_2 < \lambda_3 < \lambda_4 \ . \tag{2.47}$$

Obviously if a process has independent increments with a zero mean value and (2.46) is true, the process also has orthogonal increments. Thus processes with independent increments form a subclass of o.i. processes.

A process $y(\lambda)$ with orthogonal increments defines a measure $F(\Delta)$ on the half-intervals $\Delta = [\lambda_0, \lambda_1)$ of the real axis, that is a *set function* which associates a non-negative real value $F(\Delta)$ satisfying the additive condition

$$F(\Delta_1 \cup \Delta_2) = F(\Delta_1) + F(\Delta_2) \tag{2.48}$$

for disjoint intervals Δ_1, Δ_2, to every Δ.

In order to show this, we can take any λ_0 and define

$$\alpha(\lambda_2) = \begin{cases} E\left\{\left|y_{\lambda_2} - y_{\lambda_0}\right|^2\right\} & \lambda_2 \geq \lambda_0 \\ -E\left\{\left|y_{\lambda_2} - y_{\lambda_0}\right|^2\right\} & \lambda_2 < \lambda_0 \end{cases} . \tag{2.49}$$

Given the interval Δ two cases occur

i) $\quad \lambda_1 < \lambda_0 \leq \lambda_2$

$$E\left\{\left|y_{\lambda_2} - y_{\lambda_1}\right|^2\right\} = E\left\{\left|y_{\lambda_2} - y_{\lambda_0} - \left(y_{\lambda_1} - y_{\lambda_0}\right)\right|^2\right\}$$

$$= E\left\{\left|y_{\lambda_2} - y_{\lambda_0}\right|^2\right\} + E\left\{\left|y_{\lambda_1} - y_{\lambda_0}\right|^2\right\}$$

$$= \alpha\left(\lambda_2\right) - \alpha\left(\lambda_1\right)$$

ii) $\quad \lambda_0 \leq \lambda_1 < \lambda_2$

$$y_{\lambda_2} - y_{\lambda_0} = y_{\lambda_2} - y_{\lambda_1} + y_{\lambda_1} - y_{\lambda_0}$$

$$E\left\{\left|y_{\lambda_2} - y_{\lambda_0}\right|^2\right\} = E\left\{\left|y_{\lambda_2} - y_{\lambda_1}\right|^2\right\} + E\left\{\left|y_{\lambda_1} - y_{\lambda_0}\right|^2\right\}$$

$$\alpha\left(\lambda_2\right) = E\left\{\left|y_{\lambda_2} - y_{\lambda_1}\right|^2\right\} + \alpha\left(\lambda_1\right)$$

$$E\left\{\left|y_{\lambda_2} - y_{\lambda_1}\right|^2\right\} = \alpha\left(\lambda_2\right) - \alpha\left(\lambda_1\right) \ .$$

In either case we have $\alpha\left(\lambda_2\right) - \alpha\left(\lambda_1\right) \geq 0$ for $\lambda_2 > \lambda_1$ which implies that $\alpha\left(\lambda\right)$ is a monotone non-decreasing function. The set function $F(\Delta) = \alpha\left(\lambda_2\right) - \alpha\left(\lambda_1\right)$, with $\Delta = [\lambda_1, \lambda_2)$, defines a Stieltjes measure on $\mathbb{R}$.

We maintain that the covariance function $B\left(\lambda_1, \lambda_2\right)$ of an o.i process $y(\lambda)$ is given by

$$B\left(\lambda_1, \lambda_2\right) = \alpha\left(\lambda_1 \wedge \lambda_2\right) \tag{2.50}$$

where

$$\left(\lambda_1 \wedge \lambda_2\right) = \min\left(\lambda_1, \lambda_2\right) \ . \tag{2.51}$$

To show this take $0 < \lambda_1 < \lambda_2$, then

$$B\left(\lambda_1, \lambda_2\right) = E\left\{y_{\lambda_1} \overline{y_{\lambda_2}}\right\} \ . \tag{2.52}$$

Notice that the process $y'_\lambda = y_\lambda + y_{\lambda_0}$ has orthogonal increments if $\{y_\lambda\}$ has. Therefore it also results

$$B\left(\lambda_1, \lambda_2\right) = E\left\{\left(y'_{\lambda_1} - y'_{\lambda_0}\right)\overline{\left(y'_{\lambda_2} - y'_{\lambda_0}\right)}\right\}$$

$$= E\left\{\left(y'_{\lambda_1} - y'_{\lambda_0}\right)\overline{\left[\left(y'_{\lambda_2} - y'_{\lambda_1}\right) + \left(y'_{\lambda_1} - y'_{\lambda_0}\right)\right]}\right\} \tag{2.53}$$

$$= E\left\{\left|y'_{\lambda_1} - y'_{\lambda_0}\right|^2\right\} = \alpha\left(\lambda_1\right) \ .$$

Similarly,

$$B\left(\lambda_1, \lambda_2\right) = \alpha\left(\lambda_2\right) \tag{2.54}$$

if $0 \leq \lambda_2 < \lambda_1$.

2.2.3. Brownian Motion or Wiener Process

A well-known process with independent increments is the *Brownian Motion* (BM) process, also called the *Wiener process.*

In this case it is supposed that $y_{\lambda_2} - y_{\lambda_1}$ is real and normally distributed, with

$$E\left\{y_{\lambda_2} - y_{\lambda_1}\right\} = 0 \qquad (2.55)$$

$$E\left\{\left|y_{\lambda_2} - y_{\lambda_1}\right|^2\right\} = \sigma^2 \left|\lambda_2 - \lambda_1\right|, \qquad (2.56)$$

where $\sigma > 0$ is a fixed parameter.

Definition 2.4 -   The process $\left\{y(\lambda), \ \lambda \in \Lambda \subset \mathbb{R}\right\}$ is defined to be a *Wiener process* if
  i)   the process has independent increments;
  ii)   the increments are Gaussian r.v.'s, such that for $\lambda_1, \lambda_2 \in \Lambda$

$$E\left\{y(\lambda_2) - y(\lambda_1)\right\} = 0 \ , \qquad (2.57)$$

$$E\left\{\left|y(\lambda_2) - y(\lambda_1)\right|^2\right\} = \sigma^2 \left|\lambda_2 - \lambda_1\right| . \qquad (2.58)$$

The process is also stationary (wide-sense) since the covariance function only depends on the difference $\lambda_2 - \lambda_1$, with orthogonal increments.

From the properties of o.i. processes it is easy to verify that the covariance function $B(\lambda_1, \lambda_2)$ is given by

$$B(\lambda_1, \lambda_2) = \sigma^2 (\lambda_1 \wedge \lambda_2) . \qquad (2.59)$$

2.2.4. White Noise

Formally we can define a process $\zeta(t)$, $t \in T$ by the following properties:

a) $\zeta(t)$ is a normal process;

b) $E\left\{|\zeta(t)|^2\right\} = \infty$;

c) $E\left\{\zeta(t)\overline{\zeta(s)}\right\} = 0$, $t \neq s$.

Obviously this process does not belong to the space of square-integrable processes. This fictitious process $\zeta(t)$ is called *white noise* (WN). An explicit model of this process cannot be given since, due to the zero correlation at immediately neighboring points, the process is not quadratic mean continuous. Indeed a s.p. $\{x_t\}$ is m.s. continuous at t if and only if $E\{x_t\overline{x}_s\} = B(t,s)$ is continuous at the diagonal point (t,t) (see e.g. [3]).

However a normal process ζ_a with a covariance function of the form

$$B_a(t,s) = \frac{1}{2}ae^{-a|t-s|} \tag{2.60}$$

exists, and as $a \to \infty$, the function

$$B_\infty(t,s) = \delta(|t - s|) \tag{2.61}$$

has the properties b), c), so that white noise $\zeta(t)$ can be viewed as the limit of a sequence $\{\zeta_a\}$ of differentiable processes.

Having defined the white noise in the limit sense we can give

$$\omega_t = \int_0^t \zeta_s ds \tag{2.62}$$

the same meaning, as will be shown shortly.

For $s < t$, remembering that $\delta(-x) = \delta(x)$, we have

$$\begin{aligned}
E\{\omega_t\omega_s\} &= E\left\{\int_0^t \zeta_u du \int_0^s \zeta_v dv\right\} \\
&= \int_0^s \int_0^t E\{\zeta_u\zeta_v\} dudv \\
&= \int_0^s \int_0^t \delta(u - v) dudv \\
&= \int_0^s dv \int_0^t \delta(u - v) du \tag{2.63} \\
&= \int_0^s dv \int_{-v}^{t-v} \delta(\tau) d\tau \\
&= \int_0^s dv \\
&= s
\end{aligned}$$

where the new variable $\tau = u - v$ has been defined with $0 \leq v \leq s < t$.

Similarly,

$$E\left\{\omega_t\omega_s\right\} = t \tag{2.64}$$

if $t < s$. Hence

$$B\left(t,s\right) = \sigma^2\left(t \wedge s\right), \tag{2.65}$$

i.e. the covariance function of a BM process.

Thus, although we cannot represent white noise itself mathematically, BM may be formally regarded as the indefinite integral of white noise.

2.2.5. Stochastic Measure

The *stochastic measure* is a set function that associates to an open interval $\Delta = [\lambda_0, \lambda_1)$ of the real axis $\mathbb{R}$ a complex-valued random variable $\Phi(\Delta)$ satisfying the orthogonality condition

$$E\left\{\Phi(\Delta_1)\overline{\Phi(\Delta_2)}\right\} = 0 \tag{2.66}$$

and the additivity property

$$\Phi(\Delta_1 \cup \Delta_2) = \Phi(\Delta_1) + \Phi(\Delta_2), \tag{2.67}$$

for disjoint intervals Δ_1, Δ_2. In a more formal way the stochastic measure is defined as follows.

Definition 2.5 -   Let $(\Omega, \mathbf{S}, \mathcal{P})$ be   a   probability   space, $L_2(\mathcal{P}) = L_2(\Omega, \mathbf{S}, \mathcal{P})$ the Hilbert space of r.v.'s, $\mathbf{S}$ the class of subsets $\Delta = [\lambda_0, \lambda_1)$ of $\mathbb{R}$. Let us assume that to every $\Delta \in \mathbf{S}$ an r.v. $\Phi(\Delta)$ corresponds, satisfying the following properties

i)

$$\Phi(\Delta) \in L_2(\mathcal{P}), \quad \Phi(\varnothing) = 0 \tag{2.68}$$

ii)

$$\Phi(\Delta_1 \cup \Delta_2) = \Phi(\Delta_1) + \Phi(\Delta_2), \quad \text{if} \ \ \Delta_1 \cap \Delta_2 = \varnothing \tag{2.69}$$

iii)

$$E\left\{\Phi(\Delta_1)\overline{\Phi(\Delta_2)}\right\} = F(\Delta_1 \cup \Delta_2) \tag{2.70}$$

where $F(\Delta)$ is an elementary measure defined on **S**.

The family of r.v.'s $\left\{\Phi(\Delta), \ \Delta \in \mathbf{S}\right\}$ satisfying the properties i)-iii) is said to be an *orthogonal stochastic measure*.

An o.i. process $\{y(\lambda)\}$ might be caused to define a stochastic measure $\Phi(\Delta)$ by assuming

$$\Phi(\Delta) = y(\lambda_1) - y(\lambda_0) \ , \qquad \Delta = [\lambda_0, \lambda_1) \tag{2.71}$$

It can be easily shown that $\Phi(\Delta)$ in (2.71) defines an orthogonal stochastic measure, according to the properties (2.68)-(2.70).

2.2.6. Stochastic Integral

As the concept of stochastic integral is of central importance for the development of the subsequent chapters, a résumé of this subject is reported in this Section.

Denote by $L_0(F)$ the class of all step functions

$$u(\lambda) = \begin{cases} 0 & \lambda < \lambda_1 \\ c_j & \lambda_{j-1} \leq \lambda < \lambda_j \ , \\ 0 & \lambda \geq \lambda_n \end{cases} \qquad 2 \leq j \leq n \ , \quad \lambda \in \Lambda \tag{2.72}$$

where $\lambda_1 < \ldots < \lambda_n$, and introduce the inner product on $L_0(F)$

$$\langle u, v \rangle_F = \int_\Lambda u(\lambda) \overline{v(\lambda)} F(d\lambda) \ , \qquad u, v \in L_0(F) \ , \tag{2.73}$$

where $\Lambda \subset \mathbb{R}$. The function (2.72) can also be written as

$$u(\lambda) = \sum_{j=2}^{n} c_j \chi_{\Delta_j}(\lambda) \tag{2.74}$$

where

$$\chi_{\Delta_j}(\lambda) = \begin{cases} 1 & \lambda \in \Delta_j \\ 0 & \lambda \notin \Delta_j \end{cases} \tag{2.75}$$

is the *indicator* of the set $\Delta_j = [\lambda_{j-1}, \lambda_j)$.

The *stochastic integral* for such a function is defined as

$$\varphi = \int_\Lambda u(\lambda)\Phi(d\lambda) = \sum_{j=2}^n c_j\left[y(\lambda_j) - y(\lambda_{j-1})\right] = \sum_{j=2}^n c_j\Phi(\Delta_j) \tag{2.76}$$

where $\left\{y(\lambda),\ \lambda \in \Lambda\right\}$ is a stochastic process with orthogonal increments, i.e.

$$E\left\{(y(\lambda_2) - y(\lambda_1))\overline{\left(y(\lambda_4) - y(\lambda_3)\right)}\right\} = 0\ ,\qquad \lambda_1 < \lambda_2 < \lambda_3 < \lambda_4 \tag{2.77}$$

and $\Phi(\Delta_j) = y(\lambda_j) - y(\lambda_{j-1})$ defines a stochastic measure.

Thus the stochastic integral in this case is a random variable resulting as a linear combination of the uncorrelated variables $\Phi(\Delta_j)$, i.e. the increments of $y(\lambda)$, and may also be written as

$$\varphi = \int_\Lambda u(\lambda)\,dy(\lambda)\ . \tag{2.78}$$

Additionally, since the stochastic integral associates a function $u(\lambda)$ to a random variable φ, it establishes a correspondence between $u(\lambda)$ and φ. In view of the orthogonality of the increments in (2.76) a useful property of the inner product between two r.v. φ and ψ can be derived from the equality

$$E\{\varphi\overline{\psi}\} = E\left\{\left[\int_\Lambda u(\lambda)\,dy(\lambda)\right]\left[\int_\Lambda \overline{v(\lambda')}\overline{dy(\lambda')}\right]\right\} = \sum_{j=2}^n c_j\,\overline{b}_j E\left\{\left|\Phi(\Delta_j)\right|^2\right\}\ . \tag{2.79}$$

Using the definition of stochastic integral

$$E\left\{\left[\int_\Lambda u(\lambda)\,dy(\lambda)\right]\left[\int_\Lambda \overline{v(\lambda')}\overline{dy(\lambda')}\right]\right\} =$$

$$= E\left\{\sum_{j=2}^n c_j\left[y(\lambda_j) - y(\lambda_{j-1})\right]\sum_{k=2}^n \overline{b}_k\left[\overline{y(\lambda_k) - y(\lambda_{k-1})}\right]\right\}$$

$$= E\left\{\sum_{j=2}^n \sum_{k=2}^n c_j \overline{b}_k\left[y(\lambda_j) - y(\lambda_{j-1})\right]\left[\overline{y(\lambda_k) - y(\lambda_{k-1})}\right]\right\}$$

$$= \sum_{j,k=2}^n c_j \overline{b}_k E\left\{\left[y(\lambda_j) - y(\lambda_{j-1})\right]\left[\overline{y(\lambda_k) - y(\lambda_{k-1})}\right]\right\} \tag{2.80}$$

$$= \sum_{j=2}^n c_j \overline{b}_j E\left\{\left|y(\lambda_j) - y(\lambda_{j-1})\right|^2\right\}$$

$$= \sum_{j=2}^n c_j \overline{b}_j E\left\{\left|\Phi(\Delta_j)\right|^2\right\}\ .$$

Set

$$E\left\{\left|\Phi\left(\Delta_{j}\right)\right|^{2}\right\} = E\left\{\left|y\left(\lambda_{j}\right) - y\left(\lambda_{j-1}\right)\right|^{2}\right\} = \alpha\left(\lambda_{j}\right) - \alpha\left(\lambda_{j-1}\right). \tag{2.81}$$

Thus, to every semiclosed interval $\Delta = \left[\lambda_1, \lambda_2\right)$, $a \le \lambda_1, \lambda_2 \le b$, the set function $F(\Delta) = \alpha\left(\lambda_2\right) - \alpha\left(\lambda_1\right)$ is assigned which, by virtue of orthogonality. is obviously non-negative and additive.

Therefore $F(\Delta)$ defines a Stieltjes measure on semiclosed intervals of the real line and (2.79) becomes

$$E\left\{\varphi\bar{\psi}\right\} = \sum_{j=2}^{n} c_j \bar{b}_j F(\Delta_j) = \int_{\Lambda} u(\lambda)\overline{v(\lambda)} F(d\lambda) \tag{2.82}$$

where the integral on the right-hand side represents a Stieltjes integral.

We now introduce the linear span $\mathbf{H}_0$ or $L_0(\mathcal{P})$ of the family of the random variables $\varphi \in \mathbf{H}_0$, which may be represented in the form (2.76), (this is a subset of the space $\mathbf{H}$).

Thus the relationship (2.76) establishes a correspondence between $L_0(F)$ and $L_0(\mathcal{P})$. From (2.82) it follows that the transformation (2.76), which associates a step function to a random variable, preserves inner products, i.e.

$$\langle \varphi, \psi \rangle_{\mathcal{P}} = E\left\{\varphi\bar{\psi}\right\} = \langle u, v \rangle_{F}. \tag{2.83}$$

In view of the property (2.83) this correspondence also preserves the distance.

To prove this result, let us define the distance between the two step functions u_1, u_2 as

$$\left\|u_1 - u_2\right\| = \left[\int_{\Lambda}\left|u_1(\lambda) - u_2(\lambda)\right|^2 F(d\lambda)\right]^{1/2} \tag{2.84}$$

and the distance between the corresponding r.v.'s φ_1, φ_2 as

$$\left\|\varphi_1 - \varphi_2\right\| = \left[E\left\{\left|\varphi_1 - \varphi_2\right|^2\right\}\right]^{1/2} \tag{2.85}$$

by choosing $u = v = u_1 - u_2$ in (2.83) it follows

$$E\left\{\left|\varphi_1 - \varphi_2\right|^2\right\} = \int_{\Lambda}\left|u_1 - u_2\right|^2 F(d\lambda) \tag{2.86}$$

Hence, the correspondence determines an isometric operator $\mathcal{U}$, $\varphi = \mathcal{U}u$, between $L_0(F)$ and $L_0(\mathcal{P})$.

Now suppose that a generic function $u(\lambda)$ is a limit (in the sense of the distance (2.84)) of a sequence $\{u_n\}$ of step functions of the above type. Then

$$\|u - u_n\|^2 = \int_\Lambda |u(\lambda) - u_n(\lambda)|^2 F(d\lambda) \;\; \to \;\; 0 \qquad \left(n \to \infty\right) \qquad (2.87)$$

that is,

$$\underset{n \to \infty}{\text{l.i.m.}} \; u_n = u \,. \qquad (2.88)$$

It follows, since distance is preserved, that $\underset{n \to \infty}{\text{l.i.m.}} \; \varphi_n$ also exists, defining a random variable φ. We denote by $L_2(\mathcal{P})$ the closure of $L_0(\mathcal{P})$ in the topology generated by the scalar product (2.79). The existence of a sequence of step functions that approximate an arbitrary function $u(\lambda) \in L_2(F)$ follows from the general formulation of measure theory.

Consequently, we define the stochastic integral

$$\int_\Lambda u(\lambda) dy(\lambda) \qquad (2.89)$$

as the limit φ obtained in this way.

2.3.   Canonical Representation

The representation of stochastic processes by means of mathematical models to be as general as possible, is a central issue in the theory of stochastic processes.

The method of *canonical representation* aims to represent a process in terms of a sum of the elementary random functions.

We say that an s.p. is an *elementary random function* if it can be written as

$$x(t) = \xi \, \varphi(t) \qquad (2.90)$$

where ξ is an ordinary zero-mean r.v., and $\varphi(t)$ is a non-random function.

The elementary random function owns the two distinguishing properties of a random function: randomness, associated to the random coefficient ξ, and dependence on the time, through the ordinary function $\varphi(t)$. A more general representation is given by the summation

$$x(t) = \sum_{i=1}^{M} \xi_i \, \varphi_i(t) \,. \qquad (2.91)$$

The covariance function of $x(t)$ is given by

$$B(t,s) = E\left\{x(t)\overline{x(s)}\right\} = \sum_{i=1}^{M} \varphi_i(t)\overline{\varphi_i(s)}\, E\left\{\xi_i\overline{\xi_i}\right\} + \sum_{i\neq j} \varphi_i(t)\overline{\varphi_j(s)}\, E\left\{\xi_i\overline{\xi_j}\right\}.\ (2.92)$$

The resulting expression for $B(t,s)$ can be greatly simplified provided

$$E\left\{\xi_i\overline{\xi_j}\right\} = 0 \qquad \text{for} \quad i \neq j, \tag{2.93}$$

i.e. the coefficients ξ_i of the decomposition are uncorrelated. In such a case the decomposition is said to be *canonical representation*.

Thus the idea, which lies at the bottom of canonical representation, is to represent the process as a linear combination of orthogonal random variables, with coefficients that are functions of time. Under this assumption the covariance function becomes

$$B(t,s) = \sum_{i=1}^{M} \varphi_i(t)\overline{\varphi_i(s)}\, E\left\{\xi_i^2\right\} \tag{2.94}$$

and is named *canonical representation of the covariance function*.

As will be shown later, more general canonical representations, expressed in terms of a series or integral, can be derived on the basis of the same concept of linear combination of orthogonal random variable.

A fairly general result, which will play a key role in the definition of stochastic neural networks, is given by the following analysis showing the existence of an integral canonical representation valid for a wide class of non-stationary processes.

2.3.1. *Canonical Representation of a Class of Non-Stationary Processes*

In this section we will refer to stochastic processes with covariance function expressed by

$$B(t,s) = \int_{\Lambda} \varphi(t,\lambda)\overline{\varphi(s,\lambda)}\, F(d\lambda) \tag{2.95}$$

where $\varphi(t,\lambda)$ is a family of functions of the variable $\lambda \in \Lambda$, depending on the parameter $t \in T$, and $F(\Delta\lambda)$ is a Stieltjes measure defined on the semiclosed intervals $\Delta\lambda = [\lambda_0, \lambda_1)$. Processes of this kind constitutes a class of non-stationary processes which is sufficiently wide for the purposes of subsequent chapters, embracing a huge number of stochastic processes currently used in the applications and including the well-known class of stationary processes. Here we give some examples of processes belonging to such a class.

Example 1

Let us assume the s.p. $x(t)$ is defined as

$$x(t) = a\,v(t) \quad , \qquad t \in [0, \infty) \tag{2.96}$$

where a is a real r.v. assuming the values $\lambda \in \mathbb{R}$ with pdf $p(\lambda)$ and $v(t)$ is a real-valued function. The covariance function is given by

$$B(t, s) = E\left\{a\,v(t)\,a\,v(s)\right\} = v(t)\,v(s)\,E\left\{a^2\right\} , \tag{2.97}$$

which obviously shows that the process is non-stationary. Moreover, from the definition of covariance function it also results

$$B(t, s) = \int_{\mathbb{R}} \lambda\,v(t)\,\lambda\,v(s)\,p(\lambda)\,d\lambda , \tag{2.98}$$

which can be written in the general form (2.95) by putting,

$$\begin{aligned} \varphi(t, \lambda) &\equiv \lambda\,v(t) , \\ F(d\lambda) &\equiv d\alpha(\lambda) = p(\lambda)\,d\lambda . \end{aligned} \tag{2.99}$$

Example 2

Let us define the s.p.

$$x(t) = g(t, a) \quad , \qquad t \in [0, \infty) \tag{2.100}$$

where a is a real r.v. assuming the values $\lambda \in \mathbb{R}$ with pdf $p(\lambda)$ and $g(\cdot, \cdot)$ is a real-valued function. The covariance function is

$$B(t, s) = E\left\{g(t, a)\,g(s, a)\right\} = \int_{\mathbb{R}} g(t, \lambda)\,g(s, \lambda)\,p(\lambda)\,d\lambda . \tag{2.101}$$

which has the same form of (2.95), once chosen $\varphi(t, \lambda) = g(t, \lambda)$ and $F(d\lambda) \equiv p(\lambda)\,d\lambda$.

Example 3

Let us be given the complex-valued process

$$x(t) = a\,e^{j(\omega t + \vartheta)} = a\,e^{j\omega t}\,e^{j\vartheta} \tag{2.102}$$

where ϑ is an r.v. with pdf $p(\vartheta)$, while a and ω are real constants.

The covariance function of $x(t)$ is

$$
\begin{aligned}
B(t,s) &= E\left\{x(t)\overline{x(s)}\right\} = E\left\{a\,e^{j\omega t}\,e^{j\vartheta}a\,e^{-j\omega s}\,e^{-j\vartheta}\right\} \\
&= E\left\{a^2\,e^{j\omega(t-s)}\right\} = a^2\,e^{j\omega(t-s)} = a^2\,e^{j\omega\tau} \ .
\end{aligned}
\tag{2.103}
$$

We choose

$$\varphi(t,\lambda) = e^{j\lambda t} \tag{2.104}$$

and

$$F(d\lambda) = a^2\delta(\lambda - \omega)\,d\lambda\,, \tag{2.105}$$

where $\delta(\lambda)$ is the Dirac δ-function. By virtue of the well known properties of this function it results

$$B(t,s) = \int_\Lambda e^{j\lambda\tau}a^2\delta(\lambda - \omega)\,d\lambda = a^2\,e^{j\omega\tau} \ . \tag{2.106}$$

proving that (2.106) is a particular case of (2.95).

We are now in a position to state the aforementioned theorem, due to Karhunen [10], which represents the most important result of this chapter as well as the basic concept on which the stochastic neural networks theory is built up.

Theorem 2.1

Let $\xi(t)$ be an s.p. (non-stationary in general) such that $\xi(t) \in L_2(\Omega, \boldsymbol{S}, \mathcal{P})$, $E\left\{|\xi(t)|^2\right\} < +\infty$ for all $t \in T$, whose covariance function is expressed by the integral

$$B(t,s) = \int_\Lambda \varphi(t,\lambda)\overline{\varphi(s,\lambda)}\,F(d\lambda) \tag{2.107}$$

where Λ is the real axis, $\left\{\varphi(t,\lambda),\, t \in T\right\}$ is a *complete* family (by varying the parameter $t \in T$) of functions of the variable $\lambda \in \Lambda$ in the space of measurable functions $L_2(F)$ with the measure $F(\Delta)$ defined on the intervals $\Delta = [\lambda_0, \lambda_1)$.

Under these assumptions the s.p. $\xi(t)$ admits the following canonical representation

$$\xi(t) = \int_\Lambda \varphi(t, \lambda) \Phi(d\lambda) \qquad (2.108)$$

being $\Phi(\Delta)$ a *stochastic measure* on the intervals $\Delta \in \Lambda$ with values on the Hilbert space $L_2(\mathcal{P})$ such that

$$E\left\{ \left| \Phi(\Delta) \right|^2 \right\} = F(\Delta). \qquad (2.109)$$

The proof of the theorem is quite lengthy, even though the concepts involved require only a knowledge of standard functional analysis. Nonetheless the reader is exhorted to read it since he might benefit from it in the subsequent chapters.

PROOF

The demonstration of the proposition is divided into three parts. The definitions of *complete set* of functions and *isomorphism*, that will be used in the proof, are reported for the reader's convenience in Appendix A.

a)   **Definition of an isomorphism $\mathcal{U}$ from the space $L_2(F)$ onto $\mathcal{L}(\xi)$**

We want to show that an isomorphism from the space

$$L_2(F) \quad onto \quad \mathcal{L}(\xi) \text{ (or } \mathcal{L}(\xi(t))), \qquad (2.110)$$

where $\mathcal{L}(\xi) = \text{span}\left\{ \xi(t), t \in T \right\}$ is the subspace "spanned" by the values of $\xi(t)$, can be defined.

First of all it results

$$L_2(F) = \mathcal{L}\left(\varphi(t, \lambda)\right) \qquad (2.111)$$

where $\mathcal{L}\left(\varphi(t, \lambda)\right) = \text{span}\left\{ \varphi(t, \lambda), t \in T \right\}$, since the set $\left\{ \varphi(t, \lambda), t \in T \right\}$ is complete.

In this space the *inner product* of any two functions $f_1(\lambda)$, $f_2(\lambda)$ is defined by

$$\langle f_1, f_2 \rangle_F \triangleq \int_\Lambda f_1(\lambda) \overline{f_2(\lambda)} F(d\lambda). \qquad (2.112)$$

Let us establish for every t a linear correspondence (or operator) $\mathcal{U}$ by

$$\varphi(t,\lambda) \xleftarrow{\quad \mathcal{U} \quad} \xi(t), \quad \forall t \in T \tag{2.113}$$

This correspondence is extended by linearity to finite linear combinations

$$f(\lambda) = \sum_k c_k \varphi(t_k, \lambda) \xleftarrow{\quad \mathcal{U} \quad} \eta = \sum_k c_k \xi(t_k), \quad \forall t_k \in T \tag{2.114}$$

where c_k are complex numbers.

Denoting

$$\mathcal{L}_0\left(\varphi(t,\lambda)\right) = \left\{ f(\lambda) \;\middle|\; f(\lambda) = \sum_{k=1}^n c_k \varphi(t_k, \lambda),\; t_k \in T \right\} \tag{2.115}$$

the set of all finite linear combinations of $\varphi(t_k, \lambda)$ and by

$$\mathcal{L}_0\left(\xi(t)\right) = \left\{ \eta \;\middle|\; \eta = \sum_{k=1}^n c_k \xi(t_k),\; t_k \in T \right\} \tag{2.116}$$

the set of all finite linear combinations of $\xi(t_k)$, then the operator $\mathcal{U}(f(\lambda)) = \eta$ establishes a correspondence between $\mathcal{L}_0\left(\varphi(t,\lambda)\right)$ and $\mathcal{L}_0\left(\xi(t)\right)$.

The correspondence $\mathcal{U}$ is *isometric*. Indeed for the s.p. $\xi(t)$ we have

$$\langle \xi(t), \xi(s) \rangle_{\mathcal{P}} = B(t,s) = \int_\Lambda \varphi(t,\lambda)\overline{\varphi(s,\lambda)} F(d\lambda), \tag{2.117}$$

so that the scalar products in $\mathcal{L}_0\left(\varphi(t,\lambda)\right)$ and $\mathcal{L}_0\left(\xi(t)\right)$ are equal each other

$$\langle \xi(t), \xi(s) \rangle_{\mathcal{P}} = \langle \varphi(t,\lambda), \varphi(s,\lambda) \rangle_F. \tag{2.118}$$

Obviously this result is also valid for the linear combinations

$$\begin{aligned} f_t(\lambda) &= \sum_k c_k \varphi(t_k, \lambda), \quad \eta_t = \sum_k c_k \xi(t_k) \\ f_s(\lambda) &= \sum_k c_k \varphi(s_k, \lambda), \quad \eta_s = \sum_k c_k \xi(s_k) \end{aligned} \tag{2.119}$$

and thus

$$\langle \eta_t, \eta_s \rangle_{\mathcal{P}} = \langle f_t(\lambda), f_s(\lambda) \rangle_F. \tag{2.120}$$

Due to the completeness of the set $\left\{ \varphi(t,\lambda),\, t \in T \right\}$ the isometric mapping between $\mathcal{L}_0\left(\varphi(t,\lambda)\right) \leftrightarrow \mathcal{L}_0\left(\xi(t)\right)$ can be extended to the sets $\mathcal{L}\left(\varphi(t,\lambda)\right) \leftrightarrow \mathcal{L}\left(\xi(t)\right)$, since $\mathcal{L}\left(\varphi(t,\lambda)\right)$ $\left(\mathcal{L}\left(\xi(t)\right)\right)$ is the closure of $\mathcal{L}_0\left(\varphi(t,\lambda)\right)$ $\left(\mathcal{L}_0\left(\xi(t)\right)\right)$. Now any element of $\mathcal{L}\left(\varphi(t,\lambda)\right)$ $\left(\mathcal{L}\left(\xi(t)\right)\right)$ is the m.s. limit of elements of $\mathcal{L}_0\left(\varphi(t,\lambda)\right)$ $\left(\mathcal{L}_0\left(\xi(t)\right)\right)$.

More explicitly if we have

$$\underset{n\to\infty}{\mathrm{l.i.m.}}\, f_n(\lambda) = f(\lambda)\,,\quad f_n(\lambda) \in \mathcal{L}_0\left(\varphi(t,\lambda)\right)\,,\quad f(\lambda) \in \mathcal{L}\left(\varphi(t,\lambda)\right) \qquad (2.121)$$

for the completeness of $\mathcal{L}\left(\varphi(t,\lambda)\right)$, where $f_n(\lambda)$ is a sequence and $\eta(t_n)$ is the corresponding sequence, then due to the isometry a s.p. $\eta \in \mathcal{L}\left(\xi(t)\right)$ exists such that

$$\underset{n\to\infty}{\mathrm{l.i.m.}} \int_\Lambda \left|f(\lambda) - f_n(\lambda)\right|^2 F(d\lambda) = \underset{n\to\infty}{\mathrm{l.i.m.}}\, E\left\{\left|\eta - \eta_n\right|^2\right\} \qquad (2.122)$$

The correspondence $\mathcal{U}$ is *one-to-one*.

Indeed, let us assume two functions $f_1(\lambda), f_2(\lambda) \in \mathcal{L}\left(\varphi(t,\lambda)\right)$ such that

$$\mathcal{U}f_1(\lambda) = \mathcal{U}f_2(\lambda) \qquad (2.123)$$

exists. By linearity of $\mathcal{U}$

$$\left\|\mathcal{U}f_1(\lambda) - \mathcal{U}f_2(\lambda)\right\|_p = 0 = \left\|\mathcal{U}\left(f_1(\lambda) - f_2(\lambda)\right)\right\|_p = \left\|f_1(\lambda) - f_2(\lambda)\right\|_F \qquad (2.124)$$

which implies

$$f_1(\lambda) = f_2(\lambda)\,. \qquad (2.125)$$

In conclusion the transformation $\mathcal{U}$ defines an isomorphism between $\mathcal{L}\left(\varphi(t,\lambda)\right)$ and $\mathcal{L}\left(\xi(t)\right)$.

b)   **Definition of a stochastic measure on $\mathcal{L}\left(\xi(t)\right)$**

We want to prove that a stochastic measure defined on the sets $B \in \mathbf{S}$ (the open intervals $\Delta = \left[\lambda_0, \lambda_1\right)$), and with values in $\mathcal{L}\left(\xi(t)\right)$, exists.

For any $B \in \mathbf{S}$ the indicator

$$\chi_B(\lambda) = \begin{cases} 1 & \lambda \in B \\ 0 & \text{otherwise} \end{cases}. \qquad (2.126)$$

is an element of $L_2(F)$, $\chi_B(\lambda) \in L_2(F)$.

Let us define the r.v. $\Phi(B)$ which corresponds to $\chi_B(\lambda)$ through $\mathcal{U}$

$$\chi_B(\lambda) \xrightarrow{\;\;\mathcal{U}\;\;} \Phi(B), \quad \Phi(B) \in \mathcal{L}(\xi(t)). \tag{2.127}$$

$\Phi(B)$ exists for every B because an isomorphism between $L_2(F)$ and $\mathcal{L}(\xi(t))$ has been established. Now it is straightforward to state that $\Phi(B)$ is a stochastic measure on $\mathcal{L}(\xi(t))$ by checking these properties

1) $\Phi(B) \in \mathcal{L}(\xi(t)), \quad \Phi(\varnothing) = 0$;

2) $\begin{matrix} \chi_{B_1} \leftrightarrow \Phi(B_1) \\ \chi_{B_2} \leftrightarrow \Phi(B_2) \end{matrix} \;\Rightarrow\; \chi_{B_1} + \chi_{B_2} \leftrightarrow \Phi(B_1) + \Phi(B_2) \quad \text{with} \quad B_1 \cap B_2 = \varnothing \quad \text{(by}$

linearity of $\mathcal{U}$),

3) $E\left\{\Phi(B_1)\overline{\Phi(B_2)}\right\} = \int_\Lambda \chi_{B_1}(\lambda)\overline{\chi_{B_2}(\lambda)}\,F(d\lambda) = F(B_1 \cap B_2)$,

this property follows from the isometry

$$\left\langle \Phi(B_1), \Phi(B_2) \right\rangle_P = \left\langle \chi_{B_1}, \chi_{B_2} \right\rangle_F. \tag{2.128}$$

c)   The operator $\mathcal{U}$ as stochastic integral

Having previously proven that a stochastic measure on $\mathcal{L}(\xi(t))$ exists, we define the s.p. $\tilde{\xi}(t)$ by the stochastic integral

$$\tilde{\xi}(t) = \int_\Lambda \varphi(t,\lambda)\Phi(d\lambda), \quad t \in T. \tag{2.129}$$

We want to show that the s.p. $\tilde{\xi}(t)$ is identical to $\xi(t)$.

To this end let $-A = \lambda_1 < \lambda_2 < \ldots < \lambda_{n+1} = A$ be a partition of the interval $(-A, A)$. The random variable defined by

$$\zeta(t) = \sum_{j=1}^n \varphi(t,\lambda_j)\Phi(\Delta_j), \quad \Delta_j = [\lambda_j, \lambda_{j+1}), \quad t \in T \tag{2.130}$$

is in $\mathcal{L}(\xi(t))$ being a linear combination of the stochastic measure $\Phi(\Delta_j) \in \mathcal{L}(\xi(t))$.

As a consequence of

$$\chi_{\Delta_j}(\lambda) \leftrightarrow \Phi(\Delta_j), \tag{2.131}$$

to the r.v. $\zeta(t)$ corresponds in $L_2(F)$ the function

$$h(t,\lambda) = \sum_{j=1}^n \varphi(t,\lambda_j)\chi_{\Delta_j}(\lambda), \tag{2.132}$$

defined as

$$h(t,\lambda) = \begin{cases} \varphi\big(t,\lambda_j\big) & \text{for } \lambda_j \le \lambda < \lambda_{j+1} \\ 0 & \text{otherwise} \end{cases}, \qquad (j = 1,\dots,n). \qquad (2.133)$$

which is a *step-function* .

Therefore

$$\sum_{j=1}^{n} \varphi\big(t,\lambda_j\big)\chi_{\Delta_j}(\lambda) \xleftarrow{\quad \mathcal{U} \quad} \sum_{j=1}^{n} \varphi\big(t,\lambda_j\big)\Phi\big(\Delta_j\big). \qquad (2.134)$$

Being $\varphi(t,\lambda)$ an $L_2(F)$-measurable function, it is known from functional analysis that, as $A \to \infty$ while at the same time $\Delta_j \to 0$, the step-function will converge in m.s. to $\varphi(t,\lambda)$, in formulae

$$\underset{\substack{A\to\infty \\ \Delta_j\to 0}}{\text{l.i.m.}} \sum_{j=1}^{n} \varphi\big(t,\lambda_j\big)\chi_{\Delta_j}(\lambda) = \varphi(t,\lambda) \qquad (2.135)$$

From the definition of stochastic integral we also have

$$\underset{\substack{A\to\infty \\ \Delta_j\to 0}}{\text{l.i.m.}} \sum_{j=1}^{n} \varphi\big(t,\lambda_j\big)\Phi\big(\Delta_j\big) = \int_\Lambda \varphi(t,\lambda)\Phi(d\lambda). \qquad (2.136)$$

In view of the isomorphism between $L_2(F)$ and $\mathcal{L}(\xi(t))$ the following correspondence holds

$$\varphi(t,\lambda) \xleftarrow{\quad \mathcal{U} \quad} \int_\Lambda \varphi(t,\lambda)\Phi(d\lambda) , \qquad (2.137)$$

on the other hand the definition of $\mathcal{U}$ implies

$$\varphi(t,\lambda) \xleftarrow{\quad \mathcal{U} \quad} \xi(t) \qquad (2.138)$$

Combining (2.137) and (2.138) it finally results

$$\xi(t) = \int_\Lambda \varphi(t,\lambda)\Phi(d\lambda) \qquad (2.139)$$

and the proof of the theorem is completed.

Q.E.D.

The formula (2.108) has the meaning of continuous linear combinations of random variables $\Phi(d\lambda)$ with the coefficients $\varphi(t,\lambda)$, while the measure $F(d\lambda)$ describes the variance distribution of the various components $\Phi(d\lambda)$ on the real axis of λ values.

The result given by (2.108) may be generalized in the case of a covariance function given by

$$B(t,s) = \int_0^{+\infty} \varphi^T(t,\lambda) \cdot \varphi(s,\lambda) dF(\lambda) \tag{2.140}$$

in which

$$\varphi(t,\lambda) = \left[g_1(t,\lambda), \ g_2(t,\lambda), \ \cdots \ \right]^T \tag{2.141}$$

is a vector-valued function (here the superscript T denotes the transpose of a vector).

The canonical representation in this case is given by

$$\xi(t) = \int_0^{\infty} \varphi^T(t,\lambda) \cdot d\eta(\lambda) \tag{2.142}$$

where $\eta(\Delta\lambda)$ is a stochastic measure vector

$$\eta(\Delta\lambda) = \left[\eta_1(\Delta\lambda), \ \eta_2(\Delta\lambda), \ \cdots \ \right]^T \tag{2.143}$$

such that

$$E\left\{ \left| \eta_1(\Delta\lambda) \right|^2 \right\} = E\left\{ \left| \eta_2(\Delta\lambda) \right|^2 \right\} = \ldots = F(\Delta) \tag{2.144}$$

$$E\left\{ \eta_i(\Delta\lambda) \overline{\eta_j(\Delta\lambda)} \right\} = 0, \qquad i \neq j \ . \tag{2.145}$$

2.3.2. Generalized Canonical Representation

A wider class of s.p. may be represented in canonical form, if the constrain on the functions $\varphi(t,\lambda)$, to be a complete set in theorem 2.1, is relaxed.

In order to generalize the canonical representation given in the previous section, let

$$B(t,s) = \int_\Lambda g(t,\lambda) \overline{g(s,\lambda)} F(d\lambda) \tag{2.146}$$

be the covariance function of the process (generally non-stationary) $\zeta(t)$, expressed in terms of the generic function $g(t, \lambda)$. Note that in this context $\{g(t, \lambda), t \in T\}$ is not necessarily a complete family of functions as it was assumed in theorem 2.1.

We want to show that the canonical representation

$$\zeta(t) = \int_\Lambda g(t, \lambda) \Phi(d\lambda) \tag{2.147}$$

exists with

$$E\left\{\left|\Phi(\Delta)\right|^2\right\} = F(\Delta) . \tag{2.148}$$

To this end, let $\{\varphi(t, \lambda), t \in T\}$ be a *complete* family (by varying the parameter $t \in T$) of functions of the variable $\lambda \in \Lambda$ in the space of measurable functions $L_2(F)$ with the measure $F(\Delta)$ defined on the intervals $\Delta = [\lambda_0, \lambda_1)$.

By virtue of completeness of $\{\varphi(t, \lambda), t \in T\}$ we can write

$$\begin{aligned}
B(t, s) &= \int_\Lambda g(t, \lambda) \overline{g(s, \lambda)} F(d\lambda) \\
&= \int_\Lambda \sum_k c_k(t) \varphi(t_k, \lambda) \sum_j \overline{c_j(s)} \ \overline{\varphi(t_j, \lambda)} F(d\lambda) . \\
&= \sum_k \sum_j c_k(t) \overline{c_j(s)} \int_\Lambda \varphi(t_k, \lambda) \overline{\varphi(t_j, \lambda)} F(d\lambda)
\end{aligned} \tag{2.149}$$

The integral $\int_\Lambda \varphi(t_k, \lambda) \overline{\varphi(t_k, \lambda)} F(d\lambda) = B_\xi(t_k, t_j)$ defines the covariance function of the process $\xi(t)$, belonging to the space $L_2(\zeta)$, with canonical representation

$$\xi(t) = \int_\Lambda \varphi(t, \lambda) \Phi(d\lambda), \quad E\left\{\left|\Phi(\Delta)\right|^2\right\} = F(\Delta) . \tag{2.150}$$

Thus (2.149) becomes

$$\begin{aligned}
B(t, s) &= \sum_k \sum_j c_k(t) \overline{c_j(s)} B_\xi(t_k, t_j) \\
&= \sum_k \sum_j c_k(t) \overline{c_j(s)} E\left\{\xi(t_k) \overline{\xi(t_j)}\right\} \\
&= E\left\{\sum_k c_k(t) \xi(t_k) \sum_j \overline{c_j(s) \xi(t_j)}\right\}
\end{aligned} \tag{2.151}$$

Since for definition $B(t, s) = E\left\{\zeta(t) \overline{\zeta(s)}\right\}$, from (2.151) it results

$\zeta(t) = \sum_k c_k(t)\xi(t_k)$ where $\xi(t_k) = \int_\Lambda \varphi(t_k,\lambda)\Phi(d\lambda)$. Hence for the process $\zeta(t)$ the canonical representation

$$
\begin{aligned}
\zeta(t) &= \sum_k c_k(t)\int_\Lambda \varphi(t_k,\lambda)\Phi(d\lambda) \\
&= \int_\Lambda \sum_k c_k(t)\varphi(t_k,\lambda)\Phi(d\lambda) \\
&= \int_\Lambda g(t,\lambda)\Phi(d\lambda)
\end{aligned}
\tag{2.152}
$$

holds with $E\left\{|\Phi(\Delta)|^2\right\} = F(\Delta)$.

The representation (2.147), expressed in terms of a generic function $g(t,\lambda)$ instead of a complete set of functions $\left\{\varphi(t,\lambda),\, t \in T\right\}$, generalizes the canonical representation (2.108).

2.3.3. Stationary Processes

The family of stationary s.p.'s being a subset of the non-stationary processes space, their canonical representation may be considered as a particular case of (2.108). In this case the covariance function $B(t,s)$ depends on the difference $t-s$ only and, as it is well known, by using Bochner's theorem it can be represented as (see e.g. [2])

$$
B(t,s) = B(t-s) = \int_\Lambda e^{i\lambda(t-s)}F(d\lambda) = \int_\Lambda e^{i\lambda t}e^{-i\lambda s}F(d\lambda)
\tag{2.153}
$$

which once compared to the more general relationship (2.107) implies

$$
\varphi(t,\lambda) = e^{i\lambda t} \ .
\tag{2.154}
$$

Then for a stationary process $\xi(t)$ the following representation holds

$$
\xi(t) = \int_\Lambda e^{i\lambda t}\Phi(d\lambda)
\tag{2.155}
$$

together with

$$
B(\tau) = \int_\Lambda e^{i\lambda\tau}F(d\lambda) \ .
\tag{2.156}
$$

2.3.4. Inversion Formula

Having derived a mathematical representation of a wide class of stochastic processes, the main issue now is how to derive it from the process itself. In this section it will be shown that the stochastic measure $\Phi(\Delta\lambda)$, which specifies the canonical representation for a given process $x(t)$, can be related to the realisations of the process so that the statistical properties of $\Phi(\Delta\lambda)$ can be derived from those of the process $x(t)$.

We previously stated that the stochastic measure associated to an s.p. $\xi(t)$ belongs to the space $\mathcal{L}(\xi(t))$, a property that ensures $\xi(t)$ is represented in terms of the process itself, as it will be shown shortly.

Given the process $x(t)$ admitting the canonical representation

$$x(t) = \int_\Lambda \varphi(t,\lambda)\Phi(d\lambda) \; , \tag{2.157}$$

we form the linear combination

$$\int_T x(t)\psi_{\Delta\lambda}(t)dt \tag{2.158}$$

where $\psi_{\Delta\lambda}(t)$ is any function which depends on the parameters λ_0, λ_1, representing the extrema of the interval $\Delta\lambda = \left[\lambda_0, \lambda_1\right)$, $\lambda \in \mathbb{R}$.

We have

$$
\begin{aligned}
\int_T x(t)\psi_{\Delta\lambda}(t)dt &= \int_T \psi_{\Delta\lambda}(t)\left[\int_\Lambda \varphi(t,\lambda)\Phi(d\lambda)\right]dt \\
&= \int_T \int_\Lambda \psi_{\Delta\lambda}(t)\varphi(t,\lambda)\Phi(d\lambda)dt \quad . \\
&= \int_\Lambda \left[\int_T \psi_{\Delta\lambda}(t)\varphi(t,\lambda)dt\right]\Phi(d\lambda)
\end{aligned}
\tag{2.159}
$$

Now we choose $\psi_{\Delta\lambda}(t)$ in such a way the relation

$$\int_T \psi_{\Delta\lambda}(t)\varphi(t,\lambda)dt = \chi_{\Delta\lambda}(\lambda) \tag{2.160}$$

is satisfied, where $\chi_{\Delta\lambda}(\lambda)$ is the indicator of $\Delta\lambda$:

$$\chi_{\Delta\lambda}(\lambda) = \begin{cases} 1 & \lambda \in \Delta\lambda \\ 0 & \lambda \notin \Delta\lambda \end{cases} . \tag{2.161}$$

The function $\psi_{\Delta\lambda}(t)$ exists because $\chi_{\Delta\lambda}(\lambda)$ is an element of $L_2(F)$ and as such it can be represented as a linear combination of the functions $\varphi(t,\lambda)$, the set $\left\{\varphi(t,\lambda),\ t\in T\right\}$ being complete. Combining (2.159)-(2.161) we get

$$\int_T x(t)\,\psi_{\Delta\lambda}(t)\,dt = \int_\Lambda \chi_{\Delta\lambda}(\lambda)\,\Phi(d\lambda) = \Phi(\Delta\lambda)\ . \tag{2.162}$$

In conclusion the process $\Phi(\Delta\lambda)$ is given by

$$\Phi(\Delta\lambda) = \int_T x(t)\,\psi_{\Delta\lambda}(t)\,dt \tag{2.163}$$

where $\psi_{\Delta\lambda}(t)$ is defined through the integral equation

$$\int_T \psi_{\Delta\lambda}(t)\,\varphi(t,\lambda)\,dt = \chi_{\Delta\lambda}(\lambda)\ . \tag{2.164}$$

As (2.164) may be interpreted as a linear combination of the complete set $\varphi(t,\lambda)$, the function $\psi_{\Delta\lambda}(t)$ has the meaning of coefficient distribution in the representation of $\chi_{\Delta\lambda}(\lambda)$.

Eq. (2.163) together with (2.164) provides the inversion formulae of the canonical decomposition (2.157).

It is straightforward to check that $\Phi(\Delta\lambda) = \int_T x(t)\,\psi_{\Delta\lambda}(t)\,dt$ is an orthogonal increment process. Proving this property is equivalent to showing that

$$E\left\{\Phi(\Delta\lambda_1)\overline{\Phi(\Delta\lambda_2)}\right\} = 0\ . \tag{2.165}$$

Substituting $x(t)$ with the canonical representation we get

$$
\begin{aligned}
E\left\{\Phi(\Delta\lambda_1)\overline{\Phi(\Delta\lambda_2)}\right\} &= E\left\{\int_T x(t)\,\psi_{\Delta\lambda_1}(t)\,dt\int_T \overline{x(s)}\,\overline{\psi_{\Delta\lambda_2}(s)}\,ds\right\}\\
&= \int_T\int_T \psi_{\Delta\lambda_1}(t)\,\overline{\psi_{\Delta\lambda_2}(s)}\,E\left\{x(t)\overline{x(s)}\right\}dt\,ds\\
&= \int_T\int_T \psi_{\Delta\lambda_1}(t)\,\overline{\psi_{\Delta\lambda_2}(s)}B(t,s)\,dt\,ds\\
&= \int_T\int_T \psi_{\Delta\lambda_1}(t)\,\overline{\psi_{\Delta\lambda_2}(s)}\left[\int_\Lambda \varphi(t,\lambda)\overline{\varphi(s,\lambda)}\,F(d\lambda)\right]dt\,ds\\
&= \int_\Lambda\left[\int_T \psi_{\Delta\lambda_1}(t)\,\varphi(t,\lambda)\,dt\int_T \overline{\psi_{\Delta\lambda_2}(s)}\overline{\varphi(s,\lambda)}\,ds\right]F(d\lambda)\\
&= \int_\Lambda \chi_{\Delta\lambda_1}(\lambda)\,\chi_{\Delta\lambda_2}(\lambda)\,F(d\lambda)\\
&= \begin{cases} 0 & \text{if}\quad \Delta\lambda_1\cap\Delta\lambda_2 = \varnothing\\ F(d\lambda) & \text{if}\quad \Delta\lambda_1 = \Delta\lambda_2 = \Delta\lambda \end{cases}
\end{aligned}
\tag{2.166}
$$

and this complete the proof.

2.3.5. Canonical Representation of S.P.'s Defined on Finite Intervals:
Karhunen-Loève Theorem

Let $x(t)$ be a process defined on the interval $T = [a,b]$, where a and b are finite, with covariance function $B(t,s)$. In this particular case, according to the theory of integral operators, (see the Appendix B for a complete treatment of this subject), the covariance function can be expanded into a uniformly convergent series

$$B(t,s) = \sum_{\lambda \in \Lambda} \varphi(t,\lambda)\overline{\varphi(s,\lambda)}\lambda \tag{2.167}$$

where $\varphi(t,\lambda)$ and λ are the eigenfunctions and the eigenvalues, respectively, of the integral operator K defined by

$$K[u(t)] \triangleq \int_T B(t,s)u(s)\,ds \ , \tag{2.168}$$

and obtained as solutions of the integral equation

$$\int_T B(t,s)\varphi(s,\lambda)\,ds = \lambda\varphi(t,\lambda) \ . \tag{2.169}$$

Obviously the covariance function may be expressed in an integral form as

$$B(t,s) = \sum_{\lambda \in \Lambda} \varphi(t,\lambda)\overline{\varphi(s,\lambda)}\lambda = \int_\Lambda \varphi(t,\lambda)\overline{\varphi(s,\lambda)}\,F(d\lambda) \tag{2.170}$$

where F is a measure defined in Λ by

$$F(\lambda) = \lambda \ , \quad \lambda \in \Lambda \ , \tag{2.171}$$

proving that (2.167) is a particular case of the general expression (2.95).

Since the set of λ values in this case is countable it results

$$\chi_{\Delta\lambda}(\lambda) = \delta_{\lambda\mu} = \begin{cases} 1 & \lambda = \mu \\ 0 & \lambda \neq \mu \end{cases} \ , \quad \Delta\lambda = [\lambda,\mu) \quad . \tag{2.172}$$

Thus the inversion formula becomes

$$\int_T \psi_{\Delta\lambda}(t)\varphi(t,\lambda)\,dt = \delta_{\lambda\mu} \tag{2.173}$$

and, being the functions $\varphi(t,\lambda)$ orthogonal

$$\int_T \varphi(t,\mu)\varphi(t,\lambda)\,dt = \delta_{\lambda\mu} \ , \tag{2.174}$$

we get

$$\psi_{\Delta\lambda}(t) = \varphi(t,\lambda) \ . \tag{2.175}$$

In conclusion the canonical representation in the case of finite domain T, named *Karhunen-Loève representation* or *transformation* (KLT), has countable λ values and is given by

$$x(t) = \sum_{\lambda\in\Lambda}\varphi(t,\lambda)\Phi(\lambda) \tag{2.176}$$

with

$$\Phi(\lambda) = \int_a^b x(t)\varphi(t,\lambda)\,dt \tag{2.177}$$

and

$$E\left\{|\Phi(\lambda)|^2\right\} = \lambda \ . \tag{2.178}$$

A more rigorous and complete proof of this result, known as Karhunen-Loève theorem, is reported in Appendix C.

2.3.6. Stationary Processes with Finite Domain T

This is a particular case of Karhunen-Loève representation. In view of the general representation of stationary processes we have

$$\varphi(t,\lambda) = e^{i\lambda t} \tag{2.179}$$

and as a consequence the Karhunen-Loève series reduces to

$$x(t) = \sum_{\lambda}e^{i\lambda t}\Phi(\lambda) \ . \tag{2.180}$$

Additionally, since the domain T of $x(t)$ is finite, the process may also be represented by the Fourier series expansion

$$x(t) = \sum_{k}\mu_k\,e^{i\omega_k t} \tag{2.181}$$

as a linear combination of periodic functions, with ω_k assuming the values $\omega_1 = \dfrac{2\pi}{T}$, $2\omega_1$, $3\omega_1$, ... Comparing (2.180) and (2.181) in general it results

$$\mu_k \neq \Phi(\lambda) \qquad (2.182)$$

since the coefficients $\Phi(\lambda)$ are orthogonal, as predicted by KLT theorem, while the coefficients μ_k are not (see [5] for more details).

2.3.7. A Formula for the Measure $F(\Delta\lambda)$

The variance distribution $E\left\{|\Phi(d\lambda)|^2\right\}$ of the components $\Phi(d\lambda)$ in the canonical representation (2.108) characterises in a mean square sense the stochastic process $\Phi(d\lambda)$. Thus, given a process $x(t)$ it is worth deriving a relationship for $F(d\lambda)$.

From previous analysis a formula for the measure $F(d\lambda)$ associated to a s.p. $x(t)$, can be achieved as a function of the covariance function $B(t,s)$.

The variance of the stochastic measure

$$\Phi(\Delta\lambda) = \int_T x(t)\,\psi_{\Delta\lambda}(t)\,dt \qquad (2.183)$$

with $\psi_{\Delta\lambda}(t)$ given by

$$\int_T \psi_{\Delta\lambda}(t)\varphi(t,\lambda)\,dt = \chi_{\Delta\lambda}(t) \qquad (2.184)$$

can be easily derived

$$
\begin{aligned}
E\left\{|\Phi(\Delta\lambda)|^2\right\} &= E\left\{\int_T x(t)\psi_{\Delta\lambda}(t)\,dt \int_T \overline{x(s)}\,\overline{\psi_{\Delta\lambda}(s)}\,ds\right\} \\
&= \int_T\int_T \psi_{\Delta\lambda}(t)\overline{\psi_{\Delta\lambda}(s)}\,E\left\{x(t)\overline{x(s)}\right\}ds\,dt . \\
&= \int_T\int_T \psi_{\Delta\lambda}(t)\overline{\psi_{\Delta\lambda}(s)}\,B(s,t)\,ds\,dt
\end{aligned} \qquad (2.185)
$$

Since $E\left\{|\Phi(\Delta\lambda)|^2\right\} = F(\Delta\lambda)$, we obtain the desired result

$$F(\Delta\lambda) = \int_T\int_T \psi_{\Delta\lambda}(t)\overline{\psi_{\Delta\lambda}(s)}\,B(s,t)\,ds\,dt \qquad (2.186)$$

where $B(s,t)$ and $\psi_{\Delta\lambda}(t)$ are known functions.

PARTICULAR CASES

a) *Processes with finite support*

In the case of $T = [a,b]$ with a and b finite, the Karhunen-Loève representation holds and

$$\psi_{\Delta\lambda}(t) = \varphi(t,\lambda) \tag{2.187}$$

where $\Delta\lambda$ reduces to a discrete value λ in the real axis. From (2.186) it follows

$$F(\lambda) = \int_T \varphi(t,\lambda)\,dt \int_T \overline{\varphi(s,\lambda)}\,B(s,t)\,ds$$
$$= \int_T \varphi(t,\lambda)\lambda\overline{\varphi(t,\lambda)}\,dt = \lambda \tag{2.188}$$

where the property of $\varphi(t,\lambda)$, as normalized eigenfunctions, has been used.

b) *Stationary process*

In this case $\varphi(t,\lambda) = e^{i\lambda t}$ with $-\infty < \lambda < \infty$ and $\chi_{\Delta\lambda}(\lambda)$ is derived by

$$\chi_{\Delta\lambda}(\lambda) = \int_T \psi_{\Delta\lambda}(t)\varphi(t,\lambda)\,dt$$
$$= \int_T \psi_{\Delta\lambda}(t)e^{i\lambda t}\,dt \tag{2.189}$$

where $\Delta\lambda = [\lambda_1,\lambda_2)$.

Using the inverse FT

$$\psi_{\Delta\lambda}(t) = \frac{1}{2\pi}\int_\Lambda \chi_{\Delta\lambda}(\lambda)e^{-i\lambda t}\,d\lambda$$
$$= \frac{1}{2\pi}\int_{\lambda_1}^{\lambda_2} e^{-i\lambda t}\,d\lambda = \frac{1}{2\pi}\left[\frac{e^{-i\lambda t}}{-it}\right]_{\lambda_1}^{\lambda_2} \tag{2.190}$$

we finally obtain

$$\psi_{\Delta\lambda}(t) = \frac{1}{2\pi}\frac{e^{-i\lambda_2 t} - e^{-i\lambda_1 t}}{-it}. \tag{2.191}$$

Thus an explicit relationship for the stochastic measure $\Phi(\Delta\lambda)$ holds

$$\Phi(\Delta\lambda) = \int_T x(t)\psi_{\Delta\lambda}(t)\,dt$$
$$= \frac{1}{2\pi}\int_T \frac{e^{-i\lambda_2 t} - e^{-i\lambda_1 t}}{-it}x(t)\,dt \tag{2.192}$$

The double integral in (2.186) reduces in the stationary case to a simple integral by straightforward mathematics

$$F\left(\Delta\lambda\right) = \int_T \int_T \psi_{\Delta\lambda}\left(t\right) \overline{\psi_{\Delta\lambda}\left(s\right)} B\left(t-s\right) dt\, ds$$

$$= \int_T \int_T \psi_{\Delta\lambda}\left(t\right) \overline{\psi_{\Delta\lambda}\left(s\right)} \left(\int_\Lambda e^{\imath\lambda(t-s)} F\left(d\lambda\right)\right) dt\, ds$$

$$= \int_\Lambda F\left(d\lambda\right) \int_T \psi_{\Delta\lambda}\left(t\right) e^{\imath\lambda t} dt \int_T \overline{\psi_{\Delta\lambda}\left(s\right)} e^{-\imath\lambda s} ds$$

$$= \int_\Lambda F\left(d\lambda\right) \chi_{\Delta\lambda}\left(\lambda\right) \chi_{\Delta\lambda}\left(\lambda\right) = \int_\Lambda \chi_{\Delta\lambda}\left(\lambda\right) F\left(d\lambda\right) \qquad (2.193)$$

$$= \int_\Lambda \left(\int_T \psi_{\Delta\lambda}\left(t\right) e^{\imath\lambda t} dt\right) F\left(d\lambda\right)$$

$$= \int_T \left(\int_\Lambda e^{\imath\lambda t} F\left(d\lambda\right)\right) \psi_{\Delta\lambda}\left(t\right) dt$$

$$= \int_T \psi_{\Delta\lambda}\left(t\right) B\left(t\right) dt$$

so that we obtain the desired result

$$F\left(\Delta\lambda\right) = \frac{1}{2\pi} \int_T \frac{e^{-\imath\lambda_2 t} - e^{-\imath\lambda_1 t}}{-\imath t} B\left(t\right) dt \qquad (2.194)$$

which is the same expression derived in [4].

Being $F\left(\Delta\lambda\right)$ a Stieltjes measure it can be written as

$$F\left(\Delta\lambda\right) = \alpha\left(\lambda_1\right) - \alpha\left(\lambda_2\right), \qquad (2.195)$$

where $\alpha\left(\lambda\right)$ is a non decreasing function of λ. If α is absolutely continuous (see Sect.2.1.2) the derivative $\alpha'\left(\lambda\right) = f\left(\lambda\right)$ is called the *spectral density function* of the process. The function $f\left(\lambda\right)$ is given by

$$f\left(\lambda\right) = \frac{1}{2\pi} \int_T e^{-\imath\lambda t} B\left(t\right) dt . \qquad (2.196)$$

In fact (2.196) can be integrated in the interval $\Delta\lambda = \left[\lambda_1, \lambda_2\right]$

$$\int_{\lambda_1}^{\lambda_2} \alpha'\left(\lambda\right) d\lambda = \frac{1}{2\pi} \int_T \left(\int_{\lambda_1}^{\lambda_2} e^{-\imath\lambda t} d\lambda\right) B\left(t\right) dt \qquad (2.197)$$

to give (2.194). In this case eq. (2.156) reduces to

$$B\left(t\right) = \int_\Lambda e^{\imath\lambda t} f\left(\lambda\right) d\lambda . \qquad (2.198)$$

Eq. (2.196), (2.198) show that the covariance function $B\left(t\right)$ and the spectral density function $f\left(\lambda\right)$ are related by FT.

2.3.8. Examples of Canonical Representation

Here we report the canonical representations of the processes already introduced in the examples 1, 2, and 3 of Sect. 2.3.1.

Example 1

With the assumptions (2.99) the following canonical representation holds

$$x(t) = \int_{\Lambda} \lambda\, v(t)\, \Phi(d\lambda) = v(t) \int_{\Lambda} \lambda\, \Phi(d\lambda) \quad , \qquad \Lambda \equiv \mathbb{R} \qquad (2.199)$$

with

$$E\left\{\left|\Phi(d\lambda)\right|^{2}\right\} = F(d\lambda) = p(\lambda)\, d\lambda \ , \qquad (2.200)$$

or, that is the same,

$$E\left\{\left|\Phi(\Delta\lambda)\right|^{2}\right\} = F(\Delta\lambda) = \int_{\lambda_{1}}^{\lambda_{2}} p(\lambda)\, d\lambda \ . \qquad (2.201)$$

Example 2

The process $x(t)$ defined by (2.100) can be put in canonical form

$$x(t) = \int_{\Lambda} g(t, \lambda)\, \Phi(d\lambda) \quad , \qquad \Lambda \equiv \mathbb{R} \qquad (2.202)$$

with

$$E\left\{\left|\Phi(d\lambda)\right|^{2}\right\} = F(d\lambda) = p(\lambda)\, d\lambda \ . \qquad (2.203)$$

Example 3

In this case we have

$$x(t) = \int_{\Lambda} e^{\imath\lambda t}\, \Phi(d\lambda) \ , \qquad \Lambda \equiv \mathbb{R} \qquad (2.204)$$

with

$$E\left\{\left|\Phi(d\lambda)\right|^{2}\right\} = F(d\lambda) = a^{2}\delta(\lambda - \omega)\, d\lambda \ . \qquad (2.205)$$

2.3.9. Gaussian Random Processes

A real random process $\xi(t)$ is called Gaussian or Normal if the finite-dimensional distributions $f_{\xi_1,\cdots,\xi_n}\left(\xi(t_1), \cdots, \xi(t_n)\right)$ are Gaussian, that is, if the characteristic functions of the joint distributions of the values $\xi(t_1)$, ... , $\xi(t_n)$ of this random process have the form

$$\Phi_\xi(u_1,\cdots,u_n) = \exp\left[i\sum_{k=1}^{n} m(t_k)u_k - \frac{1}{2}\sum_{k=1}^{n}\sum_{j=1}^{n} B(t_k,t_j)u_k u_j\right] \qquad (2.206)$$

where $m(t) = E\{\xi(t)\}$ is the expectation and

$$B(t,s) = E\left\{[\xi(t) - m(t)][\xi(s) - m(s)]\right\} \qquad (2.207)$$

the correlation function. In matrix form it can be written

$$\Phi_\xi(\boldsymbol{u}) = \exp\left[i\,\boldsymbol{m}^T\boldsymbol{u} - \frac{1}{2}\boldsymbol{u}^T\boldsymbol{\Lambda}\boldsymbol{u}\right] \qquad (2.208)$$

where

$$\boldsymbol{m} = \left[m(t_1),\cdots,m(t_n)\right]^T = \left[E\{\xi(t_1)\},\cdots,E\{\xi(t_n)\}\right]^T, \qquad (2.209)$$

$$\boldsymbol{u} = [u_1,\cdots,u_n]^T, \qquad (2.210)$$

and $[\boldsymbol{\Lambda}]_{kj} = B_{kj}$ is the covariance matrix of $\xi(t_1)$, ... , $\xi(t_n)$ with

$$B_{kj} = E\left\{[\xi(t_k) - m(t_k)][\xi(t_j) - m(t_j)]\right\}. \qquad (2.211)$$

It is well known that a s.p. is completely characterized by specifying the joint density function

$$f_{\xi_1,\cdots,\xi_n}\left(\xi(t_1), \cdots, \xi(t_n)\right) \qquad (2.212)$$

for all finite sets $\{t_i\} \in T$. Obviously this definition may be generalized in a natural way to complex-valued s.p. $\xi(t) = \eta(t) + i\zeta(t)$.

As stated above, in a Gaussian process the jpdf's correspondent to the instants $t_1, \cdots, t_n$ are uniquely determined by $m(t)$ and $B(t,s)$. Thus a Gaussian process is completely characterized by its mean $m(t)$ and correlation function

$B(t,s)$.

In this case, since it is well-known that linear combinations of normal r.v.'s are normal, and being

$$\Phi(\Delta\lambda) = \int_T \xi(t)\,\psi_{\Delta\lambda}(t)\,dt \tag{2.213}$$

a linear combination of the values of $\xi(t)$, it thus follows that $\Phi(\Delta\lambda)$ are normal r.v.'s.

However, remembering the property of orthogonality of stochastic measure, i.e. $\Phi(\Delta\lambda_k)$ and $\Phi(\Delta\lambda_j)$ are orthogonal for disjoint intervals $\Delta\lambda_k$ and $\Delta\lambda_j$, it follows that in the stochastic integral $\Phi(\Delta\lambda)$ are independent Gaussian variables.

Thus the variance $E\left\{|\Phi(\Delta\lambda)|^2\right\}$ suffices to describe the joint pdf of r.v.'s $\Phi(\Delta\lambda_1)$, $\Phi(\Delta\lambda_2)$, ... , and since it results

$$E\left\{|\Phi(\Delta\lambda)|^2\right\} = F(d\lambda)\ , \tag{2.214}$$

from (2.186) it follows that the s.p. $\xi(t)$ is completely characterized by the covariance function $B(t,s)$.

It can be easily shown that this property is not in general true. To this end we assume that $\xi(t)$ has the covariance function

$$B(t,s) = \int_\Lambda \varphi(t,\lambda)\overline{\varphi(s,\lambda)}F(d\lambda) \tag{2.215}$$

and the canonical representation

$$\xi(t) = \int_\Lambda \varphi(t,\lambda)\Phi(d\lambda)\ . \tag{2.216}$$

Let $\tilde{\xi}(t)$ be another s.p. with covariance function

$$\widetilde{B}(t,s) = \int_\Lambda \widetilde{\varphi}(t,\lambda)\overline{\widetilde{\varphi}(s,\lambda)}F(d\lambda) \tag{2.217}$$

where

$$\widetilde{\varphi}(t,\lambda) = \varphi(t,\lambda)f(\lambda) \tag{2.218}$$

and $f(\lambda)$ is any function such that $|f(\lambda)|^2 = 1$.

Then we also have

$$\widetilde{B}(t,s) = \int_\Lambda \varphi(t,\lambda)\overline{\varphi(s,\lambda)}F(d\lambda)\ , \tag{2.219}$$

i.e. the two processes $\xi(t)$ and $\tilde{\xi}(t)$ have the same covariance function, even though they are not identical

$$\tilde{\xi}(t) = \int_\Lambda \tilde{\varphi}(t,\lambda)\Phi(d\lambda) = \int_\Lambda \varphi(t,\lambda)f(\lambda)\Phi(d\lambda) \neq \xi(t) \ . \qquad (2.220)$$

Appendix A

The Stieltjes Integral

Let $\alpha(x)$, $x \in \mathbb{R}$, denote a non-decreasing real function that is continuous from the left

$$\alpha(x) \le \alpha(y) \qquad \text{for} \qquad x < y ,$$
$$\lim_{\substack{h \to 0 \\ h > 0}} \alpha(x - h) = \alpha(x) . \tag{2.221}$$

To every semiclosed interval $I_{a,b}$ with end-points a and b is assigned the function

$$\mu(I_{a,b}) = \alpha(b) - \alpha(a) . \tag{2.222}$$

This function is obviously non-negative and additive. For example if $a < b < c$ we have

$$\mu(I_{a,b}) + \mu(I_{b,c}) = \alpha(b) - \alpha(a) + \alpha(c) - \alpha(b) = \mu(I_{a,c}) . \tag{2.223}$$

Therefore (2.222) defines a measure (known as the Stieltjes measure) on the semiclosed intervals of the real line.

Having defined the measure we may also define the Stieltjes integral of $f(s)$ over the set E as

$$\int_E f(s) \mu(ds) . \tag{2.224}$$

Some Results of Functional Analysis

DEFINITION A.1 (DENSE SET)

A subset S of a metric space $(\mathcal{M}, d)$ (d is the distance between two elements of $\mathcal{M}$) is *dense* in $\mathcal{M}$ if for any $\varepsilon > 0$ and any $\xi \in \mathcal{M}$, an element $\eta \in S$ exists such that $d(\xi, \eta) < \varepsilon$.

DEFINITION   A.2 (COMPLETE SEQUENCE)

A sequence of elements $\{u_k\}$ of a Hilbert space **H** is said to be *complete* in **H** if the linear combination $\lambda_1 u_1 + \cdots + \lambda_n u_n$ form a dense set in **H**. That is, if for any $\varepsilon > 0$ and any $\xi \in$ **H**, there is a finite linear combination $\eta = \lambda_1 u_1 + \cdots + \lambda_n u_n$ such that $d(\xi, \eta) < \varepsilon$.

The complete sequence is a particular case of a dense set whose elements are the linear combinations $\lambda_1 u_1 + \cdots + \lambda_n u_n$ of the elements $\{u_k\}$. In general a dense set is not necessarily generated by a sequence of elements $\{u_k\}$.

Isomorphism and Isometry

DEFINITION   A.3 (ISOMORPHISM)

An *isomorphism* from a Hilbert space $\mathfrak{S}$ onto a Hilbert space $\mathfrak{R}$ is:

   i)   a one-to-one linear transformation $\mathcal{U}$ from $\mathfrak{S}$ onto $\mathfrak{R}$

   and such that

   ii) $\langle \mathcal{U} x, \mathcal{U} y \rangle_{\mathfrak{R}} = \langle x, y \rangle_{\mathfrak{S}}$, $\forall x, y \in \mathfrak{S}$

   (i.e. $\mathcal{U}$ preserves the inner product).

DEFINITION   A.4 (ISOMETRY)

An *isometry* from a Hilbert space $\mathfrak{S}$ to a Hilbert space $\mathfrak{R}$ is:

   i)   a linear transformation $\mathcal{U}$ from $\mathfrak{S}$ *into* $\mathfrak{R}$ (not necessarily one-to-one)

   and such that

   ii) $\|\mathcal{U} x\| = \|x\|$.

   It follows that

$$\|\mathcal{U} x - \mathcal{U} y\| = \|\mathcal{U}(x - y)\| = \|x - y\| \tag{2.225}$$

thus an isometry preserves not only norms (distances from 0) but all *distances*.

THEOREM

A linear transformation $\mathcal{U}$ from a Hilbert space $\mathfrak{S}$ to a Hilbert space $\mathfrak{R}$ is an isomorphism if and only if it is an isometry, mapping $\mathfrak{S}$ onto $\mathfrak{R}$.

$\mathcal{U}$ isomorphism $\Leftrightarrow$ $\mathcal{U}$ is an isometry mapping $\mathfrak{S}$ onto $\mathfrak{R}$

   Proof.

   a) $\mathcal{U}$ isomorphism $\Rightarrow$ $\langle \mathcal{U} x, \mathcal{U} y \rangle = \langle x, y \rangle$; if $x = y$ $\left\| \mathcal{U} x \right\| = \|x\|$

and is a linear transformation from $\mathfrak{S}$ into $\mathfrak{R}$.

b) $\mathcal{U}$ is an isometry onto $\mathfrak{R}$.

    b.1)   We prove first that $\mathcal{U}$ is one-to-one

for any $x, y \in \mathfrak{S}$ the images $\mathcal{U}x, \mathcal{U}y \in \mathfrak{R}$ (because $\mathcal{U}$ is onto $\mathfrak{R}$).

Suppose $\mathcal{U}$ is one-to-one:

$$\mathcal{U}x = \mathcal{U}y \quad \text{per} \quad x \neq y \tag{2.226}$$

but in view of the isometry

$$\|\mathcal{U}x - \mathcal{U}y\| = 0 = \|\mathcal{U}(x - y)\| = \|x - y\| . \tag{2.227}$$

Thus the images are equal ($\mathcal{U}x = \mathcal{U}y$) only if $x = y$, which implies that $\mathcal{U}$ is one-to-one.

    b.2)   As already shown, if

$$\left\| \mathcal{U}x \right\| = \|x\| \quad \Rightarrow \quad \langle \mathcal{U}x, \mathcal{U}y \rangle = \langle x, y \rangle . \tag{2.228}$$

Appendix B

Some Results of the Theory of Integral Operators Applied to the Kernel $B(t,s)$

Here we report on some properties of the integral operator defined by eq. (2.168)

REMARK 1

Let $B(t,s)$ be the covariance function of the s.p. $\xi(t)$ then we have

$$
\begin{aligned}
\int_a^b \int_a^b |B(t,s)|^2 \, dt ds &= \int_a^b \int_a^b E\left\{\xi_t \overline{\xi_s}\right\} dt ds \\
&\leq \int_a^b \int_a^b E\left\{|\xi_t^2|\right\} E\left\{|\xi_s^2|\right\} dt ds \\
&= \int_a^b E\left\{|\xi_t^2|\right\} dt \int_a^b E\left\{|\xi_s^2|\right\} ds \\
&= E\left\{\int_a^b |\xi_t^2| \, dt\right\} E\left\{\int_a^b |\xi_s^2| \, ds\right\} < +\infty
\end{aligned}
\tag{2.229}
$$

where the inequality is true by virtue of the measurability of the process ξ_t.

DEFINITION B.1

If E, F are normed spaces, a linear operator $\mathcal{A} : E \to F$ is said to be *bounded* if $M \geq 0$ exists, such that

$$
\|\mathcal{A}x\| \leq M\|x\| \quad , \qquad \forall x \in E \ .
\tag{2.230}
$$

REMARK 2

The operator K defined by eqn. (2.168) is clearly linear. By the Cauchy-Schwartz inequality, we have, for fixed $t \in (c,d)$

$$
|Kx(t)|^2 \leq \left\{\int_a^b |B(t,s)|^2 \, ds\right\}\left\{\int_a^b |x(s)|^2 \, ds\right\} \ .
\tag{2.231}
$$

Hence

$$
\|Kx\|^2 \leq \left\{\int_c^d \int_a^b |B(t,s)|^2 \, ds dt\right\}\|x\|^2
\tag{2.232}
$$

Thus K is bounded.

REMARK 3

Let us be given the following definitions first.

DEFINITION B.2

Let $\{x_1, x_2, \cdots\}$ be a sequence of elements in a set S. By *a subsequence* we shall mean a sequence $\{x_{n_1}, x_{n_2}, \cdots\}$ where $x_{n_1}, x_{n_2}, \cdots$ are elements of the given sequence such that $n_1 < n_2 < \ldots$. For instance if $\{x_n\}$ is the sequence of positive integers, $x_n = n$, the sequence of even positive integers $\{x_{2n}\}$ is a subsequence.

DEFINITION B.3

Let E, F be normed spaces and let $\mathcal{A} : E \to F$ be a linear operator. $\mathcal{A}$ is said to be *compact* if, for every bounded sequence $\{x_n\}_1^\infty$ in E, the sequence $\{\mathcal{A}x_n\}_1^\infty$ has a convergent subsequence in F.

DEFINITION B.4

Let E, F be Hilbert spaces. A bounded linear operator $\mathcal{A} : E \to F$ is said to be *Hilbert-Schmidt* if a complete orthonormal sequence $\{x_n\}_1^\infty$ exists in E such that

$$\sum_{n=1}^{\infty} \|\mathcal{A}x_n\|^2 < \infty \tag{2.233}$$

For the Hilbert-Schmidt operators the following theorems hold:

THEOREM B.1

Hilbert-Schmidt operators are compact.

THEOREM B.2

Let $B(t,s) : (c,d) \times (a,b) \to \mathbb{C}$ be a Lebesgue measurable function such that

$$\int_c^d \int_a^b |B(t,s)| \, ds \, dt < \infty . \tag{2.234}$$

Then the integral operator

$$K : L_2(a,b) \to L_2(c,d) \tag{2.235}$$

with the kernel function $B(s,t)$ is a Hilbert-Schmidt operator and is therefore *compact*.

Proof of these theorems can be found in [13].

REMARK 4

THEOREM B.3 (SPECTRAL THEOREM FOR COMPACT HERMITIAN OPERATORS)
Let K be a compact Hermitian operator on a Hilbert space $\mathbf{H}$. A finite or infinite orthonormal sequence $\{\varphi_n\}$ of eigenvectors of K, with corresponding real eigenvalues $\{\lambda_n\}$ exists, such that for all $x \in \mathbf{H}$

$$Kx = \sum_n \lambda_n \langle x, \varphi_n \rangle \varphi_n \; . \tag{2.236}$$

The sequence $\{\lambda_n\}$, if infinite, tends to 0.

COROLLARY B.1
Let K be a compact Hermitian operator on a separable infinite-dimensional Hilbert space $\mathbf{H}$. A complete orthonormal sequence $\{e_n\}$ consisting of eigenvectors of K, exists. For any $x \in H$

$$Kx = \sum_{n=1}^{\infty} \lambda_n \langle x, e_n \rangle e_n \tag{2.237}$$

where λ_n is the eigenvalue corresponding to e_n.

Proof of these two results can be found in [13].

Appendix C

Karhunen-Loève Theorem

A measurable m.s. continuous Hilbert process $\xi(t)$, $t \in [a,b]$, a, b finite, admits the series expansion

$$\xi(t) = \sum_{k=1}^{\infty} \xi_k \varphi_k(t) , \tag{2.238}$$

which is convergent in L_2 for each $t \in [a,b]$. In this expansion, ξ_k is an orthogonal sequence of random variables, $E\left\{|\xi_k|^2\right\} = \lambda_k$, where λ_k are the eigenvalues and $\varphi_k(t)$ the eigenfunctions of the covariance of the process. The eigenvalues satisfy the inequality

$$\lambda_1 \geq \lambda_2 \geq \lambda_3 \geq \cdots > 0 . \tag{2.239}$$

Proof

a)   Its covariance is

$$B(t,s) = E\left\{\xi(t)\overline{\xi(s)}\right\} . \tag{2.240}$$

By Schwartz inequality

$$\left|E\left\{\xi(t)\overline{\xi(s)}\right\}\right|^2 \leq E\left\{|\xi(t)|^2\right\} E\left\{|\xi(s)|^2\right\} \tag{2.241}$$

it follows that   (see Remark 1 of Appendix B)

$$\int_c^b \int_a^b |B(t,s)|^2 \, dt \, ds < \infty \tag{2.242}$$

then $B(s,t)$ defines the kernel of the integral operator $K : L_2(a,b) \to L_2(c,d)$ defined by

$$K[u(t)] = \int_a^b B(t,s)u(s)\,ds \qquad c < t < d$$
$$B(t,s) : [c,d] \times [a,b] \to \mathbb{C} \tag{2.243}$$

the kernel is symmetric $B(s,t) = \overline{B(t,s)}$, positive definite, and bounded (see Remark 2 of Appendix B).

b)   The operator K is a compact Hermitian operator (see Remark 3 of Appendix B).

c)   According to the theory of integral equations, (see Remark 4 of Appendix B) the kernel $B(t,s)$ can be expanded into uniformly convergent series in terms of its eigenfunctions $\varphi_n(t)$:

$$B(t,s) = \sum_{n=1}^{\infty} \lambda_n \, \varphi_n(t) \overline{\varphi_n(t)} \qquad (2.244)$$

where

$$\varphi_n(t): \qquad \begin{array}{l} \displaystyle\int_a^b B(t,\tau)\varphi_n(\tau)\,d\tau = \lambda_n\varphi_n(t) \\[2mm] \displaystyle\int_a^b \varphi_n(t)\overline{\varphi_m(t)}\,dt = \delta_{nm} \end{array} \qquad (2.245)$$

moreover the eigenvalues are such that

$$\lambda_1 \geq \lambda_2 \geq \cdots > 0 \ . \qquad (2.246)$$

d)   Set

$$\xi_n = \int_a^b \xi(t)\overline{\varphi_n(t)}\,dt \qquad (2.247)$$

this integral exists (Theorem 1, p. 218, of [6] and Corollary p. 218 of [6])

$$E\left\{\xi_n\overline{\xi_m}\right\} = \int_a^b \int_a^b B(t,\tau)\overline{\varphi_n(t)}\varphi_m(\tau)\,dt d\tau = \lambda_n\delta_{nm} \qquad (2.248)$$

i.e. the sequence of r.v. ξ_n $(n = 1,2,\cdots)$ is orthogonal.

e)   Furthermore it results

$$\begin{aligned} E\left\{\xi(t)\overline{\xi_n}\right\} &= E\left\{\xi(t)\int_a^b \overline{\xi(\tau)}\varphi_n(\tau)\,d\tau\right\} \\ &= \int_a^b E\left\{\xi(t)\overline{\xi(\tau)}\right\}\varphi_n(\tau)\,d\tau \\ &= \int_a^b B(t,\tau)\varphi_n(\tau)\,d\tau \\ &= \lambda_n\varphi_n(t) \ . \end{aligned} \qquad (2.249)$$

It thus follows that

$$E\left\{\left|\xi\left(t\right)-\sum_{k=1}^{N}\xi_k\varphi_k\left(t\right)\right|^2\right\}=$$

$$=E\left\{\left|\xi\left(t\right)\right|^2\right\}-E\left\{2\xi\left(t\right)\sum_{k=1}^{N}\overline{\xi_k\varphi_k\left(t\right)}\right\}+E\left\{\left|\sum_{k=1}^{N}\xi_k\varphi_k\left(t\right)\right|^2\right\}$$

$$=B\left(t,t\right)-2\sum_{k=1}^{N}E\left\{\xi\left(t\right)\overline{\xi_k}\right\}\overline{\varphi_k\left(t\right)}+\sum_{k=1}^{N}\sum_{n=1}^{N}\varphi_k\left(t\right)\overline{\varphi_n\left(t\right)}E\left\{\xi_k\overline{\xi_n}\right\}E$$
$$\tag{2.250}$$

$$=B\left(t,t\right)-2\sum_{k=1}^{N}\lambda_k\varphi_k\left(t\right)\overline{\varphi_k\left(t\right)}+\sum_{k=1}^{N}\sum_{n=1}^{N}\varphi_k\left(t\right)\overline{\varphi_n\left(t\right)}\lambda_k\delta_{kn}$$

$$=B\left(t,t\right)-2\sum_{k=1}^{N}\lambda_k\left|\varphi_k\left(t\right)\right|^2+\sum_{k=1}^{N}\lambda_k\left|\varphi_k\left(t\right)\right|^2$$

$$=B\left(t,t\right)-\sum_{k=1}^{N}\lambda_k\left|\varphi_k\left(t\right)\right|^2\ .$$

Taking the limit

$$\lim_{N\to\infty}E\left\{\left|\xi\left(t\right)-\sum_{k=1}^{N}\xi_k\varphi_k\left(t\right)\right|^2\right\}=\lim_{N\to\infty}\left[B\left(t,t\right)-\sum_{k=1}^{N}\lambda_k\left|\varphi_k\left(t\right)\right|^2\ . \tag{2.251}$$

By virtue of continuity $B\left(t_1,t_2\right)$ it follows that

$$\lim_{t_2\to t}B\left(t,t_2\right)=B\left(t,t\right)=\lim_{t_2\to t}\left[\lim_{N\to\infty}\sum_{k=1}^{N}\lambda_k\varphi_k\left(t\right)\overline{\varphi_k\left(t_2\right)}\right]. \tag{2.252}$$

From standard analysis it is known that two limit operations applied to a sequence can be exchanged for each other provided the sequence is uniformly convergent. Since this is the case (2.222) can be written

$$B\left(t,t\right)=\lim_{N\to\infty}\left[\lim_{t_2\to t}\sum_{k=1}^{N}\lambda_k\varphi_k\left(t\right)\overline{\varphi_k\left(t_2\right)}\right]=\lim_{N\to\infty}\left[\sum_{k=1}^{N}\lambda_k\left|\varphi_k\left(t\right)\right|^2\right]. \tag{2.253}$$

So that it results

$$\lim_{N\to\infty}E\left\{\left|\xi\left(t\right)-\sum_{k=1}^{N}\xi_k\varphi_k\left(t\right)\right|^2\right\}=0 \tag{2.254}$$

uniformly in t.

References

[1]   Chen, G., Chen, G., & Hsu, S.-H. (1995). *Linear Stochastic Control Systems.* Boca Raton, U.S.A. : CRC Press, Inc.

[2]   Cramér, H., & Leadbetter M. R. (1967). *Stationary and Related Stochastic Processes.* New York, U.S.A. : John Wiley & Sons.

[3]   Davis, M. H. A. (1977). *Linear Estimation and Stochastic Control.* Great Britain: Chapman and Hall.

[4]   Doob, J. L. (1990). *Stochastic Processes.* New York, U.S.A. : Wiley

[5]   Dougherty, E. R. (1999). *Random Processes for Image and Signal Processing.* Bellingham, U.S.A.: SPIE Optical Engineering Press.

[6]   Gihman, I. I., & Skorohod, A.V. (1974). *The Theory of Stochastic Processes.* Berlin, Germany: Springer-Verlag.

[7]   Grimble, M. J., & Johnson, M. A. (1988). *Optimal Control and Stochastic Estimation: Theory and Applications, Vol. 2.* New York, U.S.A. : John Wiley & Sons.

[8]   Halmos, P. R. (1974). *Measure Theory.* New York, U.S.A.: Springer-Verlag.

[9]   Kingman, J. F. C., & Taylor, S. J. (1966). *Introduction to Measure and Probability.* New York, U.S.A.: Cambridge University Press.

[10] Karhunen, K. (1947). Uber lineare Methoden in der Wahrscheinlicherechnung, *Ann. Acad. Sci. Fennicae, Ser. A. Math Phys.* 37, 3-79.

[11] Koopmans, L. H. (1995). *The Spectral Analysis of the Time Series.* San Diego, U.S.A. : Academic Press.

[12] Prohorov, Y. V., & Rozanov, Y. A. (1969). *Probability Theory.* Berlin, Germany: Springer-Verlag.

[13] Young, N. (1988). *An Introduction to Hilbert Space.* Great Britain: Cambridge University Press.

Stochastic Models of Neural Networks
C. Turchetti
. IOS Press, 2004

As far as the laws of mathematics refer to reality, they are not certain; and as far as they are certain, they do not refer to reality.

Albert Einstein

CHAPTER THREE

NEURAL NETWORKS AS APPROXIMATORS OF RANDOM FUNCTIONS

Stochastic Neural Networks are built by introducing random fluctuations into the network. They are usually used for global optimization, since random fluctuations enable the networks to escape from local minima, increasing the probability of converging to a global minimum.

The aim of this chapter is to investigate the properties of stochastic networks with regard to the space of functions they generate, rather than their ability in solving global optimization problems.

From this point of view non-recurrent stochastic neural networks can be interpreted as stochastic processes themselves (and the recurrent networks as stochastic differential equations), that is as a random source of functions.

Thus it is natural to carry out the study of stochastic neural networks in the framework of stochastic processes theory.

One of the main objectives of this chapter is to demonstrate that a significant property of these networks is their ability in approximating stochastic processes belonging to certain specific classes.

3.1.   Stochastic Neural Networks

Stochastic neural networks are known in literature primarily as paradigms for solving optimization problems, due to their ability in circumventing the major inconvenience of the currently used Newton-based algorithms, i.e. trapping the solution in local minima.

Usually stochastic networks are classified as

i)   networks using the stochastic activation function (also known as *Boltzmann machines*);

ii)   networks using stochastic weights.

A *Boltzmann machine* [1]-[3] is a neural network with symmetric recurrent connections, and using a probabilistic mechanism in the firing of neurons. Each neuron has two states: the "on" or "firing" state x_i of a neuron is denoted by $x_i = 1$, and the "off" or "quiescent" state is represented by $x_i = 0$. Additionally, to the i-th neuron a *potential* u_i defined by

$$u_i = \sum_j \omega_{ij} x_j \tag{3.1}$$

is associated, where the connections ω_{ij} are such that $\omega_{ij} = \omega_{ji}$ for symmetry.

The Boltzmann machine operates by choosing a neuron of the network at random – say neuron i – and changing its state x_i depending on u_i. The new state x_i is equal to 1 with probability $f(u_i)$, and it is equal to 0 with probability $1 - f(u_i)$, being $f(u)$ given by

$$f(u) = \frac{1}{1 + \exp(-u)} . \tag{3.2}$$

The vector $x = [x_1, \cdots, x_n]^T$ is called the state of the Boltzmann machine. The state transition is mathematically described by a Markov chain with 2^n states x. When all the neurons are connected, it forms an ergodic Markov chain, having a unique stationary distribution $p(x)$. Whatever initial state the Boltzmann machine starts from, the probability of a state x converges to $p(x)$, and state x appears with relative frequency $p(x)$ over a long period of time.

The behavior of the other stochastic neural networks class, i.e. *networks using stochastic weights*, may be summarized as follows.

Let us consider a one-layer network consisting of k neural elements, which receive the same input signals $\boldsymbol{x} = [x_1, \cdots, x_n]^T$, and emit respective outputs $\boldsymbol{z} = [z_1, \cdots, z_k]^T$. Let ω_{ij} be the synaptic connection weight from the i-th input component x_i to the j-th neuron. The output of the neuron z_j of the j-th neuron is then written as

$$z_j = f\left(\sum_{i=1}^{n} \omega_{ij} x_i - h_j\right) \quad , \qquad j = 1, \cdots, k \qquad (3.3)$$

where f is a nonlinear output function and h_j is a threshold value. This is the behavior of a simple one-layer network without recurrent connections. The network transforms a vector input signal $\boldsymbol{x}$ to a vector output signal $\boldsymbol{z}$ by the transformation

$$\boldsymbol{z} = \mathrm{T}_\omega \boldsymbol{x} \ , \qquad (3.4)$$

where T_ω is the nonlinear mapping defined by (3.3) and $\boldsymbol{\omega} = \left[\omega_{ij}\right]$ is called the connection matrix.

When a network is complex, the connection weights may be regarded as if they were determined randomly and we find those properties which hold for almost all randomly generated networks under the same probability law.

It is worth noting that with reference to the networks defined above, Boltzmann machines are stochastic in their own nature, while regarding the networks of the second kind, it is effective to train them as if they were stochastic, although they behave deterministically. Nevertheless networks using stochastic weights may be viewed as input-output mapping depending on random variables. Thus they may be considered as random variables dependent on one (or more) parameter and in fact as stochastic processes in agreement with the definition given in Chapter 2.

As will appear later, studying neural networks from this point of view is particularly fruitful since they display new interesting properties when they are treated as stochastic networks in their own.

The aim of this chapter is to investigate the properties of such networks to be viewed as sources of random functions. In particular, as it is natural to ask whether approximating properties similar to those valid for deterministic function hold for random function too, this will be the main objective of this chapter.

In order to simplify the treatment of this subject, we will refer solely to the

AINN's because they exhibit a linear dependence on random coefficients that characterize their statistical behavior.

A natural extension of the theory developed here is the generalization of the results on the MLP and RBF networks, but involving further mathematical problems not easily solvable, due to the nonlinearity of such networks with respect to random coefficients.

3.2.   Stochastic Approximate Identity Neural Networks (SAINN's)

As shown in Chapter 1 neural networks belonging to the AINN class can be represented by finite sums of the form

$$S_n(t) = \sum_{i=-n}^{n} a_i k_\nu (t - t_i) \tag{3.5}$$

where $k_\nu(\bullet)$ are AI functions.

By assuming that at least one of the parameters ν, a_i, t_i is a random variable, the function $S_n(t)$ becomes a random function according to the definition given in Sect. 2.1.5. In fact for each fixed set ν, a_i, t_i eqn. (3.5) corresponds to a deterministic function (or trajectory) while by randomly varying the parameters ν, a_i, t_i a population of functions, i.e. a stochastic process, is obtained. A network of the kind expressed by (3.5) or more generally by (1.1) with some random parameters, may be defined as *stochastic neural network.*

In an attempt to investigate the properties of such networks, we may ask whether they own approximating properties similar to the ones derived for the deterministic counterpart.

However, since it is not easy to build-up such a general theory, we will restrict the analysis to stochastic networks with a linear dependence on random parameters alone.

Hence, with reference to AI networks, we assume the coefficients a_i only are r.v.'s, defining a new class of neural networks named Stochastic Approximate Identity Neural Networks (SAINN's) by

Definition 3.1 - An SAINN is a superimposition of AI functions of the form (3.5), with random coefficients a_i.

Hereinafter in order to simplify the notation, instead of (3.5) we will use

$$\eta(t) = \sum_m \eta_m u_m(t) \qquad (3.6)$$

to represent an SAINN, where η_m are r.v.'s and $u_m(t) = k_\nu(t - t_m)$ are AI functions.

The architecture of neural network corresponding to (3.6) is defined in Fig. 21, where the coefficients η_m are not constant as in (1.11) but rather r.v.'s.

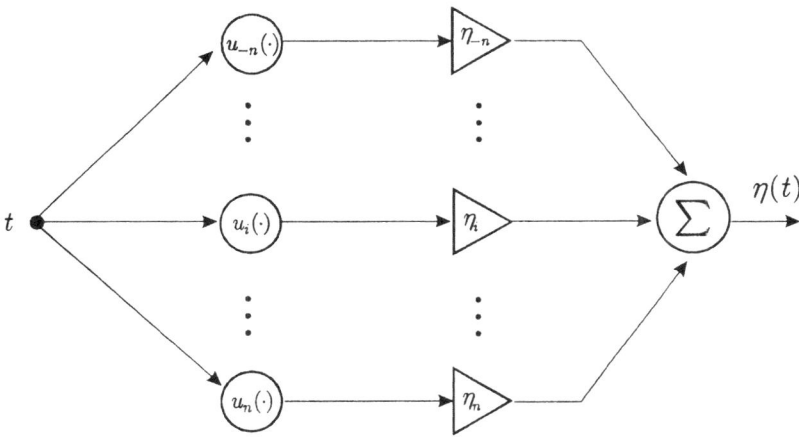

Figure 21. Architecture of an SAINN

3.3.   Approximation of Non-Stationary Stochastic Processes by SAINN's

In this Section we want to show that stochastic processes admitting the canonical representation (2.108), can be approximated in mean square by stochastic neural networks of the kind

$$\eta(t) = \sum_m \eta_m u_m(t) \qquad (3.7)$$

where η_m are random variables and $u_m(t)$ are AI functions.

For this purpose, let us be given the s.p. $\xi(t)$ whose canonical representation is

$$\xi(t) = \int_\Lambda \varphi(t,\lambda)\Phi(d\lambda) \tag{3.8}$$

where $\varphi(t,\lambda)$ is L_2-summable, i.e.

$$\int_T \int_\Lambda |\varphi(t,\lambda)|^2 F(d\lambda)\,dt < +\infty . \tag{3.9}$$

In view of Theorem 1.2, which can be naturally generalized to the two-dimensional case thanks to property P3 of AI functions, the set of functions

$$g(t,\lambda) = \sum_m a_m u_m(t) u_m(\lambda) \tag{3.10}$$

is dense in $L_2(\Lambda \times T)$, thus for $\forall \varepsilon > 0$ it results

$$d\big(g(t,\lambda),\varphi(t,\lambda)\big) < \varepsilon , \quad \forall\ t \in T,\ \lambda \in \Lambda . \tag{3.11}$$

As the stochastic measure $\Phi(\Delta)$ establishes a correspondence $\mathcal{U}$ between $L_2(F)$ and $\mathcal{L}(\xi)$

$$\varphi(t,\lambda) \xleftarrow{\ \mathcal{U}\ } \xi(t) , \quad \forall\ t \in T , \tag{3.12}$$

to the function $g(t,\lambda) \in L_2(\Lambda)$ corresponds a process $\eta(t)$ through $\mathcal{U}$ (see Fig. 22)

$$g(t,\lambda) \xleftarrow{\ \mathcal{U}\ } \eta(t) \tag{3.13}$$

with canonical representation given by

$$\eta(t) = \int_\Lambda g(t,\lambda)\Phi(d\lambda) . \tag{3.14}$$

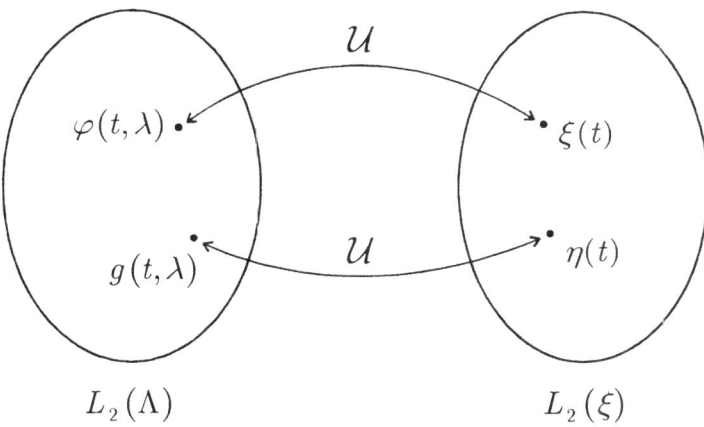

Figure 22. Correspondence of the s.p.'s $\xi(t)$, $\eta(t)$ with the functions $\varphi(t,\lambda)$, $g(t,\lambda)$ through the operator $\mathcal{U}$

Due to the isometric property of $\mathcal{U}$ the following equality holds

$$E\left\{\left|\eta(t) - \xi(t)\right|^2\right\} = \int_\Lambda \left|g(t,\lambda) - \varphi(t,\lambda)\right|^2 F(d\lambda), \quad \forall\, t \in T . \qquad (3.15)$$

By taking advantage of the dense property of the functions $g(t,\lambda)$ we have

$$\int_T \int_\Lambda \left|g(t,\lambda) - \varphi(t,\lambda)\right|^2 F(d\lambda)\, dt = \int_T \mathcal{E}^2(t)\, dt \to 0 \qquad (3.16)$$

that implies

$$\mathcal{E}^2(t) = \int_\Lambda \left|g(t,\lambda) - \varphi(t,\lambda)\right|^2 F(d\lambda) \to 0 \qquad (3.17)$$

in all T but a set belonging to T of null measure, and thus we also have

$$E\left\{\left|\xi(t) - \eta(t)\right|^2\right\} \to 0 . \qquad (3.18)$$

From what is shown above we conclude that the s.p.

$$\eta(t) = \int_\Lambda g(t,\lambda)\Phi(d\lambda) \qquad (3.19)$$

is able to approximate in mean square the given process $\xi(t)$. We may also write

$$\eta\left(t\right) = \int_{\Lambda} \sum_{m} a_m u_m\left(t\right) u_m\left(\lambda\right) \Phi\left(d\lambda\right)$$

$$= \sum_{m} a_m u_m\left(t\right) \int_{\Lambda} u_m\left(\lambda\right) \Phi\left(d\lambda\right) \ . \tag{3.20}$$

By defining the random variables

$$\eta_m = a_m \int_{\Lambda} u_m\left(\lambda\right) \Phi\left(d\lambda\right) \ , \tag{3.21}$$

we have

$$\eta\left(t\right) = \sum_{m} \eta_m u_m\left(t\right) \ . \tag{3.22}$$

Eq. (3.22) can be viewed as a stochastic neural network expressed in terms of linear combination of AI functions, through the coefficients η_m, being η_m random variables whose statistics depends on the process $\xi\left(t\right)$ to be approximated.

The similarity of (3.22) to the Karhunen-Loève representation is noticeable, although in KLT expansion the functions of time are eigenfunctions dependent on the covariance function, while in (3.22) they are AI functions.

3.4.   Learning of SAINN's from Covariance Function: Historical Learning

On the basis of what is previously proven, Eq. (3.22) defines an SAINN able to approximate, with an error given by the distance between s.p.'s $\xi\left(t\right)$ and $\eta\left(t\right)$, any given process $\xi\left(t\right)$ belonging to the class of s.p.'s (nonstationary in general) admitting a canonical form.

Learning an s.p. by means of an SAINN defined by (3.22), is equivalent to deriving both the deterministic coefficients a_m and the r.v.'s η_m. As the coefficients a_m are defined through the approximation of $\varphi(t,\lambda)$ by means of the function $g\left(t,\lambda\right) = \sum_{m} a_m u_m\left(t\right) u_m\left(\lambda\right)$, in order to perform the learning process of the neural network it is essential to know $\varphi(t,\lambda)$.

Since the functions $\varphi(t,\lambda)$ define the covariance function $B\left(t,s\right)$, knowing $\varphi(t,\lambda)$ is equivalent to have a knowledge of $B\left(t,s\right)$. Moreover the covariance function embraces much of the information achieved by gathering a population of realizations (the history of the process). For this reason learning based on the knowledge of $B(t,s)$ will be called *historical learning*.

It is convenient to treat the case of finite T separately to the case of infinite T, since it is not simple to define a unified framework for the learning purpose.

3.4.1. Finite T

In this case the set Λ is countable, as it follows from the Karhunen-Loève theory, thus (3.22) reduces to:

$$\eta(t) = \sum_m a_m u_m(t) \sum_j u_m(\lambda_j) \Phi(\lambda_j)$$
$$= \sum_m u_m(t) \sum_j a_m u_m(\lambda_j) \Phi(\lambda_j) = \sum_m \eta_m u_m(t)$$

(3.23)

with

$$\eta_m = a_m \sum_j u_m(\lambda_j) \Phi(\lambda_j) .$$

(3.24)

Moreover we may write

$$\eta(t) = \sum_j \left[\sum_m a_m u_m(t) u_m(\lambda_j) \right] \Phi(\lambda_j) .$$

(3.25)

Nevertheless the Karhunen-Loève theory establishes that $\xi(t)$ can be expanded as

$$\xi(t) = \sum_j \varphi(t, \lambda_j) \Phi(\lambda_j) .$$

(3.26)

Comparing (3.25) and (3.26), and assuming the approximation

$$\varphi(t, \lambda_j) \cong \sum_m a_m u_m(t) u_m(\lambda_j)$$

(3.27)

holds, then we have

$$\xi(t) \cong \eta(t) .$$

(3.28)

More rigorously

$$
\begin{aligned}
E\left\{ \left| \xi(t) - \eta(t) \right|^2 \right\} &= E\left\{ \left| \sum_j \left[\varphi(t,\lambda_j) - \sum_m a_m u_m(t) u_m(\lambda_j) \right] \Phi(\lambda_j) \right|^2 \right\} \\
&= E\left\{ \sum_j \left| \varphi(t,\lambda_j) - \sum_m a_m u_m(t) u_m(\lambda_j) \right|^2 \left| \Phi(\lambda_j) \right|^2 \right\} \\
&= \sum_j \left| \varphi(t,\lambda_j) - \sum_m a_m u_m(t) u_m(\lambda_j) \right|^2 E\left\{ \left| \Phi(\lambda_j) \right|^2 \right\} \\
&= \sum_j \left| \varphi(t,\lambda_j) - \sum_m a_m u_m(t) u_m(\lambda_j) \right|^2 \lambda_j^2 \to 0 ,
\end{aligned}
\tag{3.29}
$$

where the orthogonality of the stochastic measure $\Phi(\lambda_j)$ and the approximating property of the AINN's have been used.

Provided the covariance function is known from the s.p. $\xi(t)$ or it is estimated from experimental data, in the case of finite T the functions $\varphi(t,\lambda_j)$ are also known, since they are the eigenfunctions of the integral operator defined by $B(t,s)$. Therefore eq. (3.29) can be viewed as a learning relationship of the stochastic neural network, while the other learning relationship is given by

$$
\Phi(\lambda_j) = \int_T \xi(t) \varphi(t,\lambda_j) dt .
\tag{3.30}
$$

In conclusion, when T is finite, from the knowledge of the covariance function $B(t,s)$ (or an estimation of it) we may define an SAINN

$$
\eta(t) = \sum_m \eta_m u_m(t) , \quad \eta_m = a_m \sum_m u_m(\lambda_j) \Phi(\lambda_j)
\tag{3.31}
$$

that approximates the process $\xi(t)$, through the relationships

$$
\left| \varphi(t,\lambda_j) - \sum_m a_m u_m(t) u_m(\lambda_j) \right|^2 \to 0
\tag{3.32}
$$

and

$$
\Phi(\lambda_j) = \int_T \xi(t) \varphi(t,\lambda_j) dt .
\tag{3.33}
$$

It is worth noting that when $\xi(t)$ is Gaussian, $\Phi(\lambda_j)$ are independent Gaussian random variables. This case is of particular interest for the applications because the statistical behavior of $\Phi(\lambda_j)$ is completely specified by the variance $E\left\{ \left| \Phi(\lambda_j) \right|^2 \right\}$, i.e. the eigenvalue λ_j, by virtue of the relationship (2.178).

Example

As an example of the complexity of the approximating problem let us consider a stationary process $\xi(t)$ with covariance function

$$B(t,s) = a\,e^{-a|t-s|} \tag{3.34}$$

on the interval $[0,T]$. The eigenvalue equation in this case is

$$\int_0^T a\,e^{-a|t-s|}\varphi(s)\,ds = \lambda\,\varphi(t) . \tag{3.35}$$

In order to solve this integral equation it is useful to rewrite the integral as the convolution over the entire real axis $(-\infty, +\infty)$

$$h(t) * \varphi(t) = \lambda\,\varphi(t) \tag{3.36}$$

with

$$h(t) = a\,e^{-a|t-s|} , \tag{3.37}$$

and constraining (3.36) to the boundary conditions as imposed by (3.35) at the end of the time interval $\left[0,\,T\right]$, so that eq. (3.36) is identical to eq.(3.35).

By Fourier-Transform eq. (3.36) becomes

$$H(j\omega)\cdot U(j\omega) = \lambda\,U(j\omega) \tag{3.38}$$

where $H(j\omega)$, $U(j\omega)$ are the Fourier-Transforms of $h(t)$, $\varphi(t)$ respectively. Since it results

$$H(j\omega) = \frac{2a^2}{a^2 + \omega^2} , \tag{3.39}$$

eq. (3.38) reduces to

$$\frac{2a^2}{a^2 + \omega^2} U(j\omega) = \lambda U(j\omega) \tag{3.40}$$

and the eigenvalues λ are given by

$$\lambda = \frac{2a^2}{a^2 + \omega^2} . \tag{3.41}$$

Applying the inverse Fourier-Transform to eq. (3.40), a differential equation results

$$\varphi''(t) + \left(\frac{2-\lambda}{\lambda}\right) a^2 \varphi(t) = 0 \ . \tag{3.42}$$

Solving this equation requires two boundary conditions on $\varphi(t)$ and its derivative $\varphi'(t)$. To take the derivative of $\varphi(t)$ we rewrite (3.35) as

$$a e^{-at} \int_0^t e^{as} \varphi(s) \, ds + a e^{at} \int_t^T e^{-as} \varphi(s) \, ds = \lambda \varphi(t) \tag{3.43}$$

then obtaining

$$-a^2 e^{-at} \int_0^t e^{as} \varphi(s) \, ds + a^2 e^{at} \int_t^T e^{-as} \varphi(s) \, ds = \lambda \varphi'(t) \ . \tag{3.44}$$

From (3.35) and (3.44) we have

$$\frac{\varphi(T)}{\varphi'(T)} = -\frac{1}{a} \quad , \qquad \frac{\varphi(0)}{\varphi'(0)} = \frac{1}{a} \ . \tag{3.45}$$

The general solution of (3.42) is given by

$$\varphi(t) = A \sin(\omega t + \alpha) \tag{3.46}$$

and the boundary conditions (3.45) take the form

$$\tan(\omega T + \alpha) = -\frac{\omega}{a} \quad , \qquad \tan \alpha = \frac{\omega}{a} \ . \tag{3.47}$$

After some manipulation eqs. (3.47) reduce to a unique equation

$$\tan(\omega_k T) = -\frac{2a\omega_k}{a^2 + \omega_k} \tag{3.48}$$

where the index k means that a countable set of values of ω_k satisfying eq. (3.48) exists.

Eq. (3.41) defines the corresponding eigenvalues λ_k, given by

$$\Delta \lambda_k = \frac{2a^2}{a^2 + \omega_k^2} \quad , \qquad k = 1, 2, \ldots \tag{3.49}$$

while the eigenfunctions are expressed as

$$\varphi_k(t) = A_k \sin(w_k t + \alpha_k) \tag{3.50}$$

where the constants A_k, α_k are determined from the orthonormalization conditions

$$\int_0^T \varphi_k(t)\varphi_l(t)\,dt = \delta_{kl} \ . \tag{3.51}$$

As far as the stochastic neural network is concerned, eqs. (3.32) and (3.33) apply in this case with $\varphi(t,\lambda_j)$ given by eq. (3.50).

3.4.2. Infinite T

In this case the set Λ is not countable, and the problem of determining a complete set of functions $\varphi(t,\lambda)$ falls in the theory of operators whose eigenvalues form a noncountable set. Since this subject is out of the scope of this book, we restrict the treatment of this case to a specific class of random processes.

Let us assume

$$\varphi(t,\lambda) = a(t)e^{i\lambda t} \tag{3.52}$$

where $a(t)$ is an arbitrary function (such that for every $\lambda \in \Lambda$, $\varphi(t,\lambda)$ is L_2-integrable), then the set of functions $\{\varphi(t,\lambda)\}$, yielded by varying the parameter $t \in T$, is a complete family in $L_2(F)$. This property can be easily proven as follows.

Any linear combination of $\varphi(t,\lambda)$ can be written as

$$\sum_k b_k \varphi(t_k,\lambda) = \sum_k b_k a(t_k)e^{i\lambda t_k} = \sum_k c_k e^{i\lambda t_k} \ . \tag{3.53}$$

Yet, from the theory of Fourier-integral it is known that the set $\left\{e^{i\lambda t}\right\}$ is complete in $L_2(F)$, meaning that linear combinations of such kind generate the entire space $L_2(F)$. As a consequence the set $\left\{\sum_k b_k \varphi(t_k,\lambda)\right\}$ also has the same property of generating the space $L_2(F)$, which is equivalent to saying that given any function $f(\lambda) \in L_2(F)$ it results

$$f(\lambda) = \lim_{N \to \infty} \sum_{k=1}^N b_k \varphi(t_k,\lambda) \ . \tag{3.54}$$

The covariance function of the process $\xi(t)$ may be written as

$$B(t,s) = \int_\Lambda \varphi(t,\lambda)\overline{\varphi(s,\lambda)}F(d\lambda) = a(t)\overline{a(s)}\int_\Lambda e^{i\lambda(t-s)}F(d\lambda) , \qquad (3.55)$$

while the canonical representation reduces to

$$\xi(t) = \int_\Lambda \varphi(t,\lambda)\Phi(d\lambda) = a(t)\int_\Lambda e^{i\lambda t}\Phi(d\lambda) = a(t)\zeta(t) , \qquad (3.56)$$

being

$$\zeta(t) = \int_\Lambda e^{i\lambda t}\Phi(d\lambda) \qquad (3.57)$$

a stationary s.p. since it admits the representation (2.155).

Hence, we conclude that the canonical representation (3.56), with $\varphi(t,\lambda)$ given by (3.52), is valid for the class of all nonstationary processes expressed in the form $\xi(t) = a(t)\zeta(t)$, being $a(t)$ an arbitrary function and $\zeta(t)$ a stationary process.

As far as the inversion formula for the process $\xi(t)$ is concerned, from (2.160) we obtain

$$\int_T \psi_{\Delta\lambda}(t)\varphi(t,\lambda)\,dt = \int_T \psi_{\Delta\lambda}(t)a(t)e^{i\lambda t}dt = \int_T c(t)e^{i\lambda t}dt = \chi_{\Delta\lambda}(\lambda) . \qquad (3.58)$$

so that the function $c(t)$ can be derived by the Fourier inverse transform

$$c(t) = \psi_{\Delta\lambda}(t)a(t) = \frac{1}{2\pi}\frac{e^{-i\lambda_2 t} - e^{-i\lambda_1 t}}{-it} . \qquad (3.59)$$

Finally from (2.163) we have

$$\Phi(\Delta\lambda) = \int_T \xi(t)\psi_{\Delta\lambda}(t)\,dt = \int_T \zeta(t)a(t)\psi_{\Delta\lambda}(t)\,dt \qquad (3.60)$$

and using (3.59) yields

$$\Phi(\Delta\lambda) = \frac{1}{2\pi}\int_T \frac{e^{-i\lambda_2 t} - e^{-i\lambda_1 t}}{-it}\zeta(t)\,dt \qquad (3.61)$$

that is the same result as the one obtained in (2.192) for a stationary process.

Eq. (3.61) establishes that the stochastic measure $\Phi(\Delta\lambda)$ is only dependent on the stationary component $\zeta(t)$ of the process $\xi(t) = a(t)\zeta(t)$.

The measure $F(\Delta\lambda)$ can be derived from the general equation (2.186)

$$F\left(\Delta\lambda\right) = \int_T \int_T \psi_{\Delta\lambda}\left(t\right)\overline{\psi_{\Delta\lambda}\left(s\right)} B\left(t,s\right) dt\, ds$$

$$= \int_T \int_T \psi_{\Delta\lambda}\left(t\right)\overline{\psi_{\Delta\lambda}\left(s\right)} a\left(t\right)\overline{a\left(s\right)} \int_\Lambda e^{\imath\lambda(t-s)} F\left(d\lambda\right) dt\, ds \qquad (3.62)$$

which, by taking into account of (3.59), reduces to

$$F\left(\Delta\lambda\right) = \frac{1}{\left(2\pi\right)^2} \int_T \int_T \left(\frac{e^{-\imath\lambda_2 t} - e^{-\imath\lambda_1 t}}{-\imath\, t}\right)\left(\frac{e^{-\imath\lambda_2 s} - e^{-\imath\lambda_1 s}}{-\imath\, s}\right) B_\zeta\left(t-s\right) dt\, ds \qquad (3.63)$$

where $B_\zeta\left(t-s\right)$ is the covariance function of $\zeta\left(t\right)$ and is defined by

$$B\left(t,s\right) = a\left(t\right)\overline{a\left(s\right)} B_\zeta\left(t-s\right) . \qquad (3.64)$$

Coming back to the problem of approximating the s.p. $\xi\left(t\right) = a\left(t\right)\zeta\left(t\right)$, it is equivalent to approximating the deterministic function $\varphi\left(t,\lambda\right) = a\left(t\right)e^{\imath\lambda t}$ with the AINN, i.e.

$$a\left(t\right)e^{\imath\lambda t} \cong \sum_m a_m u_m\left(t\right) u_m\left(\lambda\right) . \qquad (3.65)$$

Indeed the mean square error between the given s.p. $\xi\left(t\right)$ and the approximating process

$$\eta\left(t\right) = \int_\Lambda g\left(t,\lambda\right)\Phi\left(d\lambda\right) , \qquad (3.66)$$

with

$$g\left(t,\lambda\right) = \sum_m a_m\, u_m\left(t\right) u_m\left(\lambda\right) , \qquad (3.67)$$

is given by

$$E\left\{\left|\xi\left(t\right) - \eta\left(t\right)\right|^2\right\} = E\left\{\left|\int_\Lambda \varphi\left(t,\lambda\right)\Phi\left(d\lambda\right) - \int_\Lambda g\left(t,\lambda\right)\Phi\left(d\lambda\right)\right|^2\right\}$$

$$= E\left\{\left|\int_\Lambda \left[\varphi\left(t,\lambda\right) - g\left(t,\lambda\right)\right]\Phi\left(d\lambda\right)\right|^2\right\}$$

$$= \int_\Lambda \left|\varphi\left(t,\lambda\right) - g\left(t,\lambda\right)\right|^2 F\left(d\lambda\right) \qquad (3.68)$$

$$= \int_\Lambda \left|a\left(t\right)e^{\imath\lambda t} - \sum_m a_m\, u_m\left(t\right) u_m\left(\lambda\right)\right|^2 F\left(d\lambda\right) \to 0 .$$

The stochastic neural network is defined by (3.21), (3.22), with $\Phi\left(\Delta\lambda\right)$ given by (3.61). If the process $\xi\left(t\right)$ is Gaussian the r.v.'s $\Phi\left(\Delta\lambda\right)$ are independent and completely specified by the variance $E\left\{\left|\Phi\left(\Delta\lambda\right)\right|^2\right\} = F\left(\Delta\right)$ so that $B_\zeta\left(t-s\right)$ completely characterizes the process as it follows from (3.63), (3.64).

3.5.   Real-Time Learning of Stochastic Neural Networks

The learning process discussed in the previous section requires knowledge of the covariance function $B\left(t,s\right)$ of the s.p. $\xi\left(t\right)$ to be approximated. In particular for Gaussian processes this condition is sufficient to completely represent the process, and to guarantee that the approximating process $\eta\left(t\right)$ has the same realizations of $\xi\left(t\right)$.

Since the covariance function may be estimated from a bundle of realizations, this method has been called Historical Learning to emphasize that the knowledge of past history is needed. In this section we will discuss a different learning approach by stochastic neural networks which can be directly applied to the dynamic evolution of the process and for this reason is named *real-time learning*.

Let $g\left(t,\lambda\right) = \sum_m a_m u_m\left(t\right) u_m\left(\lambda\right)$ be a set of dense functions in $L_2\left(F\right)$, which can be represented by an AINN, and define the function $\widetilde{\psi}_{\Delta\lambda}\left(t\right)$ by the integral equation

$$\int_T \widetilde{\psi}_{\Delta\lambda}\left(t\right) g\left(t,\lambda\right) dt = \widetilde{\chi}_{\Delta\lambda}\left(\lambda\right) \tag{3.69}$$

where $\widetilde{\chi}_{\Delta\lambda}\left(\lambda\right)$ approximates the indicator function $\chi_{\Delta\lambda}\left(\lambda\right)$, in view   of the approximating property of $g\left(t,\lambda\right)$. The Fig. 23 depicts a typical behavior of $\widetilde{\chi}_{\Delta\lambda}\left(\lambda\right)$ compared to $\chi_{\Delta\lambda}\left(\lambda\right)$.

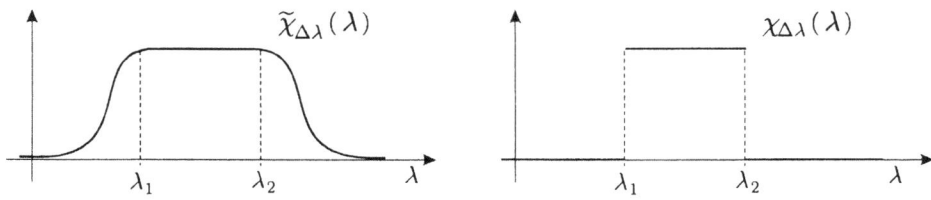

Figure 23. Typical behaviour of $\widetilde{\chi}_{\Delta\lambda}\left(\lambda\right)$ *and* $\chi_{\Delta\lambda}\left(\lambda\right)$

Given the s.p. $x\left(t\right)$, the relationship

$$\widetilde{\Phi}(\Delta\lambda) = \int_T x(t)\,\widetilde{\psi}_{\Delta\lambda}(t)\,dt \tag{3.70}$$

defines a stochastic measure on the space $\mathcal{L}(x)$, that is a random variable associated to the set $\Delta\lambda = [\lambda_1, \lambda_2)$ of the real axis. (Recall $\mathcal{L}(x) = \mathrm{span}\{x(t),\ t \in T\}$ is the subspace spanned by the values of $x(t)$).

The measure $\widetilde{\Phi}(\Delta\lambda)$ is non-orthogonal since, in general, the functions $\widetilde{\chi}_{\Delta\lambda}(\lambda)$ are such that $\widetilde{\chi}_{\Delta\lambda_1}(\lambda) \cap \widetilde{\chi}_{\Delta\lambda_2}(\lambda) \neq \varnothing$ with $\Delta\lambda_1 \cap \Delta\lambda_2 = \varnothing$.

Eq. (3.70) establishes a linear correspondence $\widetilde{\mathcal{U}}$ between the spaces $L_2(F)$ and $\mathcal{L}(x)$

$$\widetilde{\chi}_{\Delta\lambda}(\lambda) \xleftarrow{\ \widetilde{\mathcal{U}}\ } \widetilde{\Phi}(\Delta\lambda)\ . \tag{3.71}$$

Moreover from correspondence

$$\widetilde{\chi}_{\Delta\lambda}(\lambda) = \int_T \widetilde{\psi}_{\Delta\lambda}(t)\,g(t,\lambda)\,dt$$
$$\widetilde{\mathcal{U}} \updownarrow \tag{3.72}$$
$$\widetilde{\Phi}(\Delta\lambda) = \int_T \widetilde{\psi}_{\Delta\lambda}(t)\,x(t)\,dt$$

we have

$$g(t,\lambda) \xleftarrow{\ \widetilde{\mathcal{U}}\ } x(t)\ . \tag{3.73}$$

The correspondence is now extended to finite linear combinations on a partition $-A = \lambda_1 < \ldots < \lambda_{n+1} = A$ of the interval by letting

$$\sum_j g(t,\lambda_j)\,\widetilde{\chi}_{\Delta\lambda_j}(\lambda) \xleftarrow{\ \widetilde{\mathcal{U}}\ } \sum_j g(t,\lambda_j)\,\widetilde{\Phi}(\Delta\lambda_j) \tag{3.74}$$

corresponding elements by $\widetilde{\mathcal{U}}$.

Taking the limit in m.s. as $\Delta\lambda_j \to 0$ and $A \to \infty$, it results

$$\mathrm{l.i.m.} \sum_j g(t,\lambda_j)\,\widetilde{\Phi}(\Delta\lambda_j) = \int_\Lambda g(t,\lambda)\,\widetilde{\Phi}(d\lambda)$$
$$\mathrm{l.i.m.} \sum_j g(t,\lambda_j)\,\widetilde{\chi}_{\Delta\lambda_j}(\lambda) = h(t,\lambda) \tag{3.75}$$

where in general $h(t,\lambda) \neq g(t,\lambda)$, since $\widetilde{\chi}_{\Delta\lambda}(\lambda)$ is not an indicator function. (Hereinafter we will use the simplified notation l.i.m. instead of the more rigorous

$\underset{\substack{\Delta\lambda_j \to 0 \\ A \to \infty}}{\text{l.i.m.}})$

In fact, from the property of L_2-integrable functions we have

$$\text{l.i.m.} \sum_j g\left(t, \lambda_j\right) \chi_{\Delta\lambda_j}\left(\lambda\right) = g\left(t, \lambda\right), \tag{3.76}$$

so that $h\left(t, \lambda\right)$ tends to $g\left(t, \lambda\right)$ as $\tilde{\chi}_{\Delta\lambda}\left(\lambda\right) \to \chi_{\Delta\lambda}\left(\lambda\right)$. Thus at the limit the following correspondence

$$h\left(t, \lambda\right) \xleftarrow{\;\;\tilde{\mathcal{U}}\;\;} \int_\Lambda g\left(t, \lambda\right) \tilde{\Phi}\left(d\lambda\right) = \tilde{x}\left(t\right) \tag{3.77}$$

holds.

Incidentally, we remark that $\tilde{x}\left(t\right)$ is, in general, non-identical to $x\left(t\right)$ due to the correspondence

$$g\left(t, \lambda\right) = \text{l.i.m.} \sum_j f\left(t, \lambda_j\right) \tilde{\chi}_{\Delta\lambda_j}\left(\lambda\right) \xleftarrow{\;\;\tilde{\mathcal{U}}\;\;} \int_\Lambda f\left(t, \lambda\right) \tilde{\Phi}\left(d\lambda\right) \tag{3.78}$$

which implies $f\left(t, \lambda\right) \neq g\left(t, \lambda\right)$, since $\tilde{\chi}_{\Delta\lambda}\left(\lambda\right) \neq \chi_{\Delta\lambda}\left(\lambda\right)$.

Now we want to show that the s.p. $\tilde{x}\left(t\right)$ so defined approximates $x\left(t\right)$ in m.s. For, the covariance function of such a process is

$$\begin{aligned} \tilde{B}\left(t, s\right) = \langle \tilde{x}_t, \tilde{x}_s \rangle_X &= E\left\{ \int_\Lambda g\left(t, \lambda\right) \tilde{\Phi}\left(d\lambda\right) \overline{\int_\Lambda g\left(s, \mu\right) \tilde{\Phi}\left(d\mu\right)} \right\} \\ &= \int_\Lambda \int_\Lambda g\left(t, \lambda\right) \overline{g\left(s, \mu\right)} E\left\{ \tilde{\Phi}\left(d\lambda\right) \overline{\tilde{\Phi}\left(d\mu\right)} \right\} \\ &= \int_\Lambda \int_\Lambda g\left(t, \lambda\right) \overline{g\left(s, \mu\right)} F\left(d\lambda, d\mu\right) \end{aligned} \tag{3.79}$$

where

$$F\left(d\lambda, d\mu\right) = E\left\{ \tilde{\Phi}\left(d\lambda\right) \overline{\tilde{\Phi}\left(d\mu\right)} \right\} \tag{3.80}$$

defines a non-orthogonal measure on $\Lambda \times \Lambda$.

The error between $x\left(t\right)$ and $\tilde{x}\left(t\right)$ is

$$E\left\{ \left| x\left(t\right) - \tilde{x}\left(t\right) \right|^2 \right\} = E\left\{ \left| \int_\Lambda f\left(t, \lambda\right) \tilde{\Phi}\left(d\lambda\right) - \int_\Lambda g\left(t, \mu\right) \tilde{\Phi}\left(d\mu\right) \right|^2 \right\} \tag{3.81}$$

where $f\left(t, \lambda\right)$ is such that

$$g(t,\lambda) = \text{l.i.m.} \sum_j f(t,\lambda_j) \tilde{\chi}_{\Delta\lambda_j}(\lambda) \ . \tag{3.82}$$

We can write

$$
\begin{aligned}
E\left\{|x(t) - \tilde{x}(t)|^2\right\} &= \int_\Lambda \int_\Lambda f(t,\lambda) \overline{f(t,\mu)} F(d\lambda, d\mu) \\
&\quad + \int_\Lambda \int_\Lambda g(t,\lambda) \overline{g(t,\mu)} F(d\lambda, d\mu) \\
&\quad - \int_\Lambda \int_\Lambda f(t,\lambda) \overline{g(t,\mu)} F(d\lambda, d\mu) \\
&\quad - \int_\Lambda \int_\Lambda \overline{f(t,\lambda)} g(t,\mu) F(d\lambda, d\mu) \\
&= \int_\Lambda \int_\Lambda |f(t,\lambda) - g(t,\mu)|^2 F(d\lambda, d\mu) \ .
\end{aligned}
\tag{3.83}
$$

Assuming

$$\tilde{\chi}_{\Delta\lambda_j}(\lambda) \to \chi_{\Delta\lambda_j}(\lambda) \tag{3.84}$$

at the limit, implies that

$$F(d\lambda, d\mu) \to F(d\lambda) \tag{3.85}$$

and as a consequence that $g(t,\lambda)$ tends in m.s. to $f(t,\lambda)$, that is

$$\int_\Lambda \int_\Lambda |f(t,\lambda) - g(t,\mu)|^2 F(d\lambda, d\mu) = \int_\Lambda |f(t,\lambda) - g(t,\mu)|^2 F(d\lambda) \to 0 \ . \tag{3.86}$$

In conclusion, the s.p. $\tilde{x}(t)$ defined by

$$\tilde{x}(t) = \int_\Lambda g(t,\lambda) \tilde{\Phi}(d\lambda) \tag{3.87}$$

with

$$\tilde{\Phi}(\Delta\lambda) = \int_T x(t) \tilde{\psi}_{\Delta\lambda}(t) \, dt \tag{3.88}$$

and

$$\int_T \tilde{\psi}_{\Delta\lambda}(t) g(t,\lambda) \, dt = \tilde{\chi}_{\Delta\lambda}(\lambda), \tag{3.89}$$

approximates in m.s. the process $x(t)$.

The SAINN approximating the process $\xi(t)$ may be defined as

$$\eta(t) = \int_\Lambda g(t,\lambda) \tilde{\Phi}(d\lambda) = \sum_m a_m u_m(t) \int_\Lambda u_m(\lambda) \tilde{\Phi}(d\lambda) \tag{3.90}$$

with $\tilde{\Phi}(\Delta\lambda)$ given by (3.88) and (3.89).

When the process $\xi(t)$ is Gaussian, being $\tilde{\Phi}(\Delta\lambda)$ independent Gaussian r.v.'s they are completely characterized by the covariance function, so this case is very significant in applications since $B(t,s)$ suffices to represents the process.

Previous analysis enables us to define a learning scheme as follows.

From the trajectories $x(t)$ we compute

$$\tilde{\Phi}(\Delta\lambda) = \int_T x(t)\,\tilde{\psi}_{\Delta\lambda}(t)\,dt \tag{3.91}$$

where $\tilde{\psi}_{\Delta\lambda}$ is such that

$$\int_T \tilde{\psi}_{\Delta\lambda}(t)\,g(t,\lambda)\,dt = \tilde{\chi}_{\Delta\lambda}(\lambda) \tag{3.92}$$

and

$$g(t,\lambda) = \sum_m a_m\,u_m(t)\,u_m(\lambda) \tag{3.93}$$

represents an AINN.

The trajectories of the approximating process are given by

$$\eta(t) = \sum_m a_m\,u_m(t) \int_\Lambda u_m(\lambda)\,\tilde{\Phi}(d\lambda) \ . \tag{3.94}$$

Having defined the measure $\tilde{\Phi}(\Delta\lambda)$ for a finite interval $\Delta\lambda$ by (3.91), the stochastic integral in (3.94) may just be approximated by a finite summation

$$\int_\Lambda u_m(\lambda)\,\tilde{\Phi}(d\lambda) = \sum_j u_m(\lambda_j)\,\tilde{\Phi}(\Delta\lambda_j) \ . \tag{3.95}$$

During the learning stage the coefficients a_m as well as the function $\tilde{\psi}_{\Delta\lambda}(t)$ have to be chosen in such a way that the error $\mathcal{E} = x(t) - \eta(t)$ decreases.

A learning algorithm should specify a_m and $\tilde{\psi}_{\Delta\lambda}(t)$ as functions of $\mathcal{E}$, suitably chosen to guarantee convergence in mean square. For this purpose a learning scheme as that discussed in Sect. 1.7.2 is adequate. This learning scheme has several distinguishing features that make it more attractive than historical learning. It does not need knowledge of the covariance function of the process and it may be directly applied to the realizations. In other words it is not necessary to know the past history of the process. We call this kind of learning *real-time learning* of a stochastic process.

The real-time learning algorithm can be implemented as shown in the blocks scheme of Fig.24.

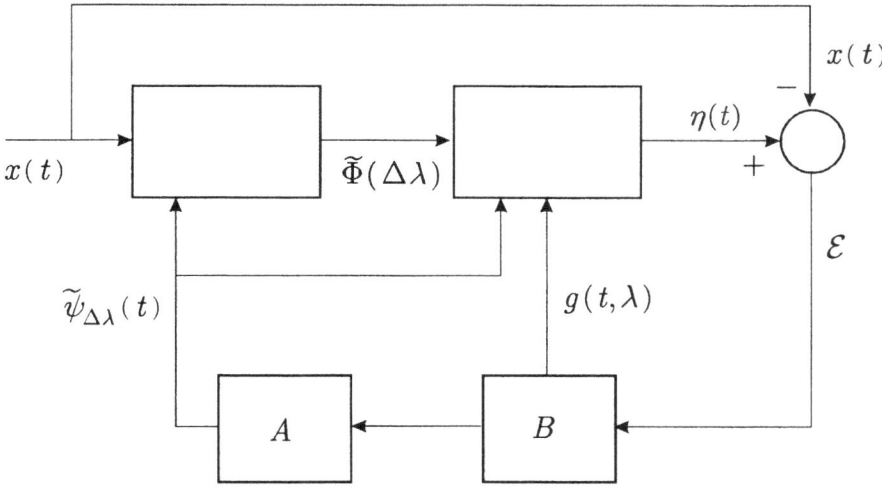

Figure 24. Blocks scheme of the real-time learning algorithm

The blocks A and B implement the functions $\widetilde{\psi}_{\Delta\lambda}(t)$, $g(t,\lambda)$ as depending on the error $\mathcal{E}$, thus the way they change with the error represents the learning algorithm.

The learning stage exhausts when the learning error tends to become close to zero, $\mathcal{E} \to 0$. Subsequently the process $\eta(t)$ can be autonomously generated with knowledge of $\widetilde{\psi}_{\Delta\lambda}(t)$, $g(t,\lambda)$ so achieved and by the random variables $\widetilde{\Phi}(\Delta\lambda)$ whose statistics can be derived from eq. (3.88).

References

[1]   Amari, S. (1990). *Mathematical Foundations of Neurocomputing.* Proceedings of the IEEE, 78 (9), 1443–1463.

[2]   Deco, G., & Parra, L. (1993). *Self-Organization in Stochastic Neural Networks.* Proceedings of International Joint Conference on Neural Networks, Vol. 1, 479–482, Nagoya, Japan, Oct. 1993.

[3]   Haykin, S. (1994). *Neural Networks – A Comprehensive Foundation.* Upper Saddle River, New Jersey: Prentice Hall.

[4]   Amari, S., & Maginu, K. (1988). *Statistical Neurodynamics of Associative Memory.* Neural Networks, 1, 63–73.

[5]   Amari, S., Kurata, K., & Nagaoka, H. (1992). *Information Geometry of Boltzmann Machine.* IEEE Transactions on Neural Networks, 3 (2), 260–271.

[6]   Zhao, J., & Shawe-Taylor, J. (1996). *A Recurrent Network with Stochastic Weights.* IEEE Proceedings of International Conference on Neural Networks, Vol. 2, 1302–1307, Washington, DC, USA, June 1996.

[7]   Simon Foo, Y.-P., & Takefuji, Y. (1988). *Stochastic Neural Networks for solving Job-Shop Scheduling: Part 1. Problem Representation.* IEEE Proceedings of International Conference on Neural Networks, Vol. 2, 275–282, San Diego, CA, USA, July 1988.

*Causality may be considered as a mode of
perception by which we reduce our sense
impressions to order*

Niels Bohr

CHAPTER FOUR

IMPLEMENTATION OF STOCHASTIC NEURAL NETWORKS

The scope of this chapter is to define some suitable architectures for the implementation of the stochastic networks.

For this purpose it is useful, preliminarily, to give a form of the canonical representation in terms of standard processes, i.e. BM and WN, which may be easily generated.

This result can be derived once the canonical representation has been decomposed into two components: a discrete component with countable values of the spectral variable λ and a component with non-countable values of the spectral variable λ.

Several application examples will show the learning capability of the stochastic networks so defined.

4.1.   Decomposition of the Canonical Representation

The spectral variable λ in the canonical representation may assume either countable or non-countable values. Here we want to show that the canonical representation decouples in general into two components, one with discrete values of λ and the other with continuous λ.

In the integral formula for the covariance function

$$B(t,s) = \int_\Lambda \varphi(t,\lambda)\overline{\varphi(s,\lambda)}\,F(d\lambda) \tag{4.1}$$

$F(A)$ represents a measure defined on the sets $A \subset \mathbb{R}$.

From measure theory it is known that ([1] p. 226, [2] p. 32) the function $F(A)$ can be decomposed into three components

$$F(A) = F_d(A) + F_c(A) + F_s(A) \ . \tag{4.2}$$

where $F_d(A)$, $F_c(A)$, and $F_s(A)$ are the discrete, continuous, and singular components, respectively.

$F_s(A)$ being a singular function with zero derivative "almost everywhere", we ignore its existence. $F_d(A)$ is the discrete component completely characterized by a function $p(\lambda)$, which results $p(\lambda) \geq 0$ for every λ and $p(\lambda) > 0$ for a discrete set of values ... , λ_{-1}, λ_0 , λ_1 , ... , so that it results

$$F_d(A) = \sum_{\lambda_j \in A} p(\lambda_j) \ . \tag{4.3}$$

The continuous component $F_c(A)$ is determined by the function $f(\lambda)$ such that $F'(\lambda) = f(\lambda)$ and we have

$$F_c(A) = \int_A f(\lambda)\,d\lambda \ . \tag{4.4}$$

Since $F_c(A)$ is a non-decreasing function, its derivative is always greater or equal to zero

$$f(\lambda) \geq 0 \ , \quad \text{for any} \quad \lambda . \tag{4.5}$$

Then for $F(A)$ the following decomposition

$$F(A) = \sum_{\lambda_j \in A} p(\lambda_j) + \int_A f(\lambda) d\lambda = F_d(A) + F_c(A) \tag{4.6}$$

holds.

For a given s.p. $\xi(t)$, a decomposition of stochastic measure, through the transformation $\mathcal{U}$, corresponds to the decomposition $F(A)$. In fact, since it results

$$F(A) \xleftarrow{\ \mathcal{U}\ } \Phi(A) , \tag{4.7}$$

also the following correspondences

$$F_d(A) \xleftarrow{\ \mathcal{U}\ } \Phi_d(A)$$
$$F_c(A) \xleftarrow{\ \mathcal{U}\ } \Phi_c(A) \tag{4.8}$$

hold. Here $\Phi_d(A)$ and $\Phi_c(A)$ are the discrete and continuous components of the stochastic measure $\Phi(A)$ respectively, satisfying the condition

$$E\left\{\Phi_d(A)\overline{\Phi_c(B)}\right\} = 0 \qquad \text{for any } A, B, \tag{4.9}$$

meaning that Φ_d and Φ_c are uncorrelated.

Now we are in position to decompose the canonical representation of the s.p. $\xi(t)$ substituting $\Phi(d\lambda) = \Phi_d(d\lambda) + \Phi_c(d\lambda)$ into (2.108).

$$\xi(t) = \int_\Lambda \varphi(t,\lambda)\Phi_d(d\lambda) + \int_\Lambda \varphi(t,\lambda)\Phi_c(d\lambda) \tag{4.10}$$

that is

$$\xi(t) = \sum_{\lambda \in \Lambda} \varphi(t,\lambda)\Phi_d(\lambda) + \int_\Lambda \varphi(t,\lambda)\Phi_c(d\lambda) = \xi_d(t) + \xi_c(t) \tag{4.11}$$

being $\Phi_d(\lambda)$ defined for discrete values $\lambda \in \Lambda$ only.

Moreover in view of the correspondence (4.8) we have the following definition for $F_c(\Delta)$ and $F_d(\lambda)$

$$E\left\{|\Phi_c(\Delta)|^2\right\} = F_c(\Delta) \quad , \qquad \Delta = [\lambda_0, \lambda_0) ,$$
$$E\left\{|\Phi_d(\lambda)|^2\right\} = F_d(\lambda) \quad , \qquad \lambda \in \Lambda . \tag{4.12}$$

According to the above decomposition $B(t,s)$ also decomposes as

$$B(t,s) = \sum_{\lambda \in \Lambda} \varphi(t,\lambda)\overline{\varphi(s,\lambda)} F_d(\lambda) + \int_\Lambda \varphi(t,\lambda)\overline{\varphi(s,\lambda)} F_c(d\lambda) . \tag{4.13}$$

4.2.   Transformation of Stochastic Measure in the Canonical Representation

The canonical representation (4.11) may be expressed in terms of standard processes, BM and WN, by means of suitable transformations of the stochastic measures $\Phi_d(\lambda)$ and $\Phi_c(\Delta)$.

With regard to the continuous component $\xi_c(t)$ let us assume the following transformation

$$\mu(\Delta) = \int_\Delta f(\lambda)\Phi_c(d\lambda) \quad , \qquad f(\lambda) \in L_2(\Lambda) \,, \quad f(\lambda) > 0 \,. \qquad (4.14)$$

We have

$$E\left\{\left|\mu(\Delta)\right|^2\right\} = \int_\Delta \left|f(\lambda)\right|^2 F(d\lambda) = G(\Delta) \,. \qquad (4.15)$$

Eq. (4.14) establishes a transformation of stochastic measure

$$\mu(d\lambda) = f(\lambda)\Phi_c(d\lambda) \qquad (4.16)$$

that can also be written as

$$\Phi_c(d\lambda) = c(\lambda)\mu(d\lambda) \quad , \qquad c(\lambda) = 1/f(\lambda) \,. \qquad (4.17)$$

Using this transformation the canonical representation for $\xi_c(t)$ becomes

$$\begin{aligned} \xi_c(t) &= \int_\Lambda \varphi(t,\lambda)\Phi_c(d\lambda) = \int_\Lambda \varphi(t,\lambda)c(\lambda)\mu(d\lambda) \\ &= \int_\Lambda \psi(t,\lambda)\mu(d\lambda) \,. \end{aligned} \qquad (4.18)$$

Also the expression for the covariance function modifies as

$$B(t,s) = \int_\Lambda \varphi(t,\lambda)\overline{\varphi(s,\lambda)}\,F(d\lambda) = \int_\Lambda \psi(t,\lambda)\overline{\psi(s,\lambda)}\,G(d\lambda) \,. \qquad (4.19)$$

In the general case of a vector-valued function $\varphi(t,\lambda)$, (4.18) and (4.19) become

$$\xi_c(t) = \int_\Lambda \Psi^T(t,\lambda)\boldsymbol{\mu}(d\lambda) \qquad (4.20)$$

and

$$B(t,s) = \int_\Lambda \mathbf{\Psi}^T(t,\lambda) \cdot \overline{\mathbf{\Psi}(s,\lambda)} G(d\lambda) \tag{4.21}$$

where $\boldsymbol{\mu}(d\lambda)$ is a vector-valued stochastic measure.

A similar transformation can be used for the discrete component

$$\zeta(\lambda) = p(\lambda)\Phi_d(\lambda) \quad , \qquad p(\lambda) > 0 \tag{4.22}$$

$$\Phi_d(\lambda) = q(\lambda)\zeta(\lambda) \quad , \qquad q(\lambda) = 1/p(\lambda) \tag{4.23}$$

so that the $\xi_d(t)$ representation reduces to

$$\begin{aligned}
\xi_d(t) &= \sum_{\lambda \in \Lambda} \varphi(t,\lambda)\Phi_d(\lambda) = \sum_{\lambda \in \Lambda} \varphi(t,\lambda)q(\lambda)\zeta(\lambda) \\
&= \sum_{\lambda \in \Lambda} \gamma(t,\lambda)\zeta(\lambda)
\end{aligned} \tag{4.24}$$

where $\zeta(\lambda)$ is the stochastic measure defined by (4.22) and such that

$$E\left\{\left|\Phi_d(\lambda)\right|^2\right\} = \left[p(\lambda)\right]^2 E\left\{\left|\zeta(\lambda)\right|^2\right\} . \tag{4.25}$$

In view of the above analysis we assume the following decomposition of the canonical representation

$$\xi(t) = \xi_d(t) + \xi_c(t) = \sum_{\lambda \in \Lambda} \varphi(t,\lambda)q(\lambda)\zeta(\lambda) + \int_\Lambda \varphi(t,\lambda)c(\lambda)dy(\lambda) \tag{4.26}$$

where $y(\lambda)$ is a *Brownian Motion* defined by

$$y(\lambda_2) - y(\lambda_1) = \mu(\Delta\lambda) \tag{4.27}$$

with

$$E\left\{\left|y(\lambda_2) - y(\lambda_1)\right|^2\right\} = \sigma_c^2 \left|\lambda_2 - \lambda_1\right| , \tag{4.28}$$

and $\zeta(\lambda)$ is a *White Noise* such that

$$E\left\{\left|\zeta(\lambda)\right|^2\right\} = \sigma_d^2 . \tag{4.29}$$

With these assumptions the canonical decomposition becomes

$$\xi(t) = \sum_{\lambda \in \Lambda} \gamma(t,\lambda)\zeta(\lambda) + \int_\Lambda \psi(t,\lambda)dy(\lambda) \tag{4.30}$$

with

$$\gamma(t,\lambda) = \varphi(t,\lambda) q(\lambda) ,$$
$$\psi(t,\lambda) = \varphi(t,\lambda) c(\lambda) . \tag{4.31}$$

Putting $\mu(\Delta\lambda) = y(\lambda_2) - y(\lambda_1)$ where $y(\lambda)$ is a BM such that

$$E\left\{ \left| y(\lambda_2) - y(\lambda_1) \right|^2 \right\} = \sigma_c^2 \left| \lambda_2 - \lambda_1 \right| , \tag{4.32}$$

we have

$$E\left\{ \left| \Phi_c(d\lambda) \right|^2 \right\} = \left[c(\lambda) \right]^2 \sigma_c^2 d\lambda = F_c(d\lambda) . \tag{4.33}$$

With regard to the discrete component, if $\zeta(\lambda)$ is a WN with

$$E\left\{ \left| \zeta(\lambda) \right|^2 \right\} = \sigma_d^2 \tag{4.34}$$

it results

$$E\left\{ \left| \Phi_d(\lambda) \right|^2 \right\} = \left[q(\lambda) \right]^2 \sigma_d^2 = F_d(\lambda) . \tag{4.35}$$

Thus, the integral expression for the covariance function becomes

$$
\begin{aligned}
B(s,t) &= \int_\Lambda \varphi(t,\lambda) \overline{\varphi(s,\lambda)} F(d\lambda) \\
&= \sum_{\lambda \in \Lambda} \varphi(t,\lambda) \overline{\varphi(s,\lambda)} F_d(\lambda) + \int_\Lambda \varphi(t,\lambda) \overline{\varphi(s,\lambda)} F_c(d\lambda) \\
&= \sum_{\lambda \in \Lambda} \varphi(t,\lambda) \overline{\varphi(s,\lambda)} \left[q(\lambda) \right]^2 \sigma_d^2 + \int_\Lambda \varphi(t,\lambda) \overline{\varphi(s,\lambda)} \left[c(\lambda) \right]^2 \sigma_c^2 d\lambda
\end{aligned}
\tag{4.36}
$$

$$B(s,t) = \sum_{\lambda \in \Lambda} \gamma(t,\lambda) \overline{\gamma(s,\lambda)} \sigma_d^2 + \int_\Lambda \psi(t,\lambda) \overline{\psi(s,\lambda)} \sigma_c^2 d\lambda . \tag{4.37}$$

From the general relationship describing an SAINN (3.20)

$$\eta(t) = \sum_k a_k u_k(t) \int_\Lambda u_k(\lambda) \Phi(d\lambda) \tag{4.38}$$

an approximation of the discrete component $\xi_d(t) = \sum_{\lambda \in \Lambda} \gamma(t,\lambda) \zeta(\lambda)$ is given by

$$\eta_d(t) = \sum_k a_k u_k(t) \sum_{\lambda \in \Lambda} u_k(\lambda) \zeta(\lambda) \tag{4.39}$$

where a_k is such that

$$E\left\{\left|\xi_d\left(t\right)-\eta_d\left(t\right)\right|^2\right\}\to 0\ . \tag{4.40}$$

For the continuous component the following approximation

$$\eta_c\left(t\right)=\sum_j b_j u_j\left(t\right)\int_\Lambda u_j\left(\lambda\right)dy\left(\lambda\right) \tag{4.41}$$

holds, with b_j satisfying

$$E\left\{\left|\xi_c\left(t\right)-\eta_c\left(t\right)\right|^2\right\}\to 0\ . \tag{4.42}$$

Therefore also the SAINN can be decomposed as

$$\eta\left(t\right)=\eta_d\left(t\right)+\eta_c\left(t\right) \tag{4.43}$$

where

$$\eta_d\left(t\right)=\sum_k a_k u_k\left(t\right)\sum_{\lambda\in\Lambda}u_k\left(\lambda\right)\zeta\left(\lambda\right)\quad,\qquad E\left\{\left|\zeta\left(\lambda\right)\right|^2\right\}=\sigma_d^2\ , \tag{4.44}$$

$$\eta_c\left(t\right)=\sum_j b_j u_j\left(t\right)\int_\Lambda u_j\left(\lambda\right)dy\left(\lambda\right)\quad,\qquad E\left\{\left|dy\left(\lambda\right)\right|^2\right\}=\sigma_c^2\,d\lambda\ . \tag{4.45}$$

Finally, the s.p. $\eta\left(t\right)$ can be rewritten as

$$\eta\left(t\right)=\sum_k \eta_k^d u_k\left(t\right)+\sum_j \eta_j^c u_j\left(t\right) \tag{4.46}$$

with

$$\eta_k^d=a_k\sum_{\lambda\in\Lambda}u_k\left(\lambda\right)\zeta\left(\lambda\right)\ , \tag{4.47}$$

$$\eta_j^d=b_j\int_\Lambda u_j\left(\lambda\right)dy\left(\lambda\right)\ . \tag{4.48}$$

4.3.   The Architecture of the Stochastic Approximate Identity Neural Networks with BM Process Source

The theory presented in Chap. 3 extends the results known in literature regarding the capability of neural networks in approximating deterministic nonlinear functions, to the case of stochastic processes in which sample functions randomly occur.

In the SAINN's described by the sums (4.46) the coefficients η_k^d, η_j^c are random variables. As a consequence the architecture of such networks must necessarily include some random generator blocks.

The architecture of the neural network defined by (4.46)-(4.48) assumes the form depicted in Fig. 25, where both the discrete and continuous components of the process $\eta(t)$ are singled out.

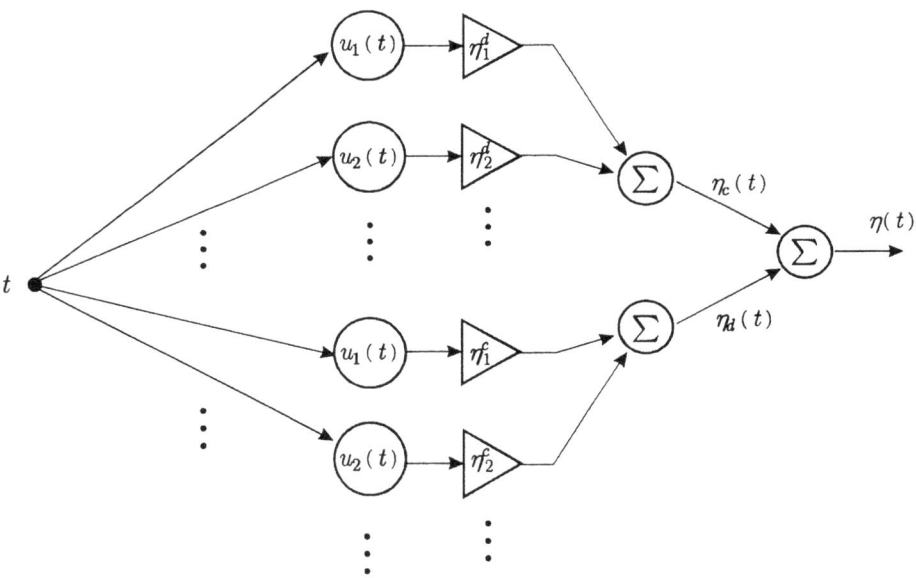

Figure 25. Architecture of the stochastic neural network given by (4.46)-(4.48)

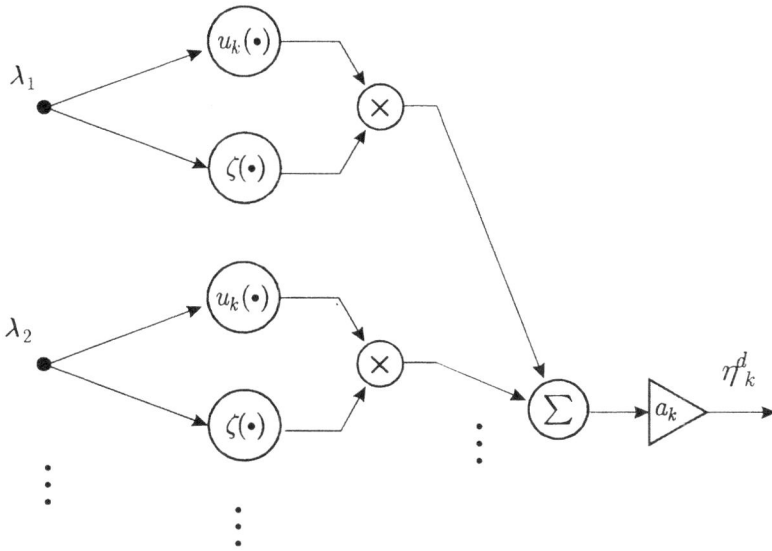

Figure 26. Block scheme for generating the coefficients η_k^d of the discrete components of $\eta(t)$

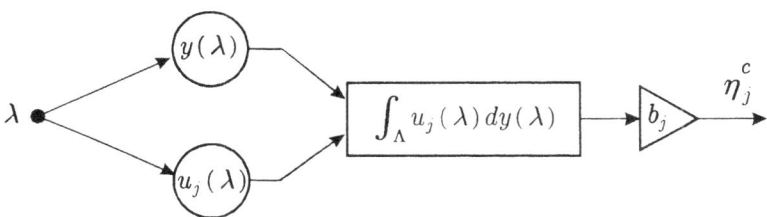

Figure 27. Block scheme for generating the coefficients η_j^c of the continuous components of $\eta(t)$

With regard to the discrete component, being the coefficient η_k^d a linear combination of the WN $\zeta(\lambda)$, they can be easily implemented as is shown in Fig. 26. Conversely, implementing the continuous component requires caution because the coefficients η_j^c are expressed as stochastic integrals. For this purpose a device able to implement a stochastic integral by a BM $y(\lambda)$ would be necessary (see Fig. 27), but at present no such device exists. Instead, referring to the stochastic integral definition, let us consider the following approximation

$$\int_\Lambda u_j(\lambda)\,dy(\lambda) \cong \sum_k u_j(\lambda_k)\mu(\Delta_k) \tag{4.49}$$

being

$$\mu(\Delta_k) = y(\lambda_k) - y(\lambda_{k-1}) . \tag{4.50}$$

This implies that the coefficients η_j^c reduce to

$$\eta_j^c = b_j \sum_k u_j(\lambda_k)\mu(\Delta_k) . \tag{4.51}$$

Restricting the analysis to the continuous component alone, two architectures are proposed here for the implementation of the coefficients η_j^c.

The first solution for a 1-D input network is reported in Fig. 28.

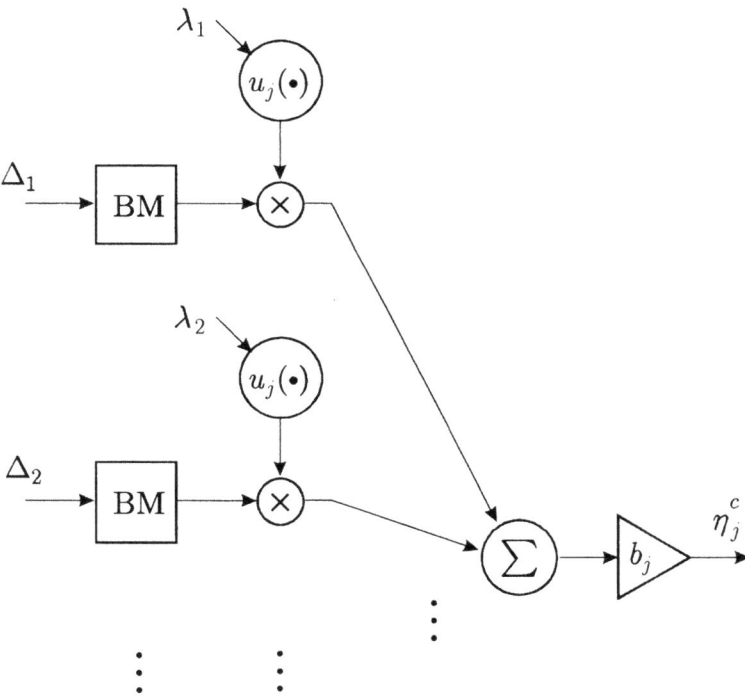

Figure 28. Implementation of the coefficients η_j^c by using different BM processes for a 1-D input network

In this case every random variable $\mu(\Delta_1)$, $\mu(\Delta_2)$, ... , is obtained from a BM process by specifying the values for σ and $\Delta_j = \lambda_j - \lambda_{j-1}$, $j = 1, 2, \dots$.

Figure 29 shows another solution for the implementation of the coefficients η_j^c , in which the random variables $\mu(\Delta_1)$, $\mu(\Delta_2)$, ... are obtained from the same BM process, but specifying different values for the increments Δ_1 , Δ_2 , ...

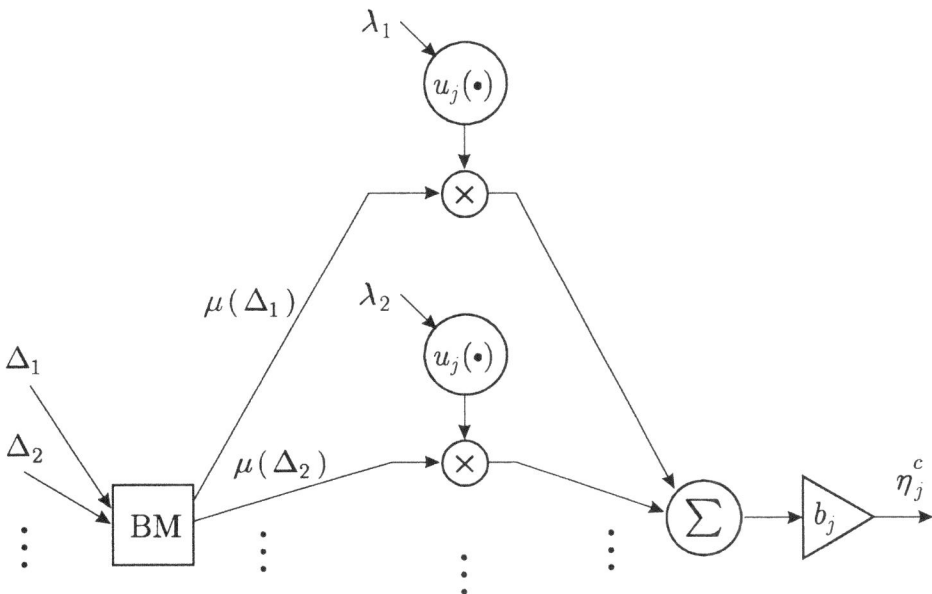

Figure 29. Implementation of the coefficients η_j^c by using one-BM process for a 1-D input network

4.4.   The Architecture of the Stochastic Approximate Identity Neural Networks with WN Process Source

The SAINN architecture shown in the previous Section is in term of BM sources. However implementing such a network using a WN as a random source in place of a BM process may be advantageous from an application point of view. WN is well approximated by thermal noise in electrical devices, or easily generated with a suitable algorithm. In view of the integral relationship between BM and WN derived in Sect. 2.2.4, the component $\xi_c(t)$ of the s.p. $\xi(t)$ may be transformed as an integral of a WN process. The component $\xi_c(t)$ is given by

$$\xi_c(t) = \int_\Lambda \Psi(t,\lambda)\, dy(\lambda) \tag{4.52}$$

where $y(\lambda)$ is a BM process.

From (2.62) we may write

$$y(\lambda) = \int_0^\lambda z(\lambda')\, d\lambda' \tag{4.53}$$

or, in differential form,

$$dy(\lambda) = z(\lambda)\, d\lambda \tag{4.54}$$

where $z(\lambda)$ is a WN process with $E\left\{|z(\lambda)|^2\right\} = q(\lambda)$.

Formally, substituting (4.54) into (4.52) gives

$$\xi_c(t) = \int_\Lambda \Psi(t,\lambda)\, z(\lambda)\, d\lambda \ . \tag{4.55}$$

Hence, the continuous component $\eta_c(t)$ of the SAINN may be rewritten as

$$\eta_c(t) = \sum_j \eta_j^c u_j(t) \tag{4.56}$$

where

$$\eta_j^c = b_j \int_\Lambda u_j(\lambda)\, dy(\lambda) = b_j \int_\Lambda u_j(\lambda)\, z(\lambda)\, d\lambda \ . \tag{4.57}$$

The SAINN architecture derived in the previous Section also applies to the new expression for $\eta_c(t)$, provided the BM random sources are replaced by WN random sources.

4.5.   Application Examples

For the sake of mathematical formulation ease, all the examples in this Section refer to processes defined on a finite interval, so that the realizations are of finite energy, and the theory of stochastic processes applies without any additional assumption.

4.5.1. Example 1

As an application example of the theory previously reported we refer to the process

$$\xi(t) = x(t)\cos\left(\lambda_0 t\right) \tag{4.58}$$

where λ_0 is a constant and $x(t)$ is a zero mean wide sense stationary process with covariance function given by

$$E\left\{x(t)x(s)\right\} = R_{xx}(\tau) = \exp\left(-\alpha|\tau|\right) \qquad \text{with} \qquad \tau = t - s \tag{4.59}$$

Let us recall the relationships between the covariance function of a wide sense stationary process and its power spectral density function is given by

$$R_{xx}(\tau) = \frac{1}{2}\int_{-\infty}^{+\infty}\exp(j\lambda\tau)f(\lambda)\,d\lambda \qquad f(\lambda) = \frac{1}{\pi}\int_{-\infty}^{+\infty}\exp(-j\lambda\tau)\,R_{xx}(\tau)\,d\tau \ . \tag{4.60}$$

Incidentally in our example $x(t)$ represents the well-known *random telegraph signal.*

It is easy to show that $\xi(t)$ is non-stationary being its covariance function given by

$$R_{\xi\xi}(t,s) = E\left\{x(t)x(s)\right\}\cos\left(\lambda_0 t\right)\cos\left(\lambda_0 s\right) \tag{4.61}$$

By deriving the spectral density $f(\lambda)$ it is straightforward to show that for the process $\xi(t)$ under analysis it results

$$\begin{aligned}
B(t,s) = R_{\xi\xi}(t,s) &= \int_0^{+\infty}\left[g_1(t,\lambda)g_1(s,\lambda) + g_2(t,\lambda)g_2(s,\lambda)\right]F(d\lambda) \\
&= \int_0^{+\infty}\varphi^T(t,\lambda)\cdot\varphi(s,\lambda)F(d\lambda)
\end{aligned} \tag{4.62}$$

where

$$\varphi(t,\lambda) = \left[g_1(t,\lambda),\ g_2(t,\lambda)\right]^T \tag{4.63}$$

with

$$g_1(t,\lambda) = \cos(\lambda t)\cos\left(\lambda_0 t\right) \quad , \qquad g_2(t,\lambda) = \sin(\lambda t)\cos(\lambda_0 t) \tag{4.64}$$

and

$$F(d\lambda) = \frac{1}{\pi} \frac{2\alpha}{\alpha^2 + \lambda^2} d\lambda .$$

(4.65)

Thus the vector-value function

$$\Psi(t,\lambda) = \left[h_1(t,\lambda),\, h_2(t,\lambda) \right]^T$$

(4.66)

to be approximated has the components given by

$$h_1(t,\lambda) = \frac{1}{\sigma} \sqrt{\frac{1}{\pi} \frac{2\alpha}{\alpha^2 + \lambda^2}} \cos(\lambda t) \cos(\lambda_0 t) ,$$

(4.67)

$$h_2(t,\lambda) = \frac{1}{\sigma} \sqrt{\frac{1}{\pi} \frac{2\alpha}{\alpha^2 + \lambda^2}} \sin(\lambda t) \cos(\lambda_0 t) .$$

These functions were approximated using an a SAINN represented by the sums

$$\xi(t) = \sum_{k=1}^{n} u_k(t) \sum_{j=1}^{m} b_{k1} u_k\left(\lambda_j\right) \mu_1\left(\Delta_j\right) + \sum_{k=1}^{q} u_k(t) \sum_{j=1}^{p} b_{k2} u_k\left(\lambda_j\right) \mu_2\left(\Delta_j\right).$$

(4.68)

In this case we have

$$\Psi(t,\lambda) = \left[h_1(t,\lambda), h_2(t,\lambda) \right]^T$$

(4.69)

$$\Psi_n(t,\lambda) = \left[\sum_{k=1}^{n} b_{k1} u_k(t) u_k(\lambda) ,\ \sum_{k=1}^{p} b_{k2} u_k(t) u_k(\lambda) \right]^T$$

(4.70)

$$dG(\lambda) = \sigma^2 d\lambda$$

(4.71)

and the error defined as in eq. (3.16) becomes

$$\mathcal{E} = \int_T \int_\Lambda \left| \Psi^T(t,\lambda) - \Psi_n^T(t,\lambda) \right|^2 \sigma^2 d\lambda\, dt .$$

(4.72)

Thus during the learning the weights b_{k1}, b_{k2}, Δ_j, λ_j of the neural network have to be chosen in order to minimize the error $\mathcal{E}$.

Figure 30 shows the covariance function $R_{\xi\xi}(t,s)$ of the process $\xi(t)$ as given by (4.62).

For comparison, the behaviour of the covariance function $R_{\eta\eta}(t,s)$ for the approximating process $\eta(t)$ as obtained from 200 realizations of (4.68) is reported in Fig. 31. As you can see this behaviour is very close to $R_{\xi\xi}(t,s)$.

The whole computation was executed in the Matlab/Simulink environment by varying λ in the range 0 to 400 rad/s with $\Delta\lambda = 1$ rad/s, $\Delta t = 0.0125$ s, $\alpha = 1$, and the BM's generator parameters adjusted to obtain $\sigma = 1$.

It is remarkable to note that the approximation of the covariance function $R_{\xi\xi}(t,s)$ is a necessary (not in general sufficient) condition for approximating a given process. However the behaviour of the covariance function encompasses many of the statistical properties of a process. Thus, even if the minimization of the error $\mathcal{E}$ guarantees the convergence of the process $\eta(t)$ to $\xi(t)$, a comparison of their covariance functions is useful to confirm the validity of the approach.

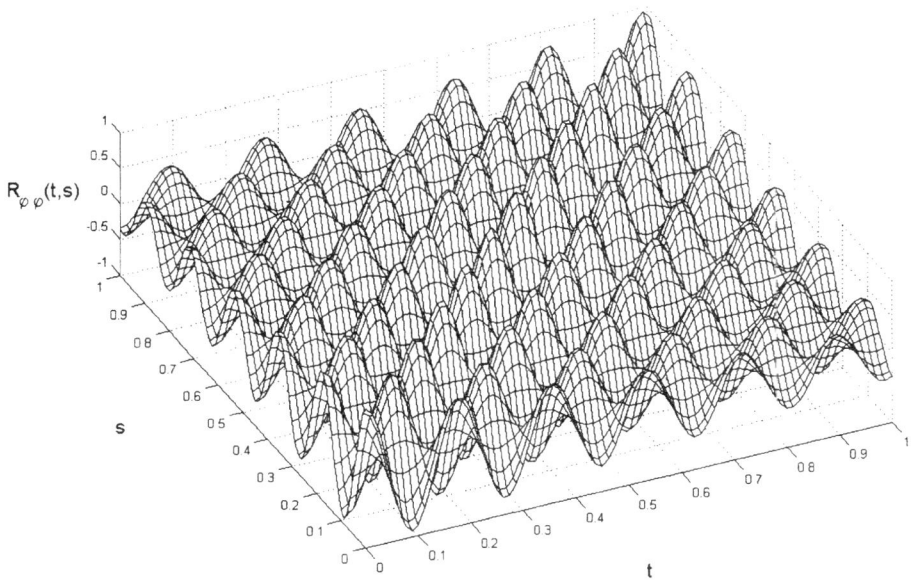

Figure 30. Covariance function $R_{\xi\xi}(t,s)$ of the process $\xi(t)$ as given by eq. (4.62)

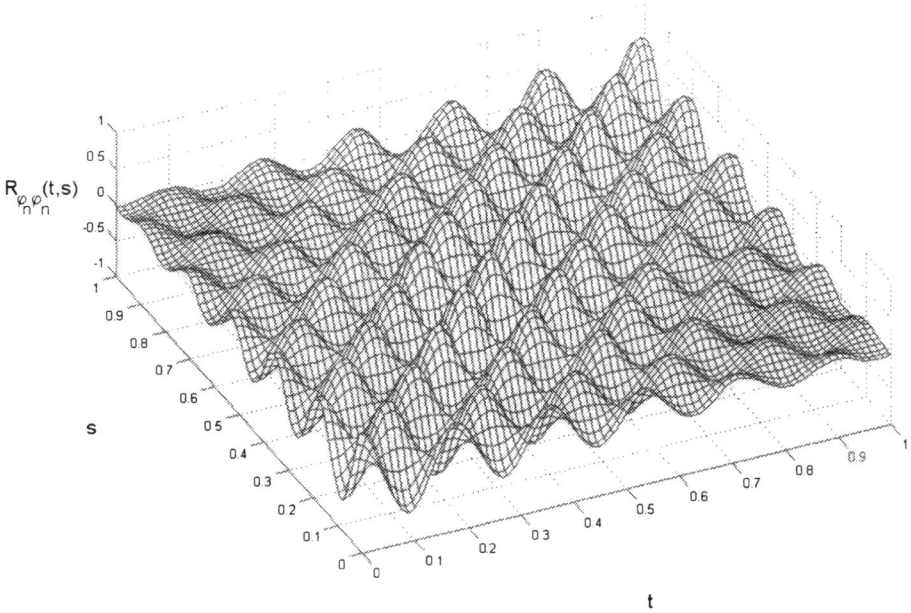

Figure 31. Covariance function $R_{\eta\eta}(t,s)$ for the approximating process $\eta(t)$ as obtained from 200 realizations of eq. (4.68)

4.5.2. Example 2

As another example, a bit more complex, we chose the following process:

$$\xi(t) = x(t)\left[\cos\left(\lambda_1 t\right) + \cos\left(\lambda_2 t\right)\right] \tag{4.73}$$

where λ_1 and λ_2 are constants and $x(t)$ is a zero mean wide sense stationary process with covariance function given by

$$E\left\{x(t)x(s)\right\} = R_{xx}(\tau) = \begin{cases} \dfrac{\sigma_1^2}{1-\dfrac{|\tau|}{\Delta}} & |\tau| \leq \Delta \\ 0 & |\tau| > \Delta \end{cases} \quad \text{with} \quad \tau = t-s . \tag{4.74}$$

In this case $x(t)$ is the well-known *binary noise*. Again $\varphi(t)$ is non-stationary, in fact its covariance function is

$$R_{\xi\xi}(t,s) = E\{x(t)x(s)\}\left[\cos\left(\lambda_1 t\right) + \cos\left(\lambda_2 t\right)\right]\left[\cos\left(\lambda_1 s\right) + \cos\left(\lambda_2 s\right)\right]. \qquad (4.75)$$

Using the spectral theory of stationary processes one can show that

$$B(t,s) = R_{\xi\xi}(t,s) = \int_0^{+\infty}\left[g_1(t,\lambda)g_1(s,\lambda) + g_2(t,\lambda)g_2(s,\lambda)\right]F(d\lambda) =$$
$$= \int_0^{+\infty}\boldsymbol{\varphi}^T(t,\lambda)\cdot\boldsymbol{\varphi}(s,\lambda)F(d\lambda) \qquad (4.76)$$

where

$$\boldsymbol{\varphi}(t,\lambda) = \left[g_1(t,\lambda), g_2(t,\lambda)\right]^T, \qquad (4.77)$$

$$g_1(t,\lambda) = \cos(\lambda t)\left[\cos\left(\lambda_1 t\right) + \cos\left(\lambda_2 t\right)\right], \qquad (4.78)$$

$$g_2(t,\lambda) = \sin(\lambda t)\left[\cos\left(\lambda_1 t\right) + \cos\left(\lambda_2 t\right)\right], \qquad (4.79)$$

and

$$F(d\lambda) = f(\lambda)d\lambda = \frac{\sigma_1^2 \Delta}{\pi}\frac{\sin^2(\lambda\Delta/2)}{(\lambda\Delta/2)^2}d\lambda_{,:} \qquad (4.80)$$

Hence, the functions to be approximated are given by

$$h_1(t,\lambda) = \sqrt{\frac{\Delta}{\pi}}\frac{\sigma_1^2}{\sigma}\frac{|\sin(\lambda\Delta/2)|}{|\lambda\Delta/2|}\cos(\lambda t)\left[\cos\left(\lambda_1 t\right) + \cos\left(\lambda_2 t\right)\right],$$
$$\qquad (4.81)$$
$$h_2(t,\lambda) = \sqrt{\frac{\Delta}{\pi}}\frac{\sigma_1^2}{\sigma}\frac{|\sin(\lambda\Delta/2)|}{|\lambda\Delta/2|}\sin(\lambda t)\left[\cos\left(\lambda_1 t\right) + \cos\left(\lambda_2 t\right)\right].$$

The covariance function $R_{\xi\xi}(t,s)$ of the process $\xi(t)$ as given by (4.75) is shown in Fig. 32. The behaviour of the covariance function $R_{\eta\eta}(t,s)$ for the approximating process $\eta(t)$ as obtained from 200 realizations of (4.68) is reported, for comparison, in Fig. 33.

Also in this case the whole computation was executed in the Matlab/Simulink environment by varying λ in the range 0 to 400 rad/s with $\Delta\lambda = 1$ rad/s, $\Delta t = 0.0125$ s, $\sigma_1 = 1$, and the BMs generator parameters were adjusted to obtain $\sigma = 1$.

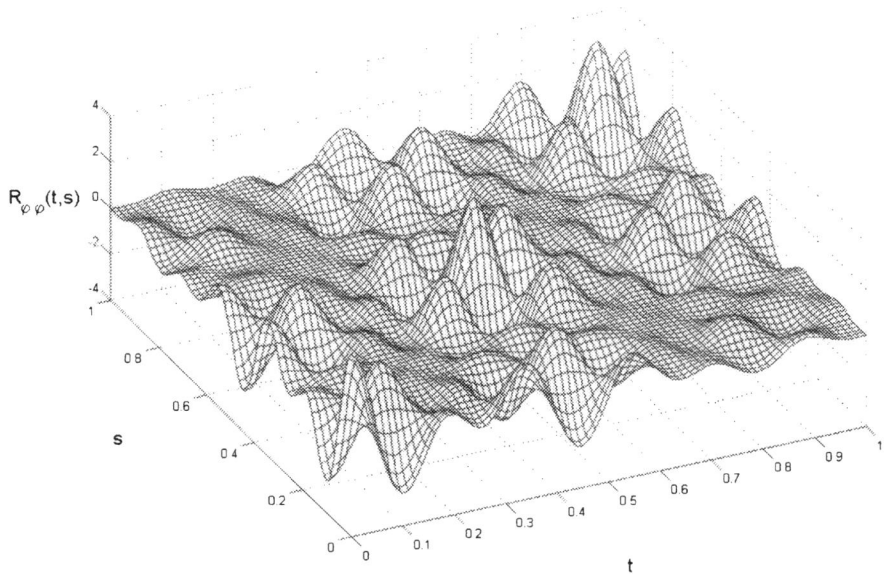

Figure 32. Covariance function $R_{\xi\xi}(t,s)$ of the process $\xi(t)$ as given by eq. (4.76)-
(4.80)

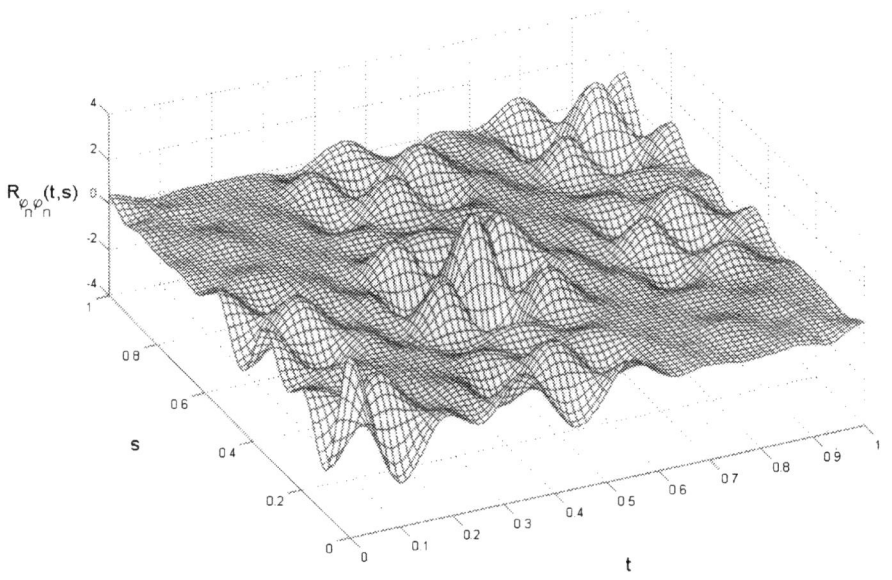

Figure 33. Covariance function $R_{\eta\eta}(t,s)$ for the approximating process $\varphi_n(t)$ as
obtained from 200 realizations of eq. (4.68)

4.5.3. Example 3

As third example of the theory previously reported we refer to the process

$$\xi(t) = x(t) \frac{\omega_0^2 t^2}{1 + \omega_0^2 t^2} \tag{4.82}$$

where ω_0 is a constant and $x(t)$ is a zero mean wide sense stationary process with covariance function given by

$$R_{xx}(\tau) = E\{x(t)x(s)\} = \exp(-\alpha|\tau|) \qquad \text{and} \qquad \tau = t - s . \tag{4.83}$$

Let us remember that the covariance function of a wide sense stationary process is related to its power spectral density function by

$$R_{xx}(\tau) = \frac{1}{2} \int_{-\infty}^{+\infty} e^{j\lambda\tau} f(\lambda) d\lambda . \tag{4.84}$$

Incidentally in our example $x(t)$ represents the well-known *random telegraph signal*.

It is easy to show that $\xi(t)$ is non-stationary being its covariance function given by

$$R_{\xi\xi}(t,s) = E\{x(t)x(s)\} \frac{\omega_0^2 t^2}{1 + \omega_0^2 t^2} \frac{\omega_0^2 s^2}{1 + \omega_0^2 s^2} . \tag{4.85}$$

By using the spectral theory of stationary processes it is straightforward to show that it results

$$B(t,s) = R_{\varphi\varphi}(t,s) = \int_0^{+\infty} \left[g_1(t,\lambda) g_1(s,\lambda) + g_2(t,\lambda) g_2(s,\lambda) \right] dF(\lambda) =$$
$$= \int_0^{+\infty} \boldsymbol{\varphi}^T(t,\lambda) \cdot \boldsymbol{\varphi}(s,\lambda) dF(\lambda) \tag{4.86}$$

where

$$\boldsymbol{\varphi}(t,\lambda) = \left[g_1(t,\lambda), g_2(t,\lambda) \right]^T \tag{4.87}$$

$$g_1(t,\lambda) = \cos(\lambda t) \frac{\omega_0^2 t^2}{1 + \omega_0^2 t^2} \quad , \quad g_2(t,\lambda) = \sin(\lambda t) \frac{\omega_0^2 t^2}{1 + \omega_0^2 t^2} \tag{4.88}$$

and

$$dF(\lambda) = f(\lambda)d\lambda = \frac{1}{\pi}\frac{2\alpha}{\alpha^2 + \lambda^2}d\lambda \ . \tag{4.89}$$

Thus the functions to be approximated $h_1(t,\lambda)$, $h_2(t,\lambda)$, i.e. the components of the vector

$$\Psi(t,\lambda) = \left[h_1(t,\lambda), h_2(t,\lambda)\right]^T \tag{4.90}$$

are given by

$$h_1(t,\lambda) = \frac{1}{\sigma}\sqrt{\frac{1}{\pi}\frac{2\alpha}{\alpha^2 + \lambda^2}}\cos(\lambda t)\frac{\omega_0^2 t^2}{1 + \omega_0^2 t^2} \ ,$$

$$\tag{4.91}$$

$$h_2(t,\lambda) = \frac{1}{\sigma}\sqrt{\frac{1}{\pi}\frac{2\alpha}{\alpha^2 + \lambda^2}}\sin(\lambda t)\frac{\omega_0^2 t^2}{1 + \omega_0^2 t^2} \ .$$

Each one of these functions were approximated using an AINN (this choice is not restrictive since other feed-forward neural networks are equally suitable) yielding the two approximating functions

$$\tilde{h}_1(t,\lambda) = \sum_{k=1}^{n} b_{k1} u_k(t) u_k(\lambda) \ , \quad \tilde{h}_2(t,\lambda) = \sum_{k=1}^{p} b_{k2} u_k(t) u_k(\lambda) \ . \tag{4.92}$$

By defining the stochastic neuron as

$$\eta_j^i(t) = b_j \sum_k u_j(\lambda_k)\left[y^i(\lambda_k) - y^i(\lambda_{k-1})\right] \ , \quad i = 1, 2, \ldots , \tag{4.93}$$

we have the representation

$$\eta(t) = \sum_{j=1}^{n} \eta_j^1 u_j(t) + \sum_{j=1}^{p} \eta_j^2 u_j(t) \tag{4.94}$$

where $\left\{y^i(\lambda), \ \lambda \in \Lambda\right\}$ are stochastic processes generated accordingly to the Ornstein-Uhlenbeck model of Brownian Motion. The covariance function $R_{\xi\xi}(t,s)$ of the process $\xi(t)$ as given by (4.85) with $\omega_0 = 20$ and $\alpha = 1$ is shown in Fig. 34.

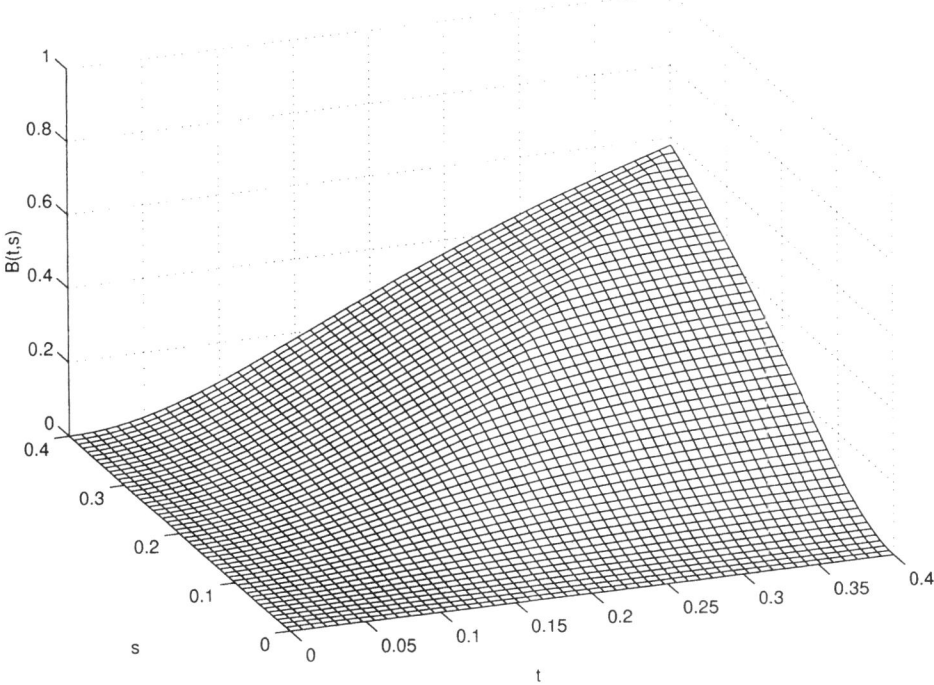

Figure 34. The covariance function $R_{\xi\xi}(t,s)$ of the process $\xi(t)$ with

$t, s \in \left[0, \ 0.4\right]$ *as given by (4.85) with $\omega_0 = 20$ and $\alpha = 1$*

Such a function can be derived by definition as the estimate of the statistical average

$$E\left\{\xi(t)\xi(s)\right\} = \frac{1}{N-1}\sum_{i=1}^{N}\xi_i(t)\xi_i(s) \tag{4.95}$$

where the terms $\xi_i(t)$, $\xi_i(s)$ are obtained as realisations of the process $\xi(t)$ from the stochastic integral

$$\xi(t) = \int_0^{\infty} \mathbf{\Psi}^T(t,\lambda) \cdot d\mathbf{y}(\lambda) \tag{4.96}$$

This integral can be easily evaluated numerically as a summation

$$\sum_i \mathbf{\Psi}^T\left(t,\lambda_i\right)\Delta \mathbf{y}\left(\lambda_i\right) \tag{4.97}$$

where the increments $\Delta y\left(\lambda_i\right)$ are obtained from a Brownian Motion process.

As you can see from Fig. 35, the covariance function achieved in this way is the same as that shown in Fig. 34. A number of 200 realisations has been used to obtain the results of Fig. 35.

Some realisations achieved from the stochastic integral (4.96) are shown in Fig. 36.

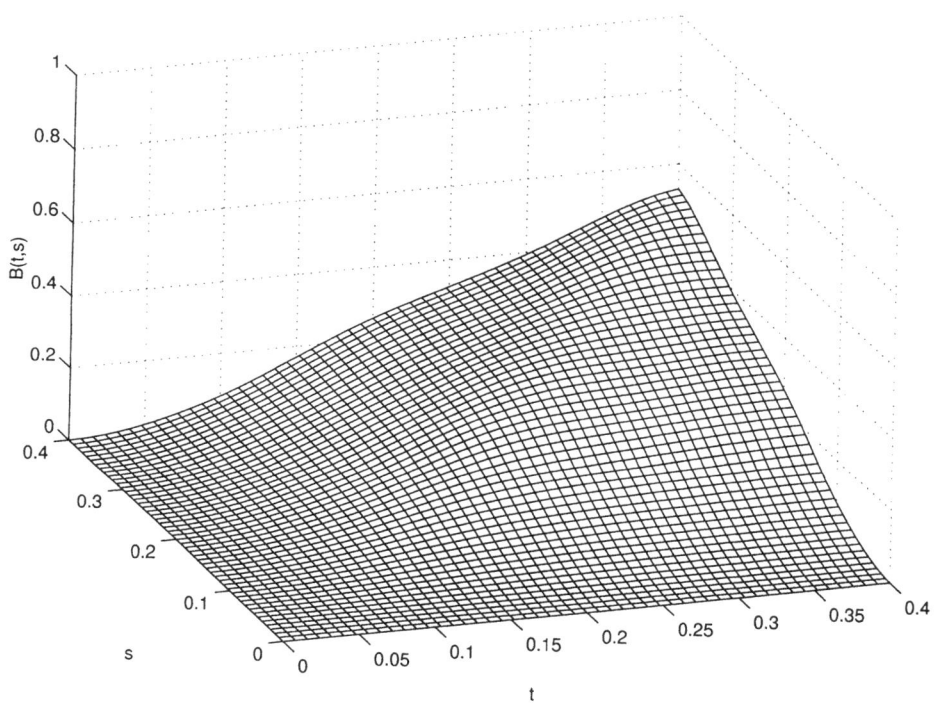

Figure 35. *The covariance function* $R_{\xi\xi}\left(t,s\right)$ *of the process* $\xi\left(t\right)$ *with* $t,s \in \left[0,\ 0.4\right]$ *as given by (4.95) and (4.96) with* $\omega_0 = 20$ *and* $\alpha = 1$

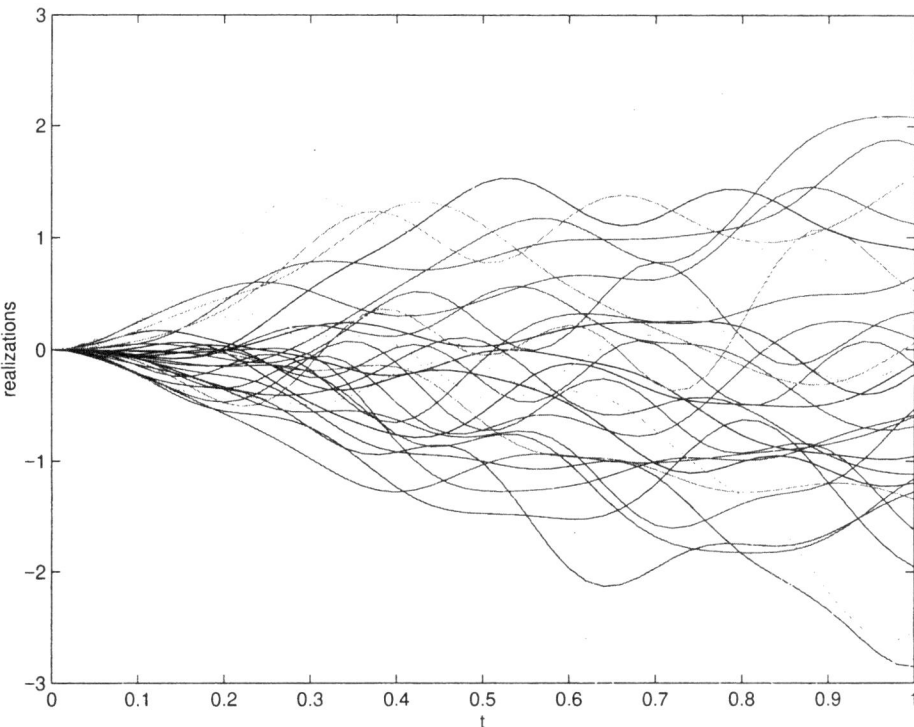

Figure 36. Some realisations derived from the stochastic integral (4.96) in which the process $y(\lambda)$ is a Brownian Motion

In order to check the validity of the approximation performed by the neural network, the functions $h_1(t,\lambda)$ and $h_2(t,\lambda)$ of eqn (4.91) are reported in Figs. 37(a) and 37(b) respectively.

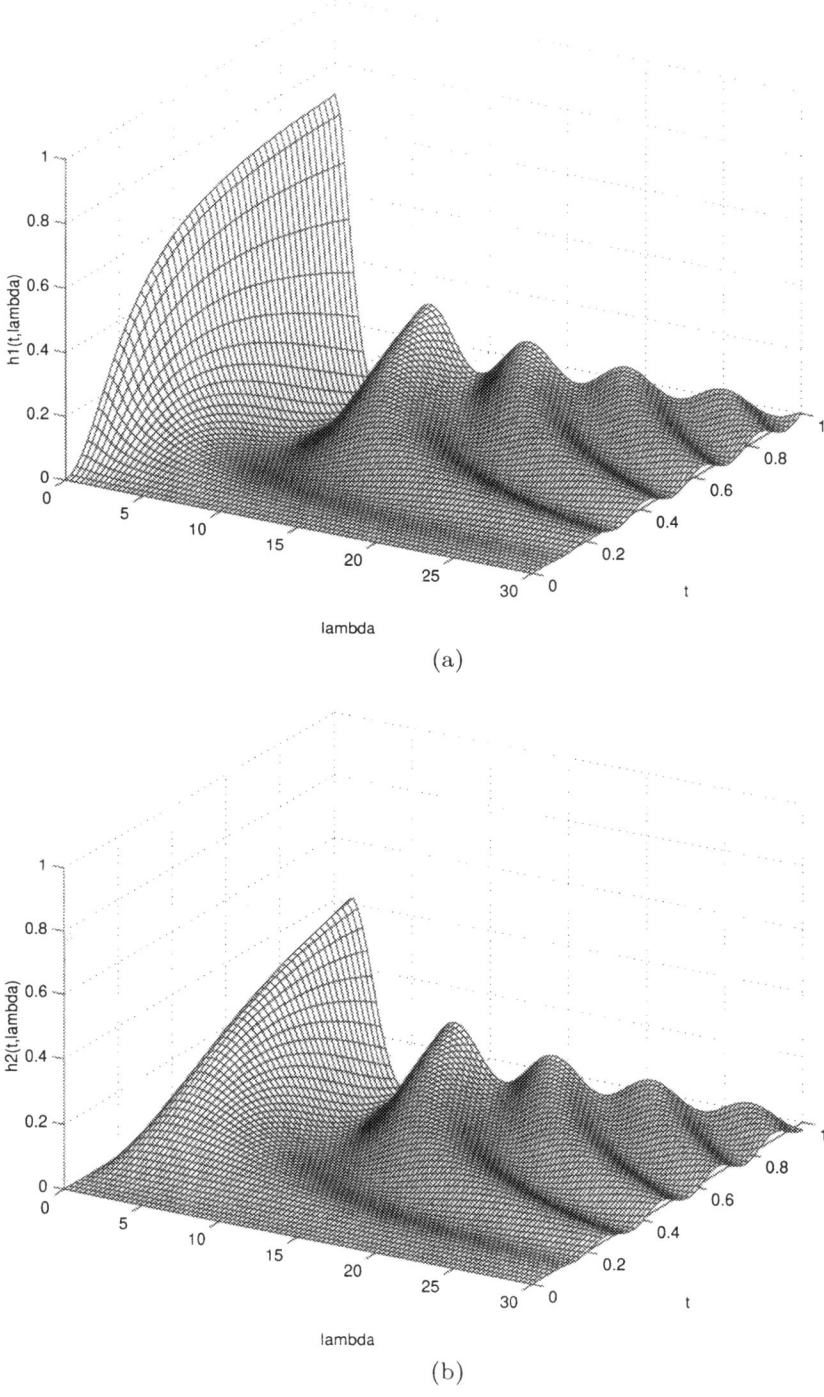

(a)

(b)

Figure 37. The functions $h_1(t,\lambda)$ and $h_2(t,\lambda)$ of eqn (4.91)

The approximation has been obtained by varying the weights w_i in order to minimise the error

$$\mathcal{E} = \int_0^{\lambda_{max}} \int_0^{t_{max}} \left[h_1(t,\lambda) - \tilde{h}_1(t,\lambda) \right]^2 + \left[h_2(t,\lambda) - \tilde{h}_2(t,\lambda) \right]^2 dt \, d\lambda \; . \qquad (4.98)$$

An AINN with two inputs, two outputs, 30 neurons and 210 weights has been used for this purpose by setting $t_{max} = 1$ and $\lambda_{max} = 30$.

For comparison the approximating functions $\tilde{h}_1(t,\lambda)$ and $\tilde{h}_2(t,\lambda)$ obtained in this way are depicted in Figs. 38(a) and 38(b).

Finally Fig. 39 reports the behaviour of the covariance function $R_{\eta\eta}(t,s)$ for the approximating process $\eta(t)$ as obtained from 200 realisations of (4.94) by using the same procedure used to obtain the results of Fig. 35. As you can see this behaviour is very close to $R_{\xi\xi}(t,s)$, thus confirming the validity of the theoretical results reported.

Additionally Fig. 40 reports some realisations of the approximating process $\eta(t)$.

The whole computation was executed in the Matlab/Simulink environment by varying λ in the range 0 to 100 rad/s with $\Delta\lambda = 0.25$ rad/s, $\Delta t = 0.01$ s, $\omega_0 = 20$, $\alpha = 1$, and the BMs generator parameters adjusted to obtain $\sigma = 1$.

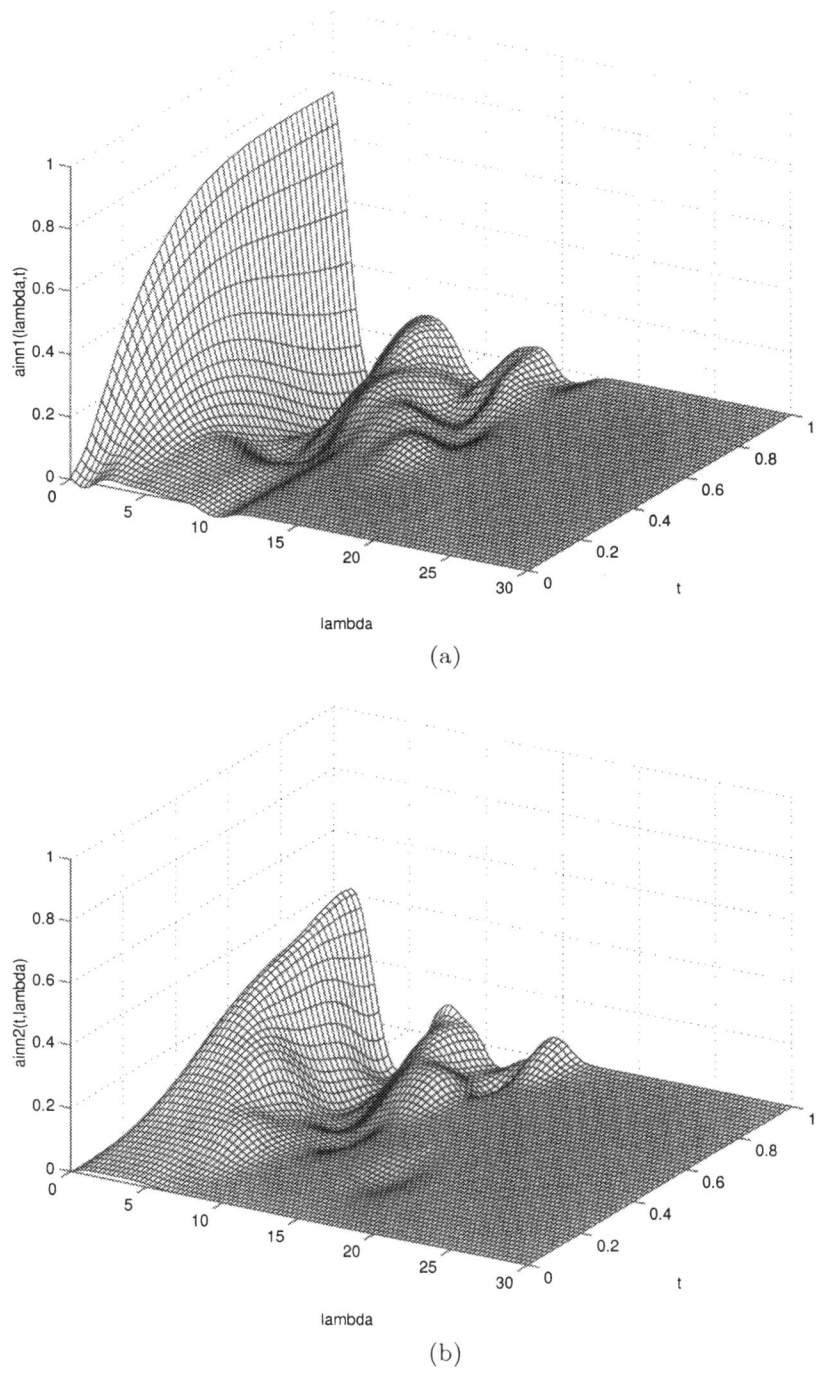

(a)

(b)

Figure 38. Output of the Approximate Identity Neural Network $\tilde{h}_1(t, \lambda)$ and $\tilde{h}_2(t, \lambda)$ which approximate $h_1(t, \lambda)$ and $h_2(t, \lambda)$ of eqn (4.91)

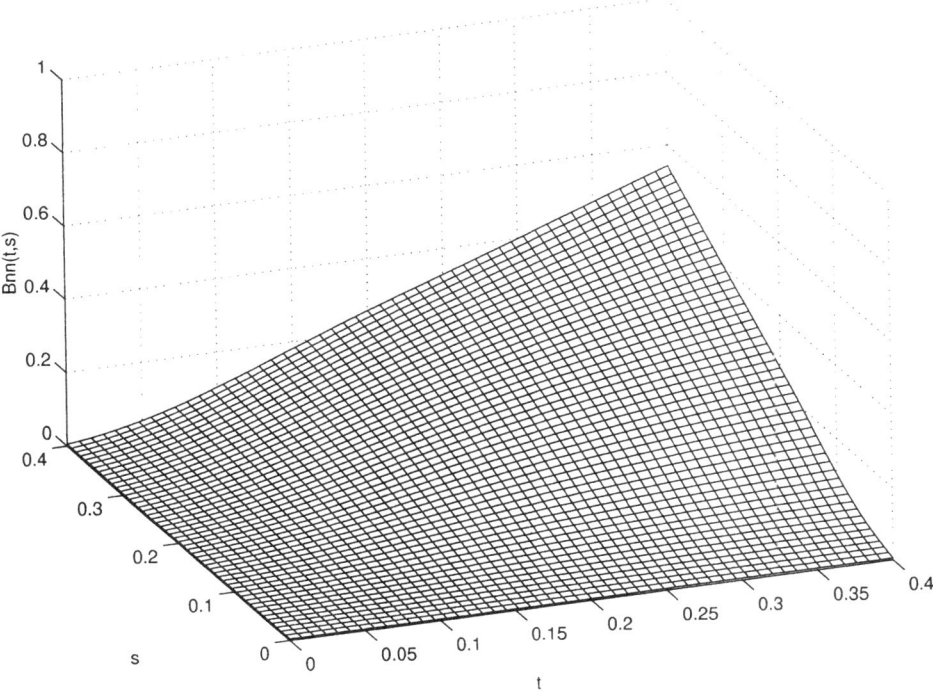

Figure 39. *The covariance function* $R_{\eta\eta}(t,s)$ *of the approximating process* $\eta(t)$ *as obtained from 200 realisations of (4.94) with* $\omega_0 = 20$ *and* $\alpha = 1$

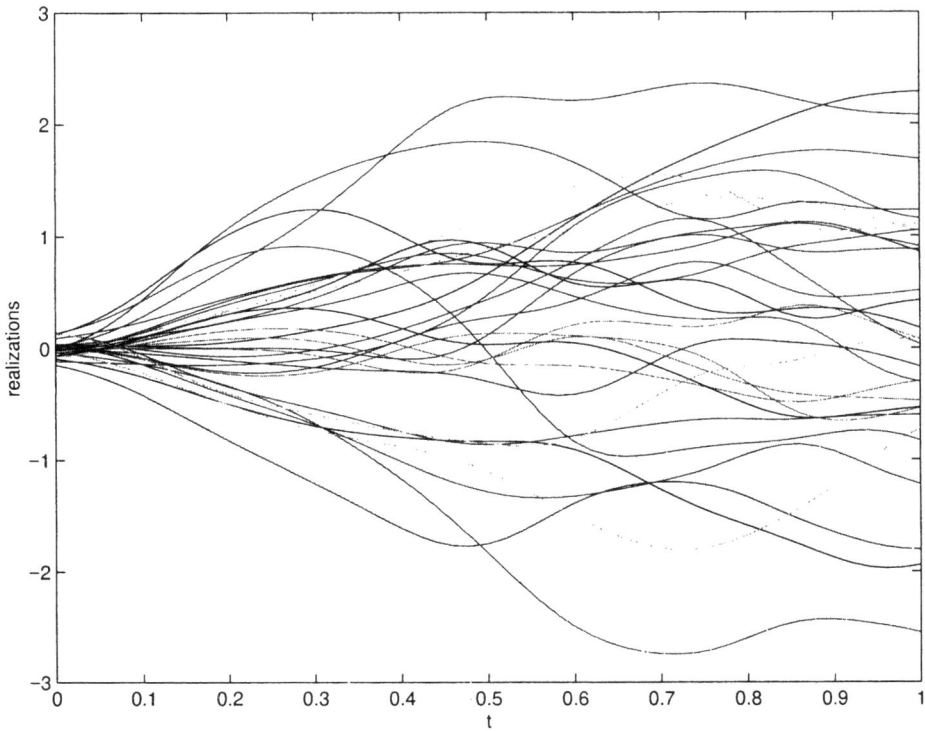

Figure 40. Some realisations of the approximating process $\eta(t)$

References

[1] Priestley, M. B. (1981). *Spectral Analysis and Time Series.* San Diego, CA, U.S.A. : Academic Press.

[2] Koopmans, L. H. (1995). *The Spectral Analysis of the Time Series.* San Diego, CA, U.S.A. : Academic Press.

[3] Turchetti, C., Conti, M., Crippa, P., & Orcioni, S. (1998). *On the Approximation of Stochastic Processes by Approximate Identity Neural Networks.* IEEE Trans. on Neural Networks, 9 (6), 1069–1085.

[4] Belli, M. R., Conti, M., Crippa, P., & Turchetti, C. (1999). *Artificial Neural Networks as Approximators of Stochastic Processes.* Neural Networks, 12, 647–658.

When I examine myself and my methods of
thought, I come to the conclusion that the gift
of fantasy has meant more to me than my
talent for absorbing positive knowledge.

Albert Einstein

CHAPTER FIVE

SAINN'S APPLICATIONS

The stochastic neural networks (SAINN's) previously defined and discussed have properties that may be useful in several applications.

In this chapter two significant case studies will be treated. The first one regards the process of modeling and memorizing physical events considered as stochastic processes. With reference to this problem the concept of stochastic memory, i.e. networks capable of memorizing s.p.'s, will be discussed.

The second case study addresses the problem of neural computing by a fundamentally different approach to the one currently adopted in digital computers. The approach is based on the composition of s.p.'s, rather than on the specification of operators as is done in the conventional mathematical approach and it is well suited for implementation by neural networks.

5.1.   Stochastic Memory

According to the Definition given in Sect. 2 a stochastic process is an indexed family of r.v.'s $\left\{\xi_t,\ t \in T\right\}$, defined on a probability space $(\Omega, \mathbf{S}, \mathcal{P})$. For each fixed $\omega \in \Omega$ the function $\xi(\cdot, \omega) = \left\{\xi(t, \omega),\ t \in T\right\}$ of the parameter $t \in T$, with values in the phase space $(X, \mathbf{B})$, is called a *trajectory or realization* (also named *sample function*) of the random process $\xi = \xi(t)$. An s.p. is therefore a collection of, in general, infinite (countable or uncountable) functions with values at instants $t_1, \dots, t_N$, constrained by the jpdf $f_{\xi_1 \xi_2 \dots} \left(\xi(t_1), \xi(t_2), \dots\right)$.

As a trivial example, recall the process

$$\xi = av(t) \tag{5.1}$$

discussed in Sect. 2.3.1, example 1. Being a an r.v. assuming the values $\lambda \in \mathbb{R}$, to each realization λ correspond a function $\lambda v(t)$. Thus if λ ranges on $\mathbb{R}$ with pdf $p(\lambda)$, an uncountable set of functions $\{\lambda v(t), \lambda \in \mathbb{R}\}$ corresponds to the s.p. $\xi(t)$.

A more concrete example showing the usefulness of this point of view may be found in the field of speech signals. Let us refer to the signals associated to a specific word, e.g. 'house', and pronounced by a single speaker. They may be considered as the realizations of a stochastic process with specific properties that distinguish them from the other signals associated to different words.

Among the main activities a neural system should be able to perform, modeling and retrieving the information on the environment it acquires through experience, are two of the most important. With regard to these aspects we maintain that a stochastic neural network of the kind discussed in Chap. 3 (SAINN) and represented by a summation

$$\eta(t) = \sum_m \eta_m u_m(t) \tag{5.2}$$

is able to approximate an s.p. $\xi(t)$, as has been proven in Sect. 3.3.

The approximation of $\xi(t)$ is accomplished by a learning stage for which one of the two methods derived in Sect. 3.4 and 3.5, the historical learning and real-time learning, may be used.

Once the learning stage is completed, the neural network (5.2) acts as a stochastic process itself, thus generating realizations whose behavior is, within the error assumed, the same as that of the process $\xi(t)$. This means that the stochastic neural network $\eta(t)$ is able to model, with a given accuracy, and to recall all the trajectories of $\xi(t)$. A network owning this property will be called a *stochastic memory*.

In view of these considerations, we maintain that a SAINN with the coefficients η_m and a_m determined through a learning stage, acts as a stochastic memory.

Let us discuss briefly the analogies and the differences of a stochastic memory in comparison to a deterministic one, which corresponds in this context to a deterministic neural network. A deterministic memory (or network) is capable of memorizing a finite set of functions. As this set is countable each function corresponds to a specific integer value. In the recalling process, once this integer value is set, just one function (or trajectory) is selected. This process occurs deterministically, or equivalently with probability 1. Conversely, in a stochastic memory there is no way to select a desired trajectory as they randomly occur. Nevertheless the amount of information it is able to memorize is larger than the one which may be memorized in the deterministic counterpart, since an infinite set (countable or uncountable) of trajectories corresponds in general to an s.p. $\xi(t)$.

How do we use and why should we use a stochastic memory instead of a deterministic one?

First of all it should be noted that neural networks (biological or artificial) operate in a non-deterministic (stochastic) environment. The behavior of such neural systems, which encompasses many different activities ranging from elementary actions to complex social behavior, is closely related to the environment in which they are forced to operate [1]. Thus the capability of memorizing stochastic processes is essential for both the human and artificial brain, in an attempt to model such an environment acting on them.

Additionally a stochastic memory has a property that is peculiar to the human brain, i.e. *generalization*. In order to explain this concept, let us refer to a set of functions (or signal in a time domain) representing a class of objects (images, speech, ...) or, more generally, a class of abstract elements (concepts, ideas, ...). Generalization means the capability of generating functions that are elements of this class, but that do not belong to the set of realizations gathered by experience [2].

This property is a direct consequence of the approximating property of a stochastic neural network. As shown in Chap. 3 a SAINN is capable of learning an s.p. $\xi(t)$ given a set of realizations (examples), by means of one of the two learning rules suggested.

Generalization is equivalent to estimating the trajectories of $\xi(t)$ not belonging to the set of examples. This property is guaranteed by the SAINN's ability of approximating a given process $\xi(t)$ with a certain accuracy.

In the human brain generalization is related to one of the most profitable activities for improving its capabilities, i.e. the ability to create new abstract concepts which may correspond to concrete actions or objects specifically synthesized on the basis of experience.

Let us refer to the example of speech signal representation to make the above statement clearer. Suppose a class of speech signals corresponding to a specific word, e.g. 'house', have been learned by the SAINN (5.2) through a set E of examples. Once the learning stage is completed, the network (5.2) should be able to generate not only the signals belonging to the set E, but also new trajectories that did not occur as examples.

A similar example in which generalization may be applied is represented by the image signals, considered as a natural extension of what is said above to two-dimensional (2-D) or three-dimensional (3-D) signals. To the same class of images learned by a finite set of examples, an infinity of different 2-D or 3-D signals corresponds, i.e. the realizations of the s.p. representing such a class.

5.1.1. Speech Signal Representation

In this section we wish to apply some of the concepts previously discussed to speech signals representation. Figure 41 reports six realizations of the Italian-language phoneme 'a' pronounced by different speakers. As you can see even if they behave similarly, the signals representing the same phoneme clearly display random fluctuations. Since the signals were achieved from measurements performed in an anechoic room, thus with a negligible noise due to the environment, randomness is an inherent characteristic of the recognizable signal itself.

Hence we assume the phoneme 'a' may be represented as an s.p. $\xi(t)$, belonging to the class of nonstationary processes defined on a finite domain T.

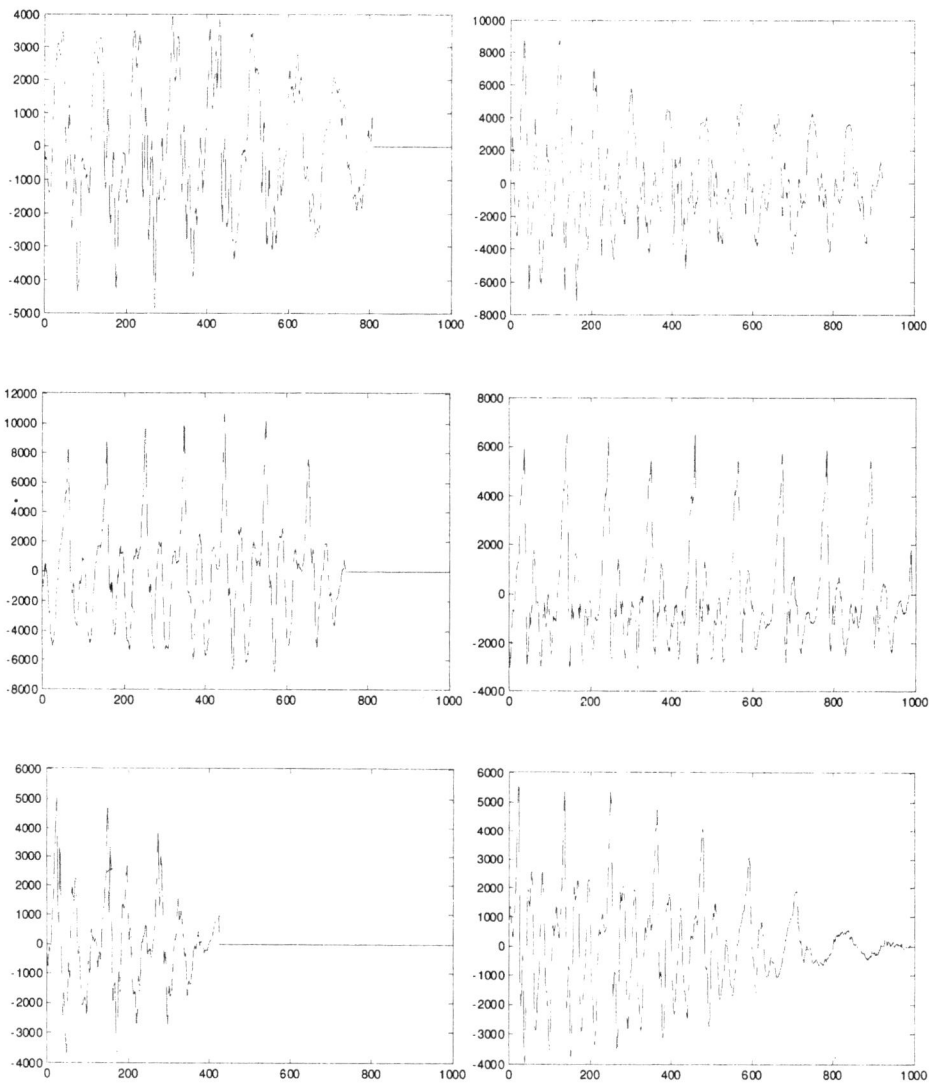

Figure 41. Examples of realizations of the Italian-language phoneme 'a' pronounced by different speakers

It is known that knowledge of the covariance function $B(t_i, t_j)$ suffices to represent a s.p. $\xi(t)$ by KLT. $B(t_i, t_j)$ can be estimated from a bundle of realizations by the relationship

$$B\left(t_i, t_j\right) = \frac{1}{n+1} \sum_{k=0}^{N} \xi^k\left(t_i\right) \xi^k\left(t_j\right) \tag{5.3}$$

where the index k represents the k-th realization and the values t_i, t_j belong to a discrete subset of the time interval T. The behavior of the covariance function for the phoneme 'a', as estimated with 22 realizations is depicted in Fig. 42.

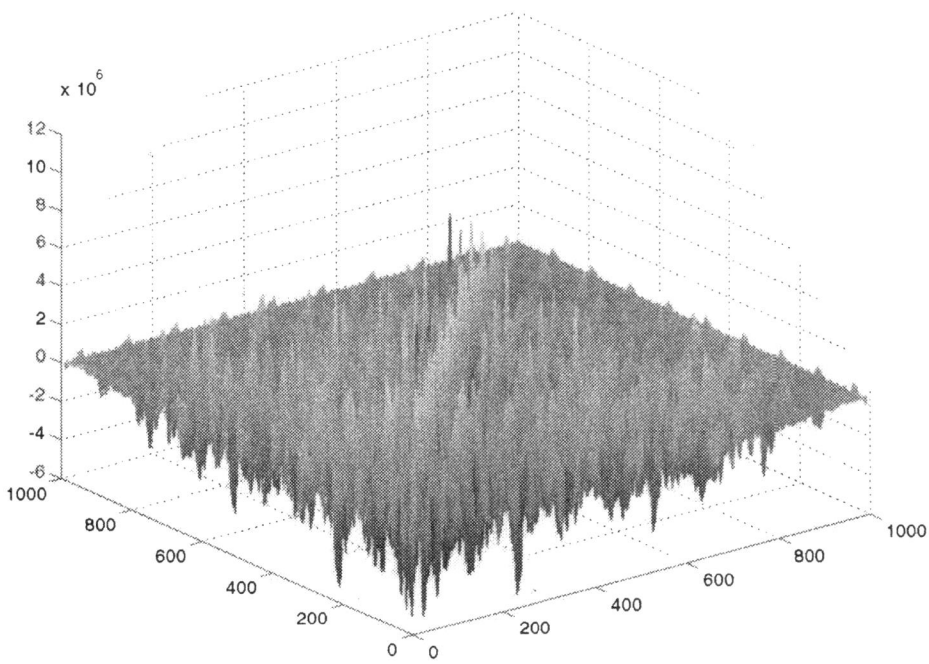

Figure 42. The covariance function for the phoneme 'a'

The eigenvalue equation (2.169) may be rewritten in the discrete case as

$$\sum_{j=1}^{N} B\left(t_i, t_j\right) \varphi\left(t_j\right) = \varphi\left(t_i\right) \tag{5.4}$$

which once solved yields to the eigenfunctions $\varphi\left(t_i\right)$, $i = 1, \dots, N$.

Some of the eigenfunctions in KLT representation of the phoneme 'a' are reported in Fig. 43, while the eigenvalues ξ_m $m = 1, 2, \dots$ for a single realization are shown in Fig. 44.

The ξ_m values rapidly decrease as the index m increases, as is predicted by the KLT theory, thus confirming that just a limited number of ξ_m values are significant.

In order to check the SAINN's capability of modelling and memorizing s.p.'s, several eigenfunctions have been approximated with AI functions.

Figure 45 shows six eigenfunctions (solid lines) as determined by KLT theory and the approximated curves (broken lines), as obtained by a superposition of 48 AI functions. As you can see the accuracy of the approximation is good even though the behaviour of the realizations is quite irregular.

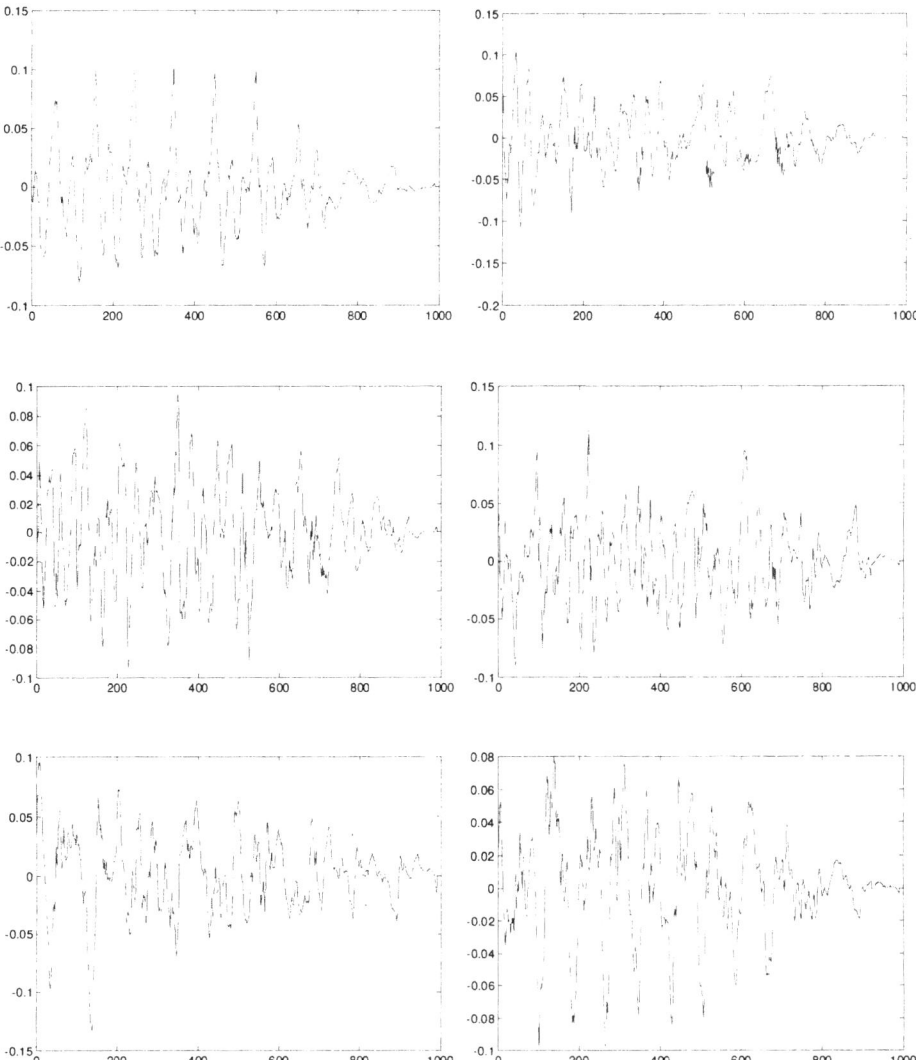

Figure 43. Six eigenfunctions (corresponding to the six highest eigenvalues) in the KLT representation of the phoneme 'a'

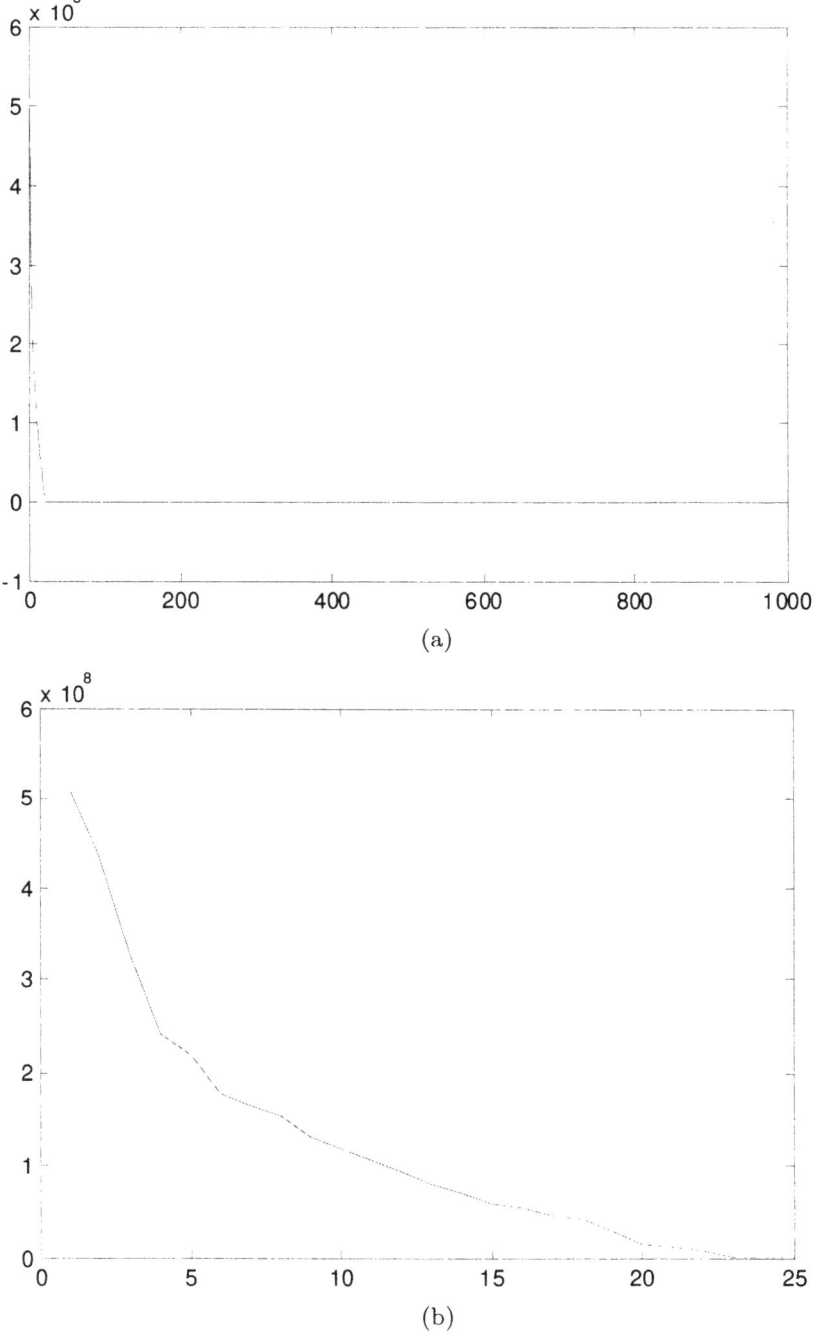

Figure 44. (a) All the eigenvalues in the KLT representation of the phoneme 'a'; (b)
the most significative eigenvalues in the KLT representation of the phoneme 'a';

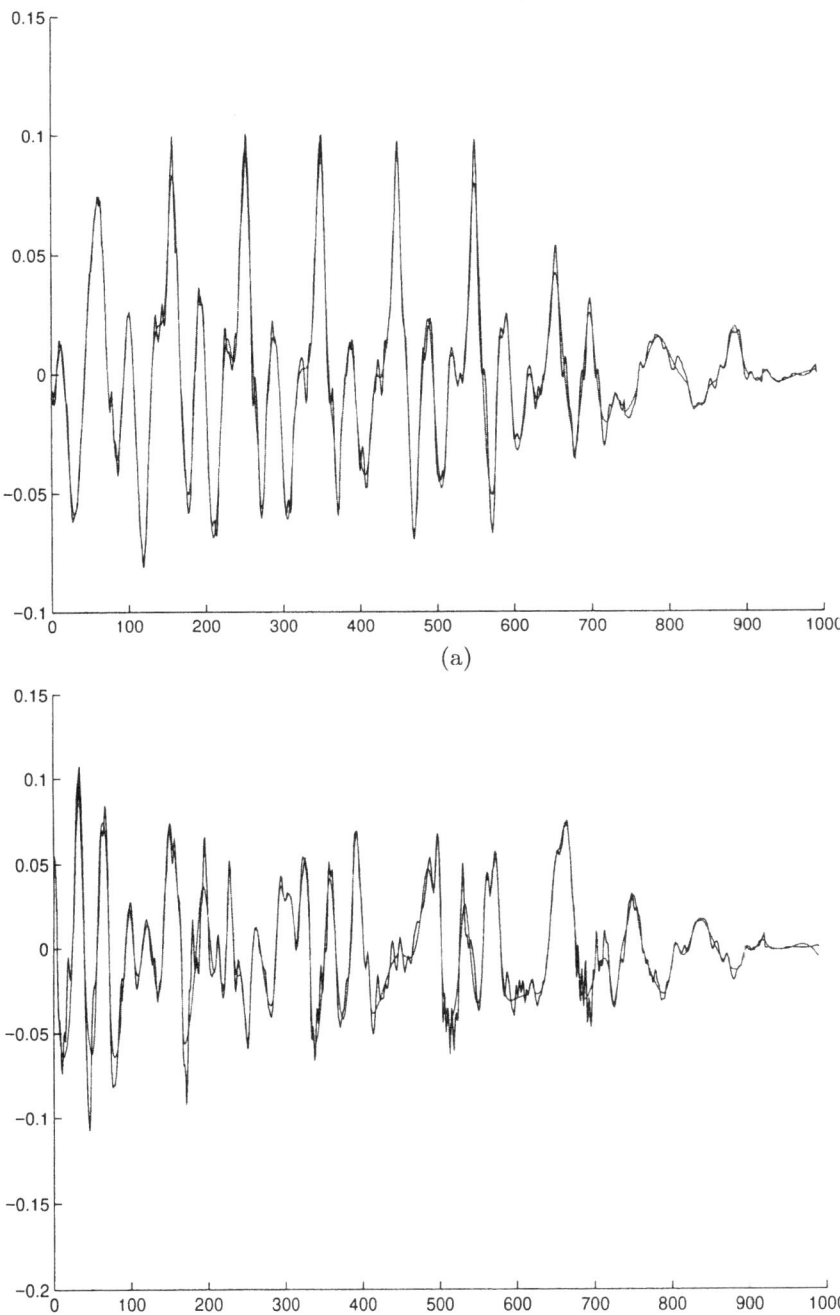

(a)

(b)

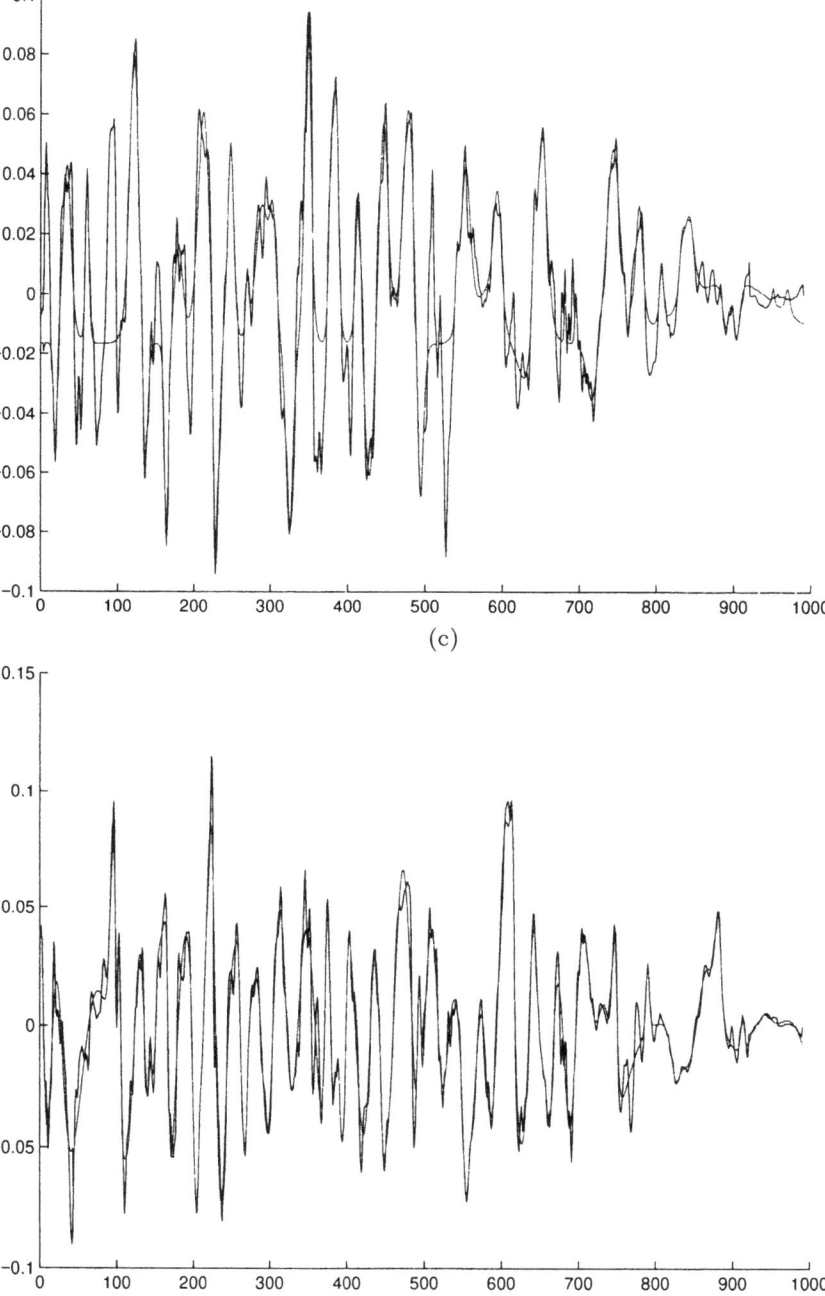

(c)

(d)

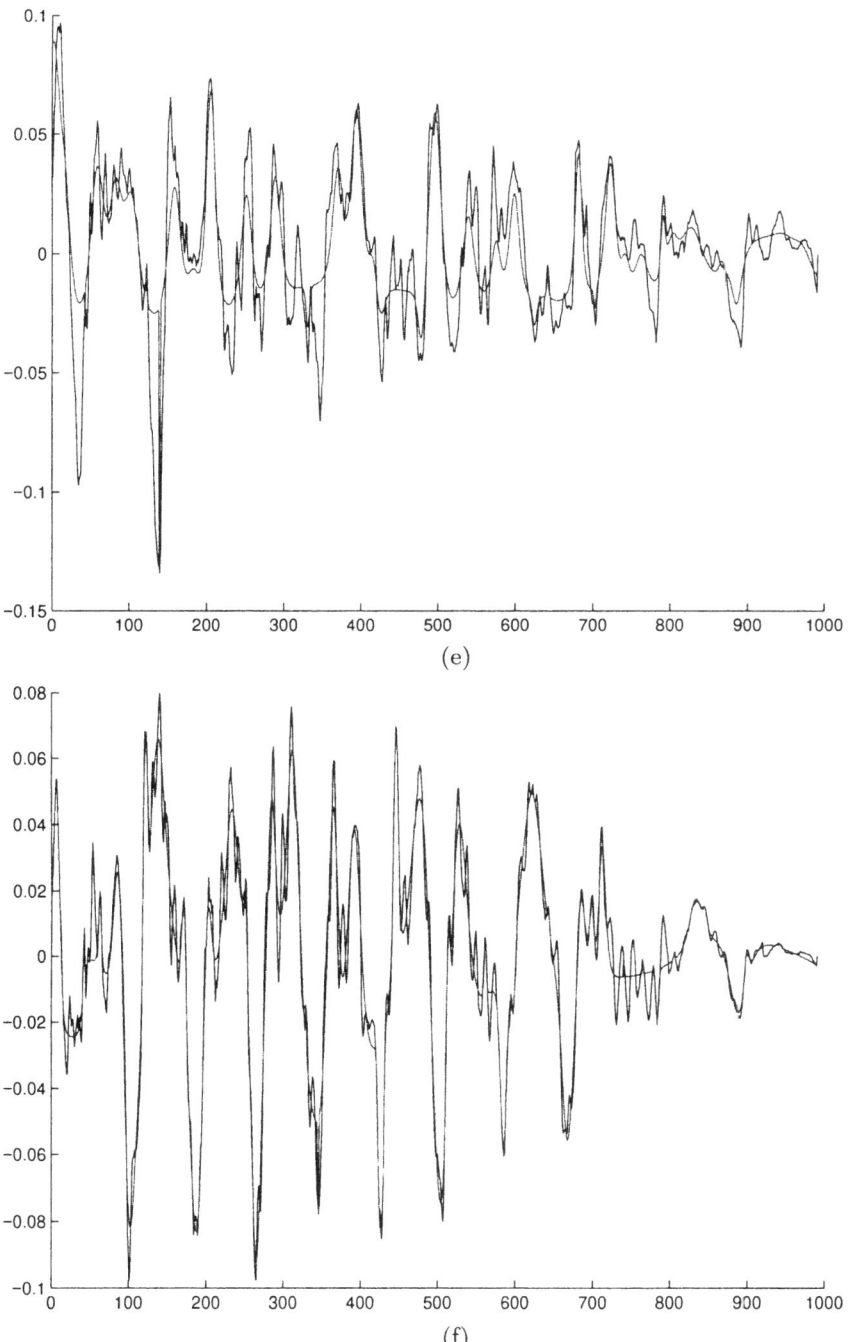

Figure 45. Approximation via SAINNs of the six eigenfunctions (corresponding to the six highest eigenvalues) of Fig. 43.

Table II: Coefficients of the SAINN (learning of first eigenfunction)

AINN	b_j	ν_j	ϑ_j	σ_j
1	0.25645	-0.14608	-2.271	0.33810
2	0.23518	0.19115	14.418	0.42865
3	0.31206	0.11847	50.762	0.42812
4	0.26277	0.20493	64.407	0.34267
5	0.15216	0.71089	78.772	0.14552
6	0.17935	0.24465	99.508	0.27574
7	-0.07766	-0.25578	118.931	1.50043
8	0.39380	0.03947	130.921	0.45836
9	0.06156	0.34133	158.593	2.13087
10	0.06772	0.34100	193.455	2.89615
11	-0.39722	0.00465	209.220	0.40961
12	0.29968	0.15069	227.228	0.40382
13	0.55433	0.19373	251.271	0.31938
14	-0.01463	1.35942	273.061	5.20324
15	0.31929	0.09210	296.916	0.37103
16	-0.17406	0.18582	303.938	0.78144
17	0.29911	0.02779	330.472	0.41740
18	0.23232	0.26501	348.643	0.49576
19	-0.06475	0.72357	370.745	0.55040
20	0.21462	0.18975	387.561	0.29687
21	-0.15656	0.28883	419.660	-0.19331
22	0.30758	0.07605	447.906	0.40584
23	0.24920	0.45532	448.386	0.25308
24	-0.15711	-0.35828	469.201	0.37550
25	0.23752	0.17936	489.107	0.38304
26	0.22654	0.24389	518.615	0.36321
27	0.14321	0.31332	530.583	0.25525
28	0.47405	0.17895	548.425	0.32356
29	0.08317	0.47392	580.618	0.60006
30	0.24086	0.24776	590.208	0.33718
31	0.19039	0.16936	618.946	0.25814
32	0.05575	0.41527	634.595	0.18023
33	0.30926	0.15254	652.535	0.27160
34	-0.06175	-0.81581	677.792	0.20548
35	0.20999	0.19388	697.019	0.26662
36	0.07979	0.30418	730.481	0.16727
37	0.11520	5.00505	741.545	0.13178
38	0.05017	0.81770	763.020	0.15787
39	0.12746	0.08379	784.823	0.21937
40	0.12352	-0.00505	806.347	0.22060
41	-0.05587	0.40547	831.839	0.17505
42	-0.06322	0.32243	842.633	0.13508
43	0.03135	0.91066	866.260	0.13933
44	0.10137	0.18590	884.862	0.23442
45	0.03223	0.87560	907.094	0.09472
46	0.04194	0.27474	925.834	0.14005
47	-0.05497	0.03290	945.407	0.15863
48	0.01874	0.06826	966.051	0.12088

5.2.   Neural Computing

Many earlier excellent papers and books [1,3-7] have underlined the differences between digital computation (i.e. computation performed by digital computers) and computation performed by biological neural systems. More precisely the following assertions make a clear distinction between neural and digital computers.

The biological neural systems do not behave like a digital computer, i.e. do not apply principles of digital computation and, as a consequence, do not implement recursive computation. This assertion is justified by the fact that neurons cannot be threshold–logic circuits, since the accuracy and stability of such circuits is not adequate to define Boolean functions. As a consequence the biological brain must use an analog mechanism for computation.

Another essential aspect that makes the difference between the two computation systems more pronounced, is the need for a preprocessing stage aimed at the logical/mathematical formulation of the problem to be solved in digital computation.

As an example, suppose we wish to estimate the trajectory of a body of mass m, with initial velocity v_0 and initial position x_0. This problem may be solved by means of the well-known dynamic laws of mechanics. From a mathematical point of view such laws, expressed as equations, represent a rigorous model of the physical event. In order that such a problem may be solved by a digital computer with high accuracy, a preprocessing stage is necessary for defining the mathematical model. However a digital computer, itself, is not able to perform at a level higher than numerical computation. Instead, this kind of processing requires the human action.

It is hard to think that a neural network is capable of processing in a short lapse of time mathematical models of the physical world with which it interacts, mathematics being an abstract formalism which has been developed over the human evolution and not a heritage of the human brain. Instead it is reasonable to think that the human brain adopts an approach to the modeling of the physical world, which is different from that currently used to yield a quantitative solution to a problem of any kind, and known as *scientific approach*.

This new computing approach should be defined on the basis of the following observations.

A digital computing machine requires a mathematical model of the problem that is solved numerically with a suitable algorithm. This is also the case of the analog computing machines which apply the same computation approach, but in a non algorithmic way, the only benefits of such machines being their high parallelism.

Conversely, in a biological neural network the model of the physical event under observation is built up by the network itself on the basis of experience (experiments or examples). Moreover, in many application problems, a solution with a high degree of accuracy is not required, thus tolerating a scarcely accurate modeling. More precisely such a modeling approach should be irrespective of the mathematical formalism (laws of composition, operators, etc.) currently adopted in the digital computation. Instead it should be directly applied to the events that occur in the environment in which the network operates.

In view of the above considerations, in the following we wish to suggest an approach to computation that is applied to elements, abstract or not, which does not need to be defined (and thus implemented) through operation of composition and/or mathematical operators.

As this approach is based on the composition of s.p.'s, we will first introduce a generalization of the concepts discussed in the previous chapter to the case of multidimensional s.p.'s.

5.2.1. Vector Stochastic Neural Networks

The purpose of this section is to generalize the treatment of Sect. 2, which was restricted to one-dimensional s.p.'s, to the canonical representation of multivariate s.p.'s.

We define a stochastic vector process as

$$\boldsymbol{\xi}(t) = \left[\xi_1(t), \dots, \xi_n(t)\right]^T \quad , \qquad t \in T \tag{5.5}$$

with zero-mean complex-valued component $\xi_j(t)$,

$$E\left\{\xi_j(t)\right\} = 0 \ , \quad j = 1, \dots, n \ , \qquad t \in T \ . \tag{5.6}$$

The covariance function matrix

$$\mathbf{B}(t,s) = \left[B_{jk}(t,s)\right] \tag{5.7}$$

of the s.p. $\boldsymbol{\xi}(t)$ is defined by

$$B_{jk}(t,s) = E\left\{\xi_j(t)\overline{\xi_k(t)}\right\} . \tag{5.8}$$

According to the theory developed in Chap. 2 we consider the class of non stationary processes such that $B_{jk}(t,s)$ may be represented in the form

$$B_{jk}(t,s) = \int_{\Lambda} \varphi_j(t,\lambda)\overline{\varphi_k(s,\lambda)} F_{jk}(d\lambda) \tag{5.9}$$

where F_{jk} is the jk-element of the spectral matrix

$$\mathbf{F}(\Delta\lambda) = \left[F_{jk}(\Delta\lambda)\right] . \tag{5.10}$$

Hence the components $\xi_j(t)$ have canonical representation

$$\xi_j(t) = \int_{\Lambda} \varphi_j(t,\lambda)\Phi_j(d\lambda) \tag{5.11}$$

where $\Phi_j(d\lambda)$ is a stochastic measure such that it results

$$E\left\{\left|\Phi_j(d\lambda)\right|^2\right\} = F_{jj}(\Delta\lambda) . \tag{5.12}$$

With reference to the vector s.p. (5.5), it is natural to generalize the definition of a SAINN to the multidimensional case. To this end we define a *vector* SAINN as the vector

$$\boldsymbol{\eta}(t) = \left[\eta_1(t), \dots, \eta_n(t)\right]^T \tag{5.13}$$

where the generic component is given by

$$\eta_j(t) = \sum_m \eta_m^j u_m(t) . \tag{5.14}$$

5.2.2. Composition of Stochastic Processes

Given the two s.p.'s $x(t)$ and $y(t)$, let us focus our attention on a composition rule of the kind

$$x(t) \perp y(t) = z(t) \tag{5.15}$$

where $\perp$ is a generic operation of composition (logic/arithmetic or any other) acting instantaneously (i.e. with no memory of the past values) on the values $x(t)$, $y(t)$ at the instant t and whose result is the s.p. $z(t)$.

We assume the s.p.'s $x(t)$, $y(t)$ and $z(t)$ may be represented in canonical form

$$x(t) = \int_\Lambda f(t,\lambda)\Sigma(d\lambda)$$
$$y(t) = \int_\Lambda g(t,\lambda)\Pi(d\lambda) \qquad (5.16)$$
$$z(t) = \int_\Lambda h(t,\lambda)\Phi(d\lambda)$$

being $\Sigma(d\lambda)$, $\Pi(d\lambda)$, and $\Phi(d\lambda)$ the stochastic measures corresponding to $x(t)$, $y(t)$ and $z(t)$ respectively. We define the vector stochastic process $\boldsymbol{\xi}(t)$ as

$$\boldsymbol{\xi}(t) = \left[x(t),\, y(t),\, z(t)\right]^T . \qquad (5.17)$$

For any interval $\Delta\lambda$ of the space Λ we also have the vector random variable

$$\left[\Sigma(\Delta\lambda),\, \Pi(\Delta\lambda),\, \Phi(\Delta\lambda)\right]^T \qquad (5.18)$$

where $\Phi(\Delta\lambda)$ is correlated both to $\Sigma(\Delta\lambda)$ and $\Pi(\Delta\lambda)$ since it results

$$\Phi(\Delta\lambda) = \int_T z(t)\,\psi_{\Delta\lambda}(t)\,dt = \int_T \{x(t)\perp y(t)\}\,\psi_{\Delta\lambda}(t)\,dt . \qquad (5.19)$$

Hence for a given $\Delta\lambda$ we may define the jpdf

$$\rho_{\Sigma\Pi\Phi}(\Sigma,\Pi,\Phi) . \qquad (5.20)$$

The trajectories of $\boldsymbol{\xi}(t)$ with stochastic measures satisfying (5.20), belong to the set of solutions of eqn. (5.15), hence the s.p. $\boldsymbol{\xi}(t)$ may be interpreted as a representation of the composition $\perp$ between the two given s.p.'s. $x(t)$, $y(t)$.

Formally we state the following

Definition 5.1 -   Given the s.p.'s $x(t)$, $y(t)$ and $z(t)$, where $z(t)$ is correlated to both x and y, we define the composition rule $\perp$ between x, y to give z as the set

$$S = \left\{\boldsymbol{\xi}(t),\ t \in T\right\} \qquad (5.21)$$

of all the realizations of $\boldsymbol{\xi}(t) = \left[x(t),\, y(t),\, z(t)\right]^T$.

Approximating $\boldsymbol{\xi}(t)$ by means of a vector SAINN $\boldsymbol{\eta}(t) = \sum_m \eta_m u_m(t)$, with stochastic measures generated according to (5.20), is equivalent to approximating the composition rule (5.15).

For a given couple of s.p.'s $x(t)$ and $y(t)$, the vector SAINN is capable of generating, within a certain error, all the trajectories belonging to the composition (5.15). Hence $\eta(t)$ may be considered as a (stochastic) representation of the composition $\perp$ between the s.p.'s $x(t)$, $y(t)$.

Note the difference of this representation with the usual definition of the (deterministic) composition $\perp$. In the latter the operation $\perp$ establishes a certain (logic/arithmetic) rule by means of which the s.p. $z(t)$ at the instant t may be computed from the values $x(t)$, $y(t)$. In the stochastic representation we don't use this rule for determining the resulting process $z(t)$, instead we randomly generate the trajectories belonging to (5.15). As a consequence such a representation does not require the implementation of the composition operation as an *ad hoc* element in a neural system, since the stochastic neural network itself is able to implement it. Nevertheless this kind of representation is not able to answer this question: given the two trajectories $x(t)$ and $y(t)$, what is the trajectory $z(t)$ resulting from (5.15)? As the network $\eta(t)$ memorizes and generates all the triples $\big(x(t), y(t), z(t)\big)$, this process may be viewed as a random searching of the solution within the set of solutions of (5.15). Finding the true solution of (5.15) is guaranteed in general only when an infinity of realizations occur, even though in the particular case the set of trajectories is finite, a finite set of realizations suffices. However, in practical cases we may need to determine an approximated solution $\tilde{\xi}(t)$ of the s.p. $\xi(t)$ accepting an error ε defined by

$$\left\| \tilde{\xi}(t) - \xi(t) \right\| < \varepsilon \ . \tag{5.22}$$

Although we cannot guarantee the constrain (5.22) is satisfied with a given error and a limited number of $\eta(t)$ realizations, the trajectory with a minimum error gives an approximated solution of the eqn. (5.15) which suffices for many practical applications.

Example 1

Let $x(t)$, $y(t)$ be periodic signals assuming only the two values $[0,1]$ and $\perp$ a binary logic operator (AND, OR, ...). In this case the s.p.'s $x(t)$, $y(t)$ and $z(t)$ are merely three random variables assuming the two values $[0,1]$, with jpdf given by (5.20). All the values achieved generating random samples of the vector ξ with jpdf given by (5.20), satisfy the composition (5.15). Hence the s.p. ξ is equivalent to the composition (5.15).

Example 2

We assume in this case the composition rule $\perp$ is simply the arithmetic product between the two real-valued signals $x(t)$, $y(t)$. Once the jpdf $\rho_{\Sigma\Pi\Phi}$ of the stochastic measures Σ, Π, Φ, has been estimated, we may generate trajectories by the processes x, y, z satisfying eqn. (5.15).

5.2.3. Representation of Transformations

Let

$$T(t_0) = \left\{ t : t \in T, \ t \geq t_0 \right\} \tag{5.23}$$

be the set of time instants truncated at the instant t_0 and $u(t)$ an s.p. defined in $T(t_0)$.

Consider a transformation

$$\Gamma \xi(t) = u(t), \qquad t \in T(t_0) \tag{5.24}$$

where Γ is an operator (non-random) and $\xi(t_0)$ an r.v. with a given pdf specifying the initial condition of the process $\xi(t)$, i.e. the solution of the eqn. (5.24).

Eqn. (5.24) is a stochastic equation due to randomness of $u(t)$, as well as of the initial condition. Here we are interested in the so-called inverse problem, i.e. given Γ, $u(t)$, $t \in T(t_0)$, and the pdf of $\xi(t_0)$, determine the s.p. $\xi(t)$.

Assuming the covariance function of $\xi(t)$ is given by

$$B(t,s) = \int_\Lambda \varphi(t,\lambda)\overline{\varphi(s,\lambda)}\, F(d\lambda) \tag{5.25}$$

then $\xi(t)$ admits the canonical representation

$$\xi(t) = \int_\Lambda \varphi(t,\lambda)\Phi(d\lambda) \tag{5.26}$$

Under this condition the solution of eqn. (5.24) may be represented by a SAINN on the basis of the theory developed in the previous chapters..

Linear case

As in general it is not straightforward to derive conditions for $\xi(t)$ to be represented in canonical form when Γ is nonlinear, this is not the case for linear operators Γ.

Assuming for $u(t)$ the representation

$$u(t) = \int_{\Lambda} \psi(t,\lambda)\Phi(d\lambda) \tag{5.27}$$

and by hypothesis

$$\xi(t) = \int_{\Lambda} \varphi(t,\lambda)\Phi(d\lambda) . \tag{5.28}$$

Thus we have

$$\Gamma\xi(t) = \int_{\Lambda} \Gamma_t\varphi(t,\lambda)\Phi(d\lambda) = \int_{\Lambda} \psi(t,\lambda)\Phi(d\lambda) \tag{5.29}$$

which reduces for all $\lambda \in \Lambda$, but a set with zero measure, to the equation

$$\Gamma_t\,\varphi(t,\lambda) = \psi(t,\lambda) \tag{5.30}$$

The function $\varphi(t,\lambda)$ is given by the solution (if exists) of eqn. (5.30), where the subscript t indicates that the operator Γ acts on the variable t.

5.2.4. Linear Differential Equations with Random Initial Conditions

A- Equations with no forced term

Let us be given the linear differential equation

$$\dot{x}(t) = A(t)x(t) \tag{5.31}$$

with random initial condition

$$x(t_0) = x_0 . \tag{5.32}$$

The general solution of (5.31) has the form

$$x(t) = \Phi(t,t_0)x_0 \tag{5.33}$$

with covariance function

$$B\left(t,s\right) = E\left\{\boldsymbol{x}\left(t\right)\overline{\boldsymbol{x}^T\left(s\right)}\right\} = E\left\{\boldsymbol{\Phi}\left(t,t_0\right)\boldsymbol{x}_0\,\overline{\boldsymbol{x}_0^T\,\boldsymbol{\Phi}^T\left(s,t_0\right)}\right\}$$
$$= \boldsymbol{\Phi}\left(t,t_0\right)E\left\{\boldsymbol{x}_0\,\overline{\boldsymbol{x}_0^T}\right\}\overline{\boldsymbol{\Phi}^T\left(s,t_0\right)}\ . \tag{5.34}$$

It is straightforward to show that (5.33) is equivalent to the discrete component of the canonical representation (see f.i. (4.37)).

Example

As an example let us consider the equation

$$\ddot{x}\left(t\right) + \omega^2 x\left(t\right) = 0 \quad , \qquad 0 \le t < \infty \tag{5.35}$$

with

$$\begin{cases} x\left(0\right) = x_0 \\ \dot{x}\left(0\right) = \dot{x}_0 \end{cases} \tag{5.36}$$

uncorrelated Gaussian r.v.'s.

Eqn.(5.35) may be put in the normal form (5.31) by choosing $x_1\left(t\right) = x\left(t\right)$, $x_2\left(t\right) = \dot{x}\left(t\right)$.

It is easy to show that the solution of (5.35)is given by

$$\begin{bmatrix} x\left(t\right) \\ \dot{x}\left(t\right) \end{bmatrix} = \begin{bmatrix} \cos\omega t & \left(1/\omega\right)\sin\omega t \\ -\omega\,\cos\omega t & \cos\omega t \end{bmatrix}\begin{bmatrix} x_0 \\ \dot{x}_0 \end{bmatrix} \tag{5.37}$$

and, thus, the resulting s.p. $x\left(t\right)$ may be approximated with a SAINN $\eta\left(t\right) = \sum_k \eta_k u_k\left(t\right)$ as:

$$x\left(t\right) = x_0\cos\omega t + \dot{x}_0\left(1/\omega\right)\sin\omega t$$
$$\simeq \sum_k \eta_k u_k\left(t\right) \tag{5.38}$$
$$= a\sum_k c_k u_k\left(t\right) + b\sum_j \overline{c}_j u_j\left(t\right)$$

a and b being r.v.'s.

B – Equations with forced term

Inserting a forced term $u(t)$ in (5.31), yields the more general linear equation

$$\dot{x}(t) = A(t)x(t) + B(t)u(t) \tag{5.39}$$

with random initial condition $x(t_0) = x_0$.

It is well-known from system theory that the solution of eqn. (5.39) is

$$\dot{x}(t) = \Phi(t,t_0)x(t_0) + \int_{t_0}^{t} h(t,\tau)u(\tau)d\tau \tag{5.40}$$

$h(t,\tau)$ being the impulse response of the system represented by eqn.(5.39).

Assuming $u(t)$ admits the canonical representation

$$u(t) = \int_{\Lambda} \psi(t,\lambda)\Phi(d\lambda) \tag{5.41}$$

then we have

$$\begin{aligned}
x(t) &= \Phi(t,t_0)x(t_0) + \int_{t_0}^{t} h(t,\tau)\left(\int_{\Lambda}\psi(t,\lambda)\Phi(d\lambda)\right)d\tau \\
&= \Phi(t,t_0)x(t_0) + \int_{\Lambda}\left[\int_{t_0}^{t} h(t,\tau)\psi(\tau,\lambda)d\tau\right]\Phi(d\lambda)
\end{aligned} \tag{5.42}$$

By putting

$$\varphi(t,\lambda) = \int_{t_0}^{t} h(t,\tau)\psi(\tau,\lambda)d\tau \tag{5.43}$$

we obtain

$$x(t) = \Phi(t,t_0)x(t_0) + \int_{\Lambda}\varphi(t,\lambda)\Phi(d\lambda) \tag{5.44}$$

showing that $x(t)$ has the same form as the general expression (4.11) with

$$\begin{aligned}
x_d(t) &= \Phi(t,t_0)x(t_0) , \\
x_c(t) &= \int_{\Lambda}\varphi(t,\lambda)\Phi(d\lambda) .
\end{aligned} \tag{5.45}$$

5.2.5. Inverse Problem Solution

Previous analysis showed that in the linear case the canonical representation of $\xi(t)$ may be derived by solving the deterministic equation (5.30) or, as demonstrated in the examples, by directly solving the stochastic equation (5.24).

Thus a SAINN approximating the behavior of $\xi(t)$ may be derived by applying the results of chapter 3. Nevertheless, in the general case of a nonlinear operator this approach is not viable. Anyway in order to solve the equation

$$\Gamma\xi(t) = u(t) , \qquad t \in T(t_0) , \tag{5.46}$$

i.e. the inverse problem associated to the operator Γ, it is necessary to know the operator Γ, other than $u(t)$ and the pdf of $\xi(t_0)$. In a neural network this requirement corresponds to the capability of the network to derive and implement such an operator. Unfortunately, while some general methods to implement an operator in a digital computer exist, the problem of deriving a mathematical operator from experimental data, has not been solved yet.

Here we want to suggest a procedure to solve the inverse problem stated by eq. (5.46) without using a mathematical model of the operator Γ.

To this end we assume that eq. (5.46) represents a physical system, $u(t)$ is the stimulus (or the input), and $\xi(t)$ is the effect (or the output) of such a stimulus.

Both the signals $u(t)$ and $\xi(t)$ will be considered as observable (or measurable) so that a population of realizations may be gathered by measurements accomplished on the physical system.

Without affecting the generality of the results, we restrict the following analysis to the case of a finite domain T. As a first step the covariance functions of the process $\xi(t)$ and $u(t)$ may be derived from their realizations. Thus from KLT theory we have the canonical representations

$$u(t) = \sum_{\lambda \in \Lambda} f(t,\lambda)\Pi(\lambda) ,$$
$$\xi(t) = \sum_{\lambda \in \Lambda} g(t,\lambda)\Phi(\lambda) , \tag{5.47}$$

$\Pi(\lambda)$ and $\Phi(\lambda)$ being the stochastic measures corresponding to $u(t)$ and $\xi(t)$ respectively. We define the vector stochastic process $\zeta(t)$ as

$$\zeta(t) = \left[u(t), \xi(t)\right]^T . \tag{5.48}$$

For any $\lambda \in \Lambda$ we also have the vector random variable

$$\left[\Pi(\lambda), \Phi(\lambda)\right]^T \tag{5.49}$$

where $\Phi(\lambda)$ is correlated to $\Pi(\lambda)$ since it results

$$\Phi(\lambda) = \int_T \xi(t) g(t,\lambda) dt = \int_T \Gamma^{-1} u(t) g(t,\lambda) dt \ , \tag{5.50}$$

Γ^{-1} being the inverse of the operator Γ.

Hence for a given $\lambda \in \Lambda$ we may define the jpdf

$$\rho_{\Pi\Phi}(\Pi,\Phi) \ . \tag{5.51}$$

Similarly to the composition of s.p.'s discussed in Sect. 5.2.2, the trajectories of $\zeta(t)$ with stochastic measures satisfying (5.51) are all solutions of the eqn. (5.46)

Finding the solution to (5.46) with initial condition $\xi(t_0)$, is equivalent, in this scheme, to the random searching in the set of the trajectories generated by the s.p. $\xi(t)$, the one satisfying the condition $\xi(t_0) = \xi_0$. Finding the true solution to (5.46) is guaranteed, provided an infinity of realizations occur. However in practical cases we may need to determine, among the trajectories satisfying eqn. (5.46), the solution $\tilde{\xi}(t)$ that guarantees the minimum error ε on the initial condition

$$\left\| \tilde{\xi}(t_0) - \xi(t_0) \right\| < \varepsilon \ . \tag{5.52}$$

As already discussed in Sect. 5.2.2 a vector SAINN may be used to represent the s.p. $\zeta(t)$, and thus to solve, within a certain error, the inverse problem stated by eqn. (5.46).

It is worth noting that the speech signal representation problem discussed in Sect. 5.1.1, may also be viewed as a representation of a transformation. Indeed it is well-known that the speech signal produced by a speaker, may be assumed to be the output of passing a glottal excitation waveform $u(t)$ through a linear time-varying filter that models the characteristics of the vocal tract. Thus this model corresponds to a transformation of the kind given by eqn. (5.46).

References

[1]   Kohonen, T. (1988). *An Introduction to Neural Computing.* Neural Networks, 1, pp. 3–16.

[2]   Poggio, T. & Girosi, F. (1990). *Networks for Approximation and Learning.* Proceedings of IEEE, 78 (9), 1481–1497.

[3]   Mead, C. (1989). *Analog VLSI and Neural Systems.* Reading, MA: Addison Wesley.

[4]   Amari, S. I. (1990). *Mathematical Foundations of Neurocomputing,* Proceedings of the IEEE, 78 (9), 1443–1463.

[5]   Beale, R., & Jackson, T. (1990). *Neural Computing: An Introduction.* Institute of Physics Publishing.

[6]   Haykin, S. (1994). *Neural Networks.* Prentice-Hall, USA.

[7]   Amari, S., & Maginu, K. (1988). *Statistical Neurodynamics of Associative Memory.* Neural Networks, 1, 63–73.

Credits

Figures and Tables

Chapter 1, Fig. 7 :

Adapted with permission from "Conti, M., Orcioni, S., & Turchetti, C. (1994). *A Class of Neural Networks Based on Approximate Identity for Analog IC's Hardware Implementation.* IEICE Transactions on Fundamentals of Electronics, Communications and Computer Sciences, E77-A (6), 1069–1079".

Chapter 1, Figs. 8, 9, 10, 11, 12, 13, 14, 15, 16 and table I :

Reproduced with permission from "Conti, M., Orcioni, S., & Turchetti, C. (1994). *A Class of Neural Networks Based on Approximate Identity for Analog IC's Hardware Implementation.* IEICE Transactions on Fundamentals of Electronics, Communications and Computer Sciences, E77-A (6), 1069–1079".

Chapter 4, Figs. 30, 31,32, 33 :

Reproduced with permission from "Turchetti, C., Conti, M., Crippa, P., & Orcioni, S. (1998). *On the Approximation of Stochastic Processes by Approximate Identity Neural Networks.* IEEE Trans. on Neural Networks, 9 (6), 1069–1085".

Chapter 4, Figs. 34, 35, 36, 37, 38, 39, 40 :

Reprinted from Neural Networks, Vol. 12, Belli, M. R., Conti, M., Crippa, P., & Turchetti, C., *Artificial Neural Networks as Approximators of Stochastic Processes*, pp. 647–658, Copyright (1999), with permission from Elsevier.

Subject Index

172